Testimonials for THE SOLID GOLD MAILBOX by Walter Weintz

"A premier primer of mail order marketing and a great entertainment for practitioners."
Joan Daniels Manley
GROUP VICE PRESIDENT, TIME INC. (retired)
PUBLISHER, TIME-LIFE BOOKS (retired)

"I've read an advance copy of Walt Weintz's book about mail order and I find it fascinating . . . it's a volume any practitioner of direct mail or advertising, beginner or old hand, will enjoy reading, and thereby profit immensely."
John Caples
VICE PRESIDENT, BBDO

"I found it an engrossing tale of what makes successful direct mail from one of the truly great promoters."
Richard V. Benson
PRESIDENT
THE BENSON ORGANIZATION

"Walter Weintz's book, THE SOLID GOLD MAILBOX, is at once a big case history of successful mail order marketing and a case by case study of specific mail order challenges. His experience spans the major milestones in the industry and, in fact, he was a part of most major innovations.
The book is full of anecdotes, each of which illustrates several important principles of direct mail. The technique is effective in that the book is excellent reading and highly instructive. After each chapter he says in effect "here's what you learned from this chapter."
J. Wendell Forbes
PUBLISHER
GUIDEPOSTS MAGAZINE

"THE SOLID GOLD MAILBOX is a super book. I enjoyed it thoroughly. It's a must for anyone involved in mail order or direct advertising. I recommend it highly . . . even to those not in the business."
Duke Drake
RETIRED CHAIRMAN AND CHIEF EXECUTIVE OFFICER
THE DUN & BRADSTREET CORPORATION

THE SOLID GOLD
MAILBOX

THE SOLID GOLD MAILBOX

*How to Create Winning
Mail-Order Campaigns . . .
By The Man Who's Done It All*

WALTER H. WEINTZ

JOHN WILEY & SONS

New York / Chichester / Brisbane / Toronto / Singapore

Library of Congress Cataloging-in-Publication Data

Weintz, Walter.
  The solid gold mailbox.

  Bibliography: p.
  Includes index.
  1. Mail-order business—United States.
2. Advertising, Direct-mail—United States.
3. Success in business—United States.   I. Title.
II. Title: Solid gold mailbox.
HF5466.W45   1987   658.8'72   86-28267
ISBN 0-471-85026-8

Printed in the United States of America

10 9 8 7 6 5 4 3 2 1

Preface

The Split Personality of the Successful Mail-Order Practitioner

Al Cole, the mail-order genius whose imagination and skill carried *Reader's Digest* from a struggling "Little Magazine" to a billion-dollar enterprise, once remarked to me:

"A good mail-order man has a split personality. On the one hand, he must be creative, and creative people hate to be troubled by practical considerations like costs and profits. On the other hand, he must be a good accountant, and good accountants are pedestrian facts-and-figures guys with ice water in their veins, who are exasperated by creative flights of fancy. They like to look at the bottom line. And if you don't have a little of both of these characters in your system, you'll never be a good mail-order operator and you'd better go into some other line of business."

The question is, how does any sane individual get that way—or is any such split-personality individual sane? At one time I was a frequent performer on the chicken-a-la-king after-luncheon speaker circuit, and I had a stock story with which I used to begin my speeches, to illustrate the problem of developing a mail-order personality.

> A man was driving along a rural road, when one of his tires blew out. He pulled over beside an imposing institution with a high iron fence around it. A sign on the fence said "STATE MENTAL INSTITUTION." As the man opened his car trunk and prepared to change the tire, one of the inmates wandered down to the fence and stood watching him.

The motorist jacked up his car, pried off the hub cap and laid it aside. Then he took out his lug wrench and removed each of the four nuts that held the wheel in place, and carefully placed them in the upturned hub cap, so that they wouldn't be lost. Next he pulled off the wheel—which promptly bounced, hit the hub cap, and flipped the four lug nuts down a handy storm sewer, where they were, of course, irretrievable.

The motorist was in despair. "Now what will I do?" he moaned. "Here I am stranded in the midst of nowhere with a three-wheel car. How will I ever get home?"

The Institutional inmate then addressed him.

"Say, Bud," he said. "Come here, and I'll tell you how to solve your problem. It's perfectly simple."

The motorist glared at the inmate. "All right, go ahead," he said with great scorn. "*You* tell me."

"You have three more wheels on the car. Each wheel has four lug nuts. You take one nut off each wheel, and you use these three lug nuts to fasten your fourth wheel back in place. Then you'll have four good wheels that'll get you safely to the nearest repair shop, where you can buy four new nuts."

"My gosh," the motorist said. "Of course! Now why didn't I think of that? Isn't it strange that I should be on the outside of this fence, and you on the inside—and you are the one who solved my problem?"

"Look, Bud," the inmate replied. "They put me in here because I'm crazy—not because I'm stupid!"

I personally maintained, in my speeches, that to be in the mail-order business, and make a success of it, you have to be a little bit crazy—but not stupid. The mail-order business is a strange combination of wild ideas and caution. It is fascinating and exciting because, with a good idea you can make a fortune overnight simply by mailing out a few thousand or a few million sales letters—or, with a bad idea, poorly planned and executed, you can lose that fortune with equal ease. In fact, it's much easier to lose than win, as has been demonstrated time and time again.

How you get to be a successful mail-order operator whose wins exceed his losses is at least one of the subjects of this book, which is mainly a collection of my recollections of the years I've spent and the campaigns I've worked on, successful and otherwise, in the mail-order business, the problems and techniques that evolved, and the lessons I have learned in the process.

In those years, it has been my privilege and good luck to be involved in some of the great mail-order successes of all time: *Reader's Digest*, Time, Inc., *TV Guide*, Columbia Record Club, Book-of-the-Month Club, Rodale Press, The Foundation for Christian Living, Boys Clubs of America, The Center for The Study of Democratic Institutions, Encyclopedia Britannica, Prudential Insurance, National Liberty, the Republican Party—there isn't room here and the reader would be too bored to continue reading, if I listed all the mail-order projects and institutions I've been involved with. I spent some 12 years with *Reader's Digest*, learning about mail order; subsequently, as a mail-order consultant, I've spent another 28 years expanding my learning, and in that time I've been involved in major projects for more than 100 mail-order companies.

It has also been my good fortune in all these projects and years to work with and for some of the real giants of mail order—men and women whose perception, skill, drive, and all-around genius made these great mail-order successes possible. These people taught me the business and helped me along the way. Again, my list of friends is too long to catalog here, but I'd like to make a token acknowledgment at least to my principal instructors.

My list begins with Vic Schwab, copy chief of Schwab and Beatty, the pioneer mail-order advertising agency, who gave me my basic copy writing training, before I went with *Reader's Digest*, and Bob Beatty, the business manager of the agency, who beat basic mail-order principles into my head.

Others certainly include DeWitt Wallace, founder and editor of *Reader's Digest*; Al Cole, the *Digest's* General Manager; Frank Herbert, the original *Digest* Circulation Manager, who evolved and executed the mailing techniques that carried the *Digest* to the top; and Fred Thompson, Frank Herbert's protege and Al Cole's right-hand man, who helped those two shape the development of the magazine.

Others high on my list include John Caples, the testing genius of BBDO, who helped me replace guesswork with scientific testing in *Digest* direct mail, newsstand, and book club promotion, and taught me much about the "bottom line" end of the mail-order business.

I'm also proud to include on my list of teachers Harry Scherman, founder and president of Book-of-the-Month Club; Neal Keating of Columbia Records; and Bob Teufel of Rodale Press,

Prevention and *Organic Gardening* magazines. Again the list is too long to interest anyone but me.

Since this book is mainly my recollections of the years I've spent in the mail-order business with these men and those institutions, I suppose that, like most recollections, mine probably tend to be loquacious, rambling—and inaccurate.

For rambling and loquaciousness, I offer no defense. After all, the whole point of a book of recollections is to ramble. But I have tried to protect myself against the charge of inaccuracy, by checking records wherever they are now available to me. Some of them, unfortunately, have slipped away with the passage of time.

However, I find that as I grow older, not only do my recollections tend to place me in the center of the stage in every scene I am recalling, but also tend to make me, consistently, the hero. I am sure my contemporaries in the actions I tell about would not always agree with my present interpretation.

On the other hand, this is my book, not theirs, and I am writing it, not they; so if they disagree, let them write their own books.

I am also told that I have a tendency to exaggerate, and it may be that I do, here and there, in the pages that follow. But, as Huck Finn said about Mark Twain, "He told the truth, mainly. There was things which he stretched, but mainly he told the truth. That is nothing. I never seen anybody but lied, one time or another . . . ."

Well, I have tried to check my facts and tell the truth, as I recall it. To my many friends who played parts in the yarns that follow, if I have slighted you, or left you out, I say: It wasn't intentional. Please attribute it to forgetfulness.

Memory is a selective thing, and so is story-telling. Here follow some of the more amusing—and, I trust, instructive—of those adventures I recall, the techniques and principles that evolved, and the lessons I learned, from 40 years in the mail-order business, told as I personally recall them.

WALTER H. WEINTZ

Norwalk, Connecticut
April 1987

Contents

List of Illustrations

1

The Secrets of Mail-Order Success

The Case of Rodale Press

This chapter will illustrate, by example, some answers to the questions that would-be mail-order entrepreneurs most frequently ask me.

What does it take to start a successful mail order business? What are my chances of succeeding with a product I have in mind?

I suppose that hardly a week has gone by, since I hung out my consulting shingle in 1958, that at least one would-be entrepreneur hasn't wandered in to see me, armed with such questions.

The first answer is, very clearly, you have to have an *idea* for an appealing product that can be marketed at a profit. There are a lot of "ifs" buried in that sentence.

To be appealing to the general public, a product must satisfy a need or a desire that is harbored in the breasts of men and/or women in commercial numbers. This is Rule One in the mail-order

CARTOON BY CEM.

"After I found the *Reader's Digest* lucky penny in my
mailbox, the breaks started coming thick and fast."

Reprinted by permission of CEM.

business. I cannot explain why it is so often overlooked or ignored.

You'll find a catalog of basic human needs and wants in any
advertising textbook: the need for love, security, wealth, success,
health, religious faith, amusement and entertainment, popularity,
and whatever else it is that brings happiness. The wants include
ambition for self and children, desire for self-improvement (win

friends, broaden your education, overcome self-doubts and fears); personal accomplishment (do-it-yourself); the need for respect and praise of your family and friends. Better than any textbook, perhaps, would be a study of the table of contents listed on the cover of most any *Reader's Digest* published between 1930 and 1960.

Some random examples of products that meet a few of these basic human needs are cook books that help the amateur cook win the admiration of her family and friends, home repair manuals that help the amateur tinkerer complete admirable home workshop projects, insurance programs that protect the individual and the family against economic disaster, books like *How To Win Friends And Influence People*, diet books, beauty aids, and self-help magazines like *Reader's Digest*.

Rodale press, a client my son and partner Todd Weintz and I have worked for over a period of nineteen years, is an excellent example of a company that has become wonderfully successful because its magazines, books, and clubs fulfill the basic requirements for good mail-order products, and because these products have been promoted by the use of dramatic selling *ideas*.

Rodale's *Organic Gardening*, the magazine that helps amateur gardeners raise astounding crops of fruits and vegetables, does so *without the aid of dangerous chemical fertilizers or insecticides*. This is a unique product idea that fulfills a human need. The magazine is filled with gratifying "how to" information on how to be a successful gardener, save money, and win admiration with gardening accomplishments—through *organic* gardening, which is a unique approach to gardening. Almost single-handed, *Organic Gardening* launched a "natural growing" revolution which has swept America's gardens and farms.

Rodale's *Prevention*—the magazine that tells its readers how to avoid illness by eating natural foods, following a natural nutritional and exercise health-care program, and avoiding health-destroying drugs and artificial foods—undoubtedly has helped to bring about the natural foods and natural living health revolution that is also sweeping America. The unique product idea here is, of course, prevention of illness. The basic selling idea, capsuled in the headline "how to live it up and live longer," is just about irresistible.

RODALE BOOK CLUB ENVELOPE

A typical Rodale Press Mailing, which combines on a single envelope most of the elements that make a successful order package.

Reprinted by permission of Rodale Press.

Rodale's *Bicycling* magazine both helps fulfill the needs of the cycling hobbyist and helps promote the cycling hobby. *Bicycling* thus cashes in on the fitness craze while promoting the fitness way of life at the same time.

All Rodale Books—which not infrequently achieve hard-cover sales of millions of copies (at prices ranging up to and over $20 a copy)—answer similar basic needs for help with health or hobby. Books about vitamins, woodworking, herbal remedies, natural healing, and natural food recipes. Rodale's book clubs—the Self-Sufficiency Book Club and the Prevention Book Club—clearly answer the same kinds of basic human needs.

Summing Up. In all cases, Rodale's products satisfy specific human needs with a unique idea: natural gardening, preventive health care, do-it-yourself home projects.

And while other, more colorful, more entertaining magazines and books come and go, Rodale press, with its modest publishing ventures that unerringly answer such deep-felt human needs, has grown to be one of the largest and most prosperous magazine and book publishers in America.

Of course, a good mail-order product must also answer a basic human need *in commercially worthwhile quantities*. For example, if NASA executives are among America's most frequent flyers, the market is probably still too small and the list too specialized for profitable commercial exploitation by mail-order. On the other hand, the air-lines' lists of business "Frequent Flyers," who sign chits every time they fly, comprise large master lists which are well worth mail-order promotions. Mail order generally deals with human needs in massive numbers. You can't build a mail-order business on a list of a few hundred or even a few thousand prospects.

It is very easy to discover if the numbers are there for a product you wish to sell. Consult any reputable list broker (you can find their names in the yellow pages, or in the direct mail trade journals, or by consulting the Direct Marketing Association in New York) and ask for a "list of lists." The broker will tell you how many (if any) consumers there are on lists of men and women who would be likely to buy your product.

Another characteristic that a good mail order product should have is a *substantial mark-up*. A guide to mark-up is the "rule of three," which says that one third of the selling price of a mail order product should pay the cost of the product itself, one-third should pay the cost of promotion, and one-third should be set aside for overhead and profits.

If a product costs $10 to produce, and sells for $20, either the cost is too high, or the price is too low, because the product cost eats up half of the price, leaving only 50 percent to be split between promotion and profits.

Similarly, if a product costs $10, and the selling price is $30, but probable promotion costs are projected at $20 per sale, obviously there's nothing left for profits and the product is doomed to failure.

Incidentally, this "rule of three" explains why the mail-order field tends to be dominated by magazines, books, clubs, insurance, health and beauty products, and fund raising for worthy causes and political candidates. Printed paper, in the form of magazines and books, is one of the most inexpensive, high-mark-up of all products. Manufacturing a magazine may cost 50¢; the cover price may be $4. It's the *editorial content* of the magazine that largely sets the price.

Insurance, of course, is equally high-leverage. The customer gets something for his or her money only when a "covered" need arises; and then the customer is compensated from a monetary reserve which he or she helped fund.

Health and beauty products also tend to enjoy very high mark-ups. The actual manufacturing cost of most cosmetics is very small, compared with their perceived value and the prices that women are willing to pay to enhance their beauty.

Worthy causes operate on strict budgets. Expenditures for political campaigns are determined by how much money is raised in the first place. So these are also, or can be, "high leverage" mail-order ventures.

A good mail-order product fulfills a basic human need, for a substantial audience, and the product cost leaves sufficient room for a reasonable promotion cost and profit. The product is *unique* in some way, and it lends itself to dramatic promotional copy. However, there remains the problem of financing. Sam Josefowitz, one of the most successful and knowledgeable mail-order operators I've ever known, once told me that he started Concert Hall Society, his record club, with an investment of $5,000—the cost of a test ad. He subsequently sold this business for $3 million. Ultimately, Sam sold the mail-order conglomerate he built, from his $5,000 start, for $80 million.

"Today," said Sam, "the minimum investment required to launch a company like Concert Hall Society would probably be $100,000."

Actually, it doesn't take $100,000 to make a direct mail *test*. On some products (for instance, a financial newsletter that sells for $500, or a million-dollar executive insurance program) the initial investment would be as little as one-tenth of that amount. But there's no getting around it: An idea without the money to launch it isn't worth a Confederate dollar today.

However, inexpensive *testing* is one of the special advantages that mail-order projects enjoy, and we'll have more on this point later.

The next element necessary for the successful launching of a mail order product is a tough, realistic marketing plan and financial forecast. The budding entrepreneur needs to sit down with a pencil (so that erasures can be made) and lay out, for every step of the way, the anticipated arithmetic. How much will the product really cost? What price can it be sold for? What's the percentage of return that must be secured on a test mailing to justify going ahead? How much will a test cost, and how much money will be needed if the test is successful and the decision is made to launch the product full scale? And what assurance do you have that the product will produce a profitable income, once it's launched?

The last question is an important one, and it leads to another example out of my consulting experience—a lesson about *money*.

Early in my consulting career a woman appeared in my office in the Time-Life Building in Rockefeller Center, and announced that she had an idea for a new magazine.

I explained to her that the way to start a new magazine was to sample the market with a "dry test." Before spending a lot of money for editorial work, actually producing and publishing the magazine, she should make a test mailing and see what kind of response she got.

Such a test, I told her, would cost about $50,000, and there was no sense talking about launching a magazine unless she had $50,000 she was ready to venture with the strong possibility that she'd never see the money again. And I couldn't work on the project unless she had the $50,000 in hand.

I expected this position of mine to end the conversation, but it did not. The woman said she had the $50,000.

I then told her there would be no point in spending $50,000 for a test if she did not have another $500,000 in venture capital readily available, with which to launch the magazine, if the $50,000 test told her to "go ahead."

She assured me that she had the $500,000.

"Well," I said, "there is no point in risking $500,000 unless you have an additional $1 million in reserve to operate the business for a full year—and this would have to be $1 million that you can afford to lose and are prepared to lose."

And I explained to her that you never know, with a new magazine, whether or not you have a viable business until the end of the first year, when your charter subscribers come up for renewal.

"If they like the magazine," I said, "they'll renew. If they don't like the magazine, they won't, and you'll be out a lot of money."

The woman assured me that she had set aside a considerable sum for venture capital for the project, and was quite prepared to lose it.

I told her about the basic financial theory of starting a new magazine: The first year you lose money, the second year you break even, and the third year you make a profit. Thus, with a successful publication, in three years you get your money back and own a valuable business, free and clear. Provided your project is successful!

She had named her magazine *Atlas*, after the giant who carried the world on his shoulders, and it was to be a *reprint* magazine with a real twist: A magazine that reprinted actual articles from international publications outside the United States—from France, Japan, Russia, India, and so on. Thus, instead of getting a second-hand reading (from U.S. publications) on what the rest of the world thinks about the United States and international happenings, readers of *Atlas* would get unedited, unfiltered material, and they could form their own judgment about what was going on in the world.

This was a *unique* product idea, which seemed to me to answer a basic human desire for knowledge and for self-improvement. It sounded like a good idea.

The publisher had engaged Quincy Howe, a great and famous editor, writer and broadcast commentator on international affairs, to head up her editorial staff. She wanted only 35,000 circulation to start. I thought the project had a good chance of success, and I was eager to help her invest her dollars.

However, I entered one strong caveat. "Magazines are dependent upon advertising revenue for their very existence," I said. "The *Reader's Digest* would have gone out of business if it hadn't decided to take advertising. *Atlas* can't exist without advertising. Now that you've got me to promote your publication, what you need most is a hot-shot ad salesman. Go out and spend part of your venture capital hiring the best ad salesman money can buy, and money should be no object."

She assured me that she had already solved the advertising problem. As a unique international publication, *Atlas* was a natural medium for large, multinational organizations like IBM, W. R. Grace, du Pont, and Sun Oil. It would be a display case where such companies would be pleased to do their institutional advertising. And she had connections with such companies.

It sounded pretty reasonable to me. So we put together a test mailing. The mailing worked (it pulled an overall return of better than 5 percent, which was quite satisfactory) and we went ahead with a big mailing. I had no trouble getting *Atlas* 35,000 starting subscribers. And these were *paid* subscribers.

At the end of the year, I did a series of renewal letters for *Atlas*. These pulled very well—better than 60 percent of the starting customers renewed; this is considered good for a "first renewal" in the magazine business. With a relatively small additional promotional mailing to outside lists, it was quite possible to maintain *Atlas's* circulation at the desired 35,000 level.

The only problem was advertising. My publisher did not hire a hot-shot advertising salesman. She depended upon connections, and as often happens when the chips are down, connections are a different thing when you come asking for money.

At the end of three years she sold *Atlas*—at a substantial loss—which of course was tax deductible.

After a good product and adequate financing, one of the most important ingredients for mail-order success—an ingredient that's as important as the product itself—is the skill of the promotion, the actual mailings that are created to promote the product. (It is only natural that I should say this, because the creation of such mailings is my life's work. Nevertheless, this is an unbiased, factual statement!) A good product, offered to the right list, can be a shocking failure if the mailing that presents it to prospects is uninspired, insipid—what the political cartoonists and the newspaper editorial writers love to condemn with the blanket appellation of "junk mail."

There is no doubt about it. A lot of direct mail is junky. Fortunately, the marketplace usually sorts out the junk from the worthwhile quite readily, and most "junk mail" is self-destructive. In any case, the success or failure of any mail-order enterprise is decided ultimately by the skill, or lack of skill, involved in the promotion. And this is why knowledgeable direct mail entrepreneurs frequently pay very large sums to direct mail consultants who specialize in creating successful mailings.

I've saved until last what I consider to be the most important ingredient necessary for mail-order success—the *personality* of the person who is launching the product, as described by Al Cole in the preface.

"A good mail order man," said Al Cole, "has a split personality. On the one hand, he must be creative, and on the other hand he must be a good accountant. And if you don't have a little of both these characters in your system, you'll never be a good mail order operator and you'd better go into some other line of business."

Rodale Press is the classic example of Al Cole's mail order dictum that *both* imagination and good business judgment are needed for mail-order success, which I've been privileged to observe. In 1966, I was invited to make a speech at a Direct Mail Advertising Association convention in Boston. After the speech a young man came up and introduced himself to me. He said his name was Bob Teufel and he did circulation promotion work for Rodale Press, which published *Organic Gardening* and *Prevention* magazine, and he wanted the Weintz organization to be his consultants.

Accordingly, my son Todd and I made a pilgrimage to Emmaus, Pennsylvania, where Rodale Press had its headquarters, set down amidst the Amish cornfields. We found Mr. Teufel (he was then a very young man, although even then his hair was silvery grey) seated at a typewriter in a tiny room that was entirely painted in shocking pink. In the adjoining office (also painted shocking pink) was the editor of *Prevention* magazine. Todd and I gathered that the two of them pretty much put out *Prevention*—one wrote it and the other promoted it. The circulation was impressive—about a half million copies. Mr. Teufel also promoted *Organic Gardening* on the side; that magazine was edited by Bob Rodale, the son of Rodale Press' founder, J.I. Rodale.

J.I. Rodale was an eccentric genius, who embodied the first half of Mr. Cole's prescription for mail order success. He had great ideas, and pursued them with boundless enthusiasm. He also had an uncanny sense of what made a good magazine. He was, in his special field, the editorial equal of DeWitt Wallace, the *Reader's Digest* Editor.

However, *Organic Gardening* and *Prevention* magazines, while moderately successful, were not the marvels of the magazine publishing field until Bob Teufel came along. What Al Cole did for *Reader's Digest*, Teufel did for Rodale's publications. He provided the innovative business leadership and the hard-headed "accounting" mentality that were needed to turn J. I. Rodale's great mail-order *projects* into great mail-order *successes*.

In 1966, when Todd and I met Teufel, the Rodale company was doing a total annual volume of business of about $6 million. In the years that followed, as we continued to be Rodale's consultants, we watched the company grow by leaps and bounds. Today the business is grossing over $150 million.

In midstream (1975), J. I. Rodale died—and there is an interesting contrast here between what happened at Rodale and what happened at the Reader's Digest Association when each of these founding elders died. At J. I. Rodale's death, his son, Bob Rodale, took over as Editor and Publisher (and, principal owner) of the entire Rodale Press operation.

When the founder of a business perishes, the business is apt to lose direction and go into a tailspin. When J. I. Rodale died, the growth of Rodale Press under Bob Rodale and Bob Teufel actually accelerated. One reason for this acceleration was Bob Teufel's business judgment and drive. The other reason was Bob Rodale's firm belief in the basic *mail-order* tenets on which Rodale was founded: *helpful* do-it-yourself advice, and information that satisfied basic human needs for health, happiness, and a sense of accomplishment.

Bob Rodale understood and believed in these principles. He held his publications unswervingly to these mail order pillars of strength. He gave Bob Teufel mail-order products Bob could run with. Like Al Cole at the *Digest*, Bob Teufel did the rest.

By contrast with Rodale's development after J. I.'s death, *Reader's Digest* changed direction when DeWitt Wallace died. The new editor appeared to feel that the day of the mass self-improvement publication was past and seemed bent on turning the *Digest* into an "investigative reporting" publication modeled on the Washington *Post*.

This editor was supported by a new *Reader's Digest* President from Great Britain who (in my opinion) just didn't understand the American roots of the *Digest*. He arrived at Pleasantville via the London and Australian offices of *Reader's Digest*. Under his direction, the *Digest* started diversifying into non-mail-order fields, such as pleasure boat manufacturing, a computer data bank company, and a publication called *Families* magazine, which quickly folded, and was rumored to have lost the *Digest* $20 million.

By 1984—just a few short years after Mr. Wallace died—the *Digest* found it necessary to mail millions of letters twice a year to maintain its failing subscription circulation. The newsstand sales had dropped from the 2 million-per-month level at which I left it in 1958 down close to the 700,000 level at which I found it in 1946.

The end of that story has not yet been told. The *Digest* now has a new editor and a new president. Under their guidance the *Digest* is returning to the basic principles of editing and publishing which won the magazine its position as the marvel of the publishing industry.

What are the lessons to be learned from the *Digest's* past difficulties? First, I should say, was the fact that neither the new editor nor the new president who took the reins after Mr. Wallace died really understood or believed in the principles that made *Reader's Digest* a huge mass market success. The editor obviously wanted to "modernize" the magazine; the president wanted to "diversify." On both counts, they drifted away from Mr. Wallace's creed. Wally insisted on sticking to the publication of only one magazine, and he insisted on keeping that magazine basically an upbeat, informative, self-improvement magazine. A *mail-order* product!

2

From Selling Pigeons to Consulting for Time Inc.

Mail-Order Basics Are Always the Same

In this chapter I'll try to illustrate how the basic ingredients for mail-order success apply in every mail-order enterprise—whether you're a teen-age boy trying to make a fortune selling pigeons by mail, a paralyzed polio victim seeking to make a living or a consultant to Time Inc. wrestling with the problem of a classical music program that Time Inc. has invested millions of dollars in, and should be selling like gangbusters—but isn't.

Those simple, basic principles, outlined in the last chapter, are worth summarizing here (in case you've already forgotten them). Indeed, they are basics that are frequently forgotten or overlooked by would-be mail-order millionaires—generally with grievous results.

To be successful, a mail-order product must:

1. Fulfill a basic human need

2. Offer a *unique* answer to that need (a dramatic and different product idea)
3. Have a *substantial* audience (commercially exploitable—not too specialized)
4. Operate with a substantial profit margin (the "rule of three")
5. Be adequately financed (capital!)
6. Be backed by a careful, realistic marketing program
7. Be promotable through a *dramatic*, unique selling idea
8. Be directed and operated by a split-personality mail-order individual who possesses *both* imagination and good business judgment (good management).

Now let's take a look at a couple of illustrations.

My own mail-order experiences began in the Blue Ridge Mountains of Virginia, in a little lead-and-zinc mining town called Austinville, where my father was the mill superintendent, and I more or less grew up.

During the Civil War (what we still referred to as "The War Between the States"), Austinville supplied much of the lead that Confederates shot at the Yankees, and the Yanks eventually came down there and closed the mine. There is still an extant shot tower close by Austinville, where hot lead was poured through a screen into water fifty or so feet below, forming round musket balls for shooting at Yankees.

By the time I graced the scene, Austinville had a population of about 200. Austinville had a 3-room schoolhouse, where three young normal school graduates taught grades one through seven, plus high school grades one and two. In due course, I was graduated from Austinville High.

I like to think that two experiences I had during those early days in Austinville profoundly shaped my future life. One was my discovery of pigeons, which a man named Elmer C. Rice sold by mail order. The magazines I read as a boy were filled with mail-order ads, and the most compelling of these, to me, were always those by Elmer Rice, self-proclaimed Founder of the Squab Industry in America, and President of the Plymouth Rock Squab Company of Melrose, Massachusetts.

Mr. Rice explained in his mail-order ads, and in a handsome hard-bound book that I purchased, entitled *The National Standard Squab Book*, that raising "giant squabs" was an easy road to riches. You simply purchased a few pedigreed "homing pigeon breeders" from Mr. Rice, and they did the rest. Soon your modest backyard pigeon house would be filled with fat, marketable squabs, which you could easily market by mail-order, just as he did, and you would shortly become one of the idle rich.

I took Mr. Rice's exhortation to set myself up in the pigeon business to heart. I persuaded my father to build me a handsome pigeon house and finance the acquisition of assorted pigeons, and although my pigeons never seemed to live up to Elmer Rice's standards of production, I did become infected with an early mail-order fever which lasted the rest of my life. I knew there was money to be made via the U.S. Mails.

But the trouble with starting a mail-order business, as I quickly discovered, was the need for venture capital. I spent many happy hours calculating how quickly I would acquire immense sums of money with a few of those "starting breeders" from the Plymouth Rock Squab Company, even allowing for the cost of feed ($3 per 100 lbs). But I needed more money.

I had a Scottish aunt who was slightly more affluent than I, and I approached Aunt Gracie with the idea that we should go partners; she would put up the venture capital, and I would manage the business. Aunt Gracie was willing to consider my proposal, provided I could show her figures to back up my promise of big returns on her investment. With Scottish caution, she demanded a financial forecast.

I spent many more happy hours working out on paper, for Aunt Gracie's perusal, every detail of our projected enterprise. And I subjected her to the mail-order blandishments of the Plymouth Rock Squab Company manual.

Squabs Pay! Experience of a Customer Who Without Any Experience Erected A Plant Worth Three Thousand Dollars and Made

Money Almost From the Start—Settlements of Squab Breeders in
Iowa, California, New Jersey and Pennsylvania . . . Large Income
Made From Pigeons Squab Plants Known to be Making Money . . .
No Occupation for a Drone . . . No Exaggeration.

Aunt Gracie was entranced, and I knew I qualified.

However, she felt that a modest investment would be the
soundest way to begin, and she staked me only to one pair of
pigeons.

Unfortunately, it turned out that a mail-order business, besides
a good product, requires a good manager. Instead of buying Elmer
Rice's best Plymouth Rock Breeders, I went astray and purchased
a pair of beautiful yellow muffed tumblers, whose specialty was
turning elaborate somersaults in the air over my modest business
establishment, and who were not the industrious squab producers
that the book described in such delightful detail. My pigeons cost
more, ate more, and produced disappointingly fewer squabs than
those of Elmer C. Rice's more successful disciples.

Besides, there always seemed to be setbacks. Eggs didn't hatch,
or were broken by careless parents. Hawks discovered the Weintz
Breeding Establishment, and moved in. I continued to purchase
fancy pigeons, rather than industrious breeders, and both production and sales were slack. But I kept elaborate records—down to
the laying or hatching of a single egg—and I worked up wonderful financial forecasts including cash flow tabulations and contin-
gency reserves. My first mail-order venture turned out to be
educational (although I never seemed to understand the lessons
the business was trying to teach me). My working capital got used
up, and I was forced to turn to other sources for money.

Again, mail-order beckoned. I had seen many ads for "boy
salesmen." I was particularly intrigued by one series, in which
beautiful ponies were offered as prizes to the "boy salesman" who
sold the most magazines, and I have always regretted that I didn't
enter that contest and win a pony. But a sounder, more promising
business was offered in their ads by the Curtis Publishing Company. They were, it appeared, willing to set me up, complete with
capital and product, as a Curtis Junior Salesman, and they pro-

vided me with 100 printed business cards, one of which I still proudly carry in my wallet. It says:

WALTER WEINTZ

AUSTINVILLE, VIRGINIA

JUNIOR DEGREE MEMBER

THE LEAGUE OF CURTIS

SALESMEN

THE SATURDAY EVENING POST

THE LADIES HOME JOURNAL

THE COUNTRY GENTLEMAN

As it turned out they, too, had a contest. If I increased my sales sufficiently, I earned extra points in the national contest, and became eligible for all kinds of substantial prizes. I went at it hammer and tongs.

There were only two hang-ups. One was the fact, as I have already mentioned, that Austinville had a population of approximately 200. My market was limited. The other was the fact that the Curtis Publishing Company, for some reasons known only to their circulation manager, insisted on quotas. You had to sell a fixed ratio of *The Country Gentleman* for all your sales of *The Saturday Evening Post* and *The Ladies Home Journal*. And selling *The Country Gentleman* in a mining town like Austinville, where country gentlemen were few and far between, was difficult—even at 5¢ a copy.

I remember one of the mine's shift bosses who made the mistake of purchasing an initial copy of *The Country Gentleman* from me, as a kind of encouraging, friendly gesture. I remember, in the months thereafter, as I searched the town and hunted him down, how his face took on a drawn look when he saw me cheerily approaching with my bag of unsold *Country Gentleman* on my shoulder. He paid dearly for an initial act of kindness. He was my only regular *Country Gentleman* customer.

Still, I made good money as a junior degree member of the League of Curtis Salesmen, although I ran out of customers before I won the contest.

Eventually I went off to complete my high school education at a military prep school (Austinville High offering nothing beyond the second year) and my mother enjoyed several months of negotiations with Curtis, who kept sending me, every week, increasing avalanches of Curtis magazines that I was expected to sell—or at least pay for.

Years later, when I became the circulation manager of *Reader's Digest*, I met another former Curtis boy salesman, whose story was quite different from mine, and I tell it here because it has a moral, of sorts, and definitely illustrates all the ingredients that make up a successful mail-order enterprise.

The man's name was Arthur White, and when I met him he was a millionaire.

As a boy, back around the year 1900, Arthur lived on his parents' farm on the outskirts of Westfield, Massachusetts, a metropolis which in those days advertised itself as "Whip City," as its principal industry at that time was the manufacture of buggy whips. Like me, and, I believe, like all other Curtis junior salesmen, Arthur was ambitious, and hard-working; and so, having a larger market than I to work with (at least, that's one explanation of his success as opposed to my own failure) he built up a substantial customer list, which he cheerfully serviced by bicycle every week.

At the age of fourteen—you might say at the height of a promising career—Arthur was stricken with polio and completely incapacitated. He could not walk, stand, sit up unassisted, or even dress himself. When I later got to know Arthur, he told me that as he lay in his sick bed and contemplated the miserable, useless lifetime stretching out before him, he found the prospect intolerable. And he decided that he wanted to do something about it.

He lived on a farm, so the logical thing to do was to set up a roadside vegetable produce stand. His parents built him a little shed at the edge of the road, and each morning the hired hand would carry Arthur down to the stand and prop him up in a chair. Then he would arrange the vegetable display and go off and leave Arthur, alone with his vegetables in the broiling sun.

At the end of the day, the hired man would come out and carry Arthur back into the house.

This business prospered, on a small scale, but Arthur was ambitious. He wanted to expand. So he worked out a new scheme. Each morning at 4:00 the hired man would dress Arthur, hitch up a team of horses to a wagon, and set him in the driver's seat. And Arthur would drive into town to the wholesale produce market, where he would purchase products to add to his roadside offering: bananas and oranges and other produce.

But he soon found that sitting in the sun waiting for customers can be a slow and tiresome business, especially if you have a dynamic, energetic, eager personality and inventive brain, caged in a practically immobilized body. He began to wonder if there weren't some way he could go to his customers, as he did when he was a Curtis boy salesman, instead of making them come to him, as he was now forced to do. And he thought of the U.S. Mail.

Obviously, he couldn't sell vegetables by mail. But he could utilize his body to the extent that he could laboriously write letters by hand. And he had a *list* (the basic ingredient of all mail-order businesses!) of all the customers who had formerly purchased *The Saturday Evening Post* and *Ladies Home Journal* (and even *The Country Gentleman*) from him. So he wrote them a letter.

> You remember me. Before I was stricken by polio, I used to enjoy seeing you every week, and delivering your copy of *The Saturday Evening Post*. Now, of course, that is impossible. But I'd still like to serve you.
>
> So I have arranged with the Curtis Publishing Company to be their subscription representative, and I can have *The Saturday Evening Post* delivered to you every week by the postman. And although I can't come and see you, I will represent you with the Curtis Company, and handle your subscription, so that you get the lowest price available, and the best service. And if you ever have any problems, I'll take them up with Curtis on your behalf.
>
> Also, I'll be glad to take your order for any other magazine subscriptions that you might care to enter, and you can have all your magazine subscriptions taken care of through one source ...

As might be expected, Arthur's former customers were genuinely touched, and his laborious hand-written mailing established some kind of mail-order record, pulling at least 100 percent return;

in fact, considerably better than that, as many former Curtis customers took advantage of Arthur's kind offer and ordered other
magazines which he conveniently listed.

The trouble was, his previous boy-salesman's list was somewhat
limited. Undaunted, Arthur revised his letter, and sent it out to
the telephone directory list of Whip City residents.

> Before I was stricken with polio it was my pleasure to serve the
> residents of Westfield as a boy magazine salesman. Every week I'd
> go cheerfully from door to door, giving folks the chance to buy *The
> Saturday Evening Post* and other good magazines. Perhaps you re-
> member me visiting you. Now I can no longer visit you personally,
> but I can still serve *you* by mail, just as I am serving my former
> home delivery customers. And I'd be happy to take your order for a
> subscription to *The Saturday Evening Post*, and to any other magazine
> that you might care to order ...

This mailing established another mail-order record for percentage of returns—a record that has probably never been matched.
Again, the problem was the limited market. Westfield, although a
city of moderate size, wasn't big enough to match Arthur White's
soaring ambitions. So he wrote another letter, and mailed it off to
mail-order lists throughout the nation. This letter simply left off
the reference to Westfield, and explained that Mr. White was formerly a door-to-door salesman, but now (stricken by polio) did
business by mail, and would be happy to serve.

At the age of 20 (after he became a millionaire), Arthur White
was forced to build a substantial building to house the staff and
records of his very substantial magazine subscription sales business. He was by then one of the biggest magazine subscription
sales agents in the United States, and as such he had considerable
clout.

Shortly after my appointment as circulation manager of the
Reader's Digest was announced to the trade, I received a rather tart
letter of congratulations from Arthur. He explained that he was
probably *Reader's Digest's* largest independent sales agent (which
was true) and complained bitterly that the *Digest's* agent manager
(a fictitious character named Alan Scott) gave him, Arthur, deplor-
ably small commissions on his sales, and in view of Arthur's

importance to me as the new *Digest* circulation manager, I had better come up to Westfield and get acquainted.

I went to see him and we became fast friends. By then, Arthur was in his 60s, a frail skeleton of a man who had to be carried into the room where we held our meetings. The letters he still mailed out, by the millions, carried a four-color portrait of a cheerful, smiling young Arthur, waving a crutch at the reader, and the mailing was still very effective. However, Arthur complained that I was taking business away from him by the mailings I made for *Reader's Digest*, and that his commissions were outrageously low.

By now, Arthur had broken out from magazines into the related greeting card business.

"The advantage of gift cards over magazine subscriptions," Arthur told me, "is that you can send out a package of gift cards— unordered merchandise—and get paid for it. You can't enter unordered magazine subscriptions." So—under the *nom de plume* of White's Quaint Shop—he began selling gift cards, and then began selling related gift items.

When I left *Reader's Digest* to become a consultant, Arthur immediately called me up and retained me (at a ridiculous cut-price), and for years he was one of my most enjoyable clients. I'd visit him once a month, and mostly listen to his inexhaustible marketing ideas and learn from his profound understanding of human nature's response to properly presented mail-order enticements. Arthur's death closed a very pleasant chapter in my mail-order consulting career; certainly I learned a lot more from him than he did from me.

Obviously, Arthur White succeeded because he combined in one person and one product all the necessary elements for a successful mail-order business. He had a product that fulfilled a need—a choice selection of America's favorite magazines. He had a unique product *idea*—a *mail-order* magazine subscription service (Arthur was the pioneer in this field). His product cost him nothing: The magazine publishing companies paid the cost of fulfillment, so in effect he had absolutely no product cost, and he easily met the requirements of "the rule of three." He had an adequate market—the mailing lists of everybody in the United States. He had a selling "hook" that would be difficult to match—the sympathy generated by his own unfortunate disability. And he had the split personality, combining imagination with cool judgment, that is the root of all mail-order success!

Many years later, after I became a direct mail consultant, I was witness to a third illustration of the unchanging basic laws of mail-order, and how they govern both the humble and the proud.

At this time, BBDO, the big advertising agency which had given me tremendous help while I was learning the direct mail promotion business at *Reader's Digest*, decided to become a "full-service agency"—that is, they decided to set up a direct mail division to serve their clients who needed help in the direct result field. BBDO invited me in as their consultant, to help get their direct mail division established. And one of the first BBDO accounts they asked me to help out on was Time Inc.

Time Inc. had followed a logical progression, from selling magazines to the sale of books and records to their magazine subscribers—an evolution that I personally had gone through as circulation director at *Reader's Digest*. They had developed an impressive set of record-albums-plus-booklets, which they called "The Story of Great Music." These were records of classical music by the great masters—Beethoven, Vivaldi, Tschaikovsky. The recordings were grouped by period: one album on "The Classical Period," one on "The Baroque Period," one on "The Spanish School of Music." The thought was that each album would introduce the listener to the lives and works of the great composers and the periods in which they lived, and would lead to a deeper understanding and appreciation of the masters' works.

The only trouble with this great set was that the sales were not up to the smashing success that marked most Time Inc. mail-order promotions. The sales were good—but the Time Inc. executives figured they could be better. Anyone at RCA Victor or Columbia Records (or, in fact, any clerk in any record shop) could probably have told Time Inc. *why* the set didn't sell as well as they'd have liked. The simple explanation was that the public didn't buy classical records in commercial quantities. At that time, for example, less than 10 percent of RCA Victor's substantial sales were classical records. In fact, at that time Elvis Presley accounted for most of RCA Victor record sales.

So the sale of the Time/Life records was good, but not great. BBDO was given the job of finding out why "The Story of Great Music" wasn't a real best seller and coming up with a proposal to *make* it sell.

So BBDO set out to ascertain, scientifically, what consumers themselves might think about the Time-Life Record Albums. A "focus group" was put together, and I was invited to sit in as an observer.

This focus group consisted of some twenty carefully selected female *LIFE* Subscribers, who BBDO and *LIFE* considered to be a fair cross-section of the kind of subscribers who should have been interested in classical records. They were all young, affluent, suburban housewives. They were all college graduates, and their husbands all held executive positions at high salaries with big companies in New York City.

The group was assembled in a small meeting room, with a female interlocutor, a psychologist trained in group manipulation. In the auditing room, watching the proceedings through a one-way mirror (unknown, of course, to the participants) sat BBDO and *LIFE* representatives, a video-tape cameraman to record the proceedings, and me.

The psychologist opened the meeting by explaining that the group was assembled to discuss classical music. And so, she said, perhaps the group should begin by giving their definitions of just what classical music was. And she turned to the first of these educated, upscale suburban women and said, "Suppose you tell me what you think of when you think of classical music."

Without hesitation, the other replied:

"Music by Jackie Gleason's orchestra."

The interlocutor tried again, on a second woman.

"And what do you think about as classical music?"

"Music by Lawrence Welk."

A little unnerved, she turned to a third.

"What kind of classical music do *you* like?"

"I don't like any of it," the woman replied. "I'm into hard rock, and that's all I listen to."

But the psychologist had a job to do, and she pursued it. Turning to a fourth woman, she said sweetly:

TIME/LIFE "POPULAR CLASSICS" MAILING

A mailing that succeeded by broadening the base of the product's market.

Reproduced by permission of TIME-LIFE BOOKS, INC.

"And how would you define classical music?"

"Well," said the woman, "music by Lowenbrau!"

We subsequently did a mailing for the great music set built around the *least* classical album in the series—a "Popular Classics" Album—and it was successful—because it broadened the base of the product's market.

There was an important lesson that *LIFE* could draw from this focus group experience. Basically, the market just wasn't there in the substantial numbers Time/Life was accustomed to dealing with. If you want a mass market success, you must start with a mass market product.

So to sum up: it matters not whether you are a kid selling (or not selling) pigeons, a handicapped magazine salesman like Arthur White, or the operators of a multimillion dollar direct mail business, like Time Inc., you *must* constantly keep in mind the basic laws that govern mail-order business:

You must have a product that fulfills a basic human need.

Your product must embody a unique approach for answering that human need.

The product must appeal to a broad, economically promotable market.

It must lend itself to an attention-getting promotional concept.

You must have ample financing to get your project off the ground.

The product must have an adequate built-in profit margin.

It must be backed by a solid marketing plan.

And you yourself must have a split personality, combining wild, creative imagination with a strong dose of common sense.

Given all these ingredients, you have the making of a mail-order success.

3

Prescription for Success

The Ingredients that Made the Reader's Digest a Direct Mail Phenomenon

My mail-order career and my mail-order adventures revolve pretty largely around the *Reader's Digest*, so I think it is necessary to give here a brief background history of the *Digest*, with my own interpretation of the basic ingredients that made *Reader's Digest* such a phenomenal mail-order success.

Reader's Digest is a classic demonstration of the basic elements that make for mail-order success. It is also a working model which illustrates how each of the basic elements can be applied to turn a *potential* winner into a great mail-order enterprise. These elements—unique product concept, mass market potential, adequate financing, inspired promotion, a sound marketing program, a sizeable profit margin and the "split personality" that's necessary for mail-order success—are all present in the *Digest's* story.

But these basic ingredients did not all pop into place the day the *Digest* was conceived. In fact the development was a somewhat lengthy process, involving a great deal of learning along the way.

To begin with, in 1922, a young man named DeWitt Wallace had an idea for a magazine which would *reprint* "31 articles of lasting interest," selected from all the hundreds of articles published each month in dozens of magazines, and condensed for the busy reader. This "reading service" would enable the average person to keep up with all the interesting output of the leading periodicals— getting the best of everything that was published.

The articles would be selected on the basis of their personally helpful qualities. They would be inspirational, informative, how-to-do-it pieces; articles to help the reader expand mentally, be more interested—and interesting. Articles that would help the reader overcome personal problems, and reach desirable goals in life—popularity, success, happiness. Not a bad concept for a magazine!

This concept was unique. It reflected the personality and personal taste of Wally himself, and this was, in essence, what made the magazine successful. I didn't meet Wally until 1947—25 years or so after he founded the *Digest*—and by then the *Digest* was a huge success, as was Mr. Wallace. Yet he was still striving for self-improvement, still had feelings of inadequacy, still was looking for ways to become more successful, happier—a better person. The search was sincere; and Wally simply put his own tastes, interests and ambitions into his magazine. Wally had in him all the simple wishes, ideals, morals, and feelings of inadequacy that motivate most Americans. The magazine was successful because it reflected a great editor.

Explaining the *Digest's* success to outsiders was always a touchy subject for Digesters, because Wally himself was extremely touchy on the subject. He felt very strongly that the *Digest's* success was entirely the product of his own editorial genius—this was the one thing he was very sure of. He was less than generous in giving credit where credit was due for the parts played by Al Cole and Frank Herbert and the brilliant marketing techniques they developed that swept his unique product to success.

An illustration of Wally's sensitivity on the subject occurred after the Canadian edition was launched. The new publisher thought it would be a great idea, and one which would win him favor with Wally, to reprint the very first issue of the *Digest* in its entirety on the *Digest's* 25th anniversary. Accordingly, he printed up a few thousands copies of this issue, intended for distribution to advertisers—and sent a copy to Pleasantville, expecting an appropriate pat on the back. Instead, he received a thunderous order to gather in and burn all copies, and for a while his job security was in some jeopardy.

The reason was simple. When Wally published that first issue of the *Digest*, he believed that magazine readers would be more responsive to a female editor, and accordingly, he listed Lila Acheson Wallace, who was indeed his cofounder and coeditor, as well as his wife, on the mast-head as editor-in-chief. This misrepresentation was quickly corrected in early issues, and in later years, Wally had no desire to broadcast the impression that she, not he, was the original editor.

At one time I made a speech to an advertising club in Seattle, Washington, on the subject of the *Digest's* success. I thought that I was far enough from Pleasantville so that it was safe for me to talk about what made the *Digest* so successful, while colorful, general magazines like *The Saturday Evening Post*, and *LIFE*, and *Look* (not to mention *Liberty*) were all having a tough time. I showed the audience the front cover of the current issue of the *Digest*, which listed 31 articles of lasting interest, plus some humorous, down-to-earth or instructive short fillers such as "Life in These United States," and "My Most Unforgettable Character." And I contrasted the 31 articles, with their up-beat, optimistic tone and their practical, personally helpful answers to everybody's everyday problems—spouses and children, careers and money, health, morale, and morality—to the entertaining and perhaps edifying, but certainly not as personally helpful, stories and articles that formed the backbone of the other mass magazines. I said that it was the editorial philosophy of the *Digest* that made it successful, and I mentioned that this was a direct reflection of the mind of the *Digest's* editor, DeWitt Wallace.

A few days after I made the speech, Wally's personal assistant, Gordon Davies, called me up and said he'd heard I had made a speech, and Mr. Wallace wanted to see a copy. With some trepidation, I sent along my typewritten text, and Gordon called me back the next day.

"Mr. Wallace wanted me to tell you how much he enjoyed your

speech," said Gordon. "He thinks it was the best speech about the *Digest* that anyone ever made."

Indeed, the speech was sincere. The basic reason for the *Digest's* success was its editorial concept and direction. But there were, in fact, two additional reasons for the magnitude of the success, and the names of those reasons were Albert L. Cole and Frank M. Herbert, the two men who planned, created, and executed the mail-order promotion that ultimately turned the *Digest* into a publishing giant. Wally *did* have a great mail-order concept; but at the start he lacked most of the other elements needed for spectacular success.

Indeed, he almost failed to get his project started. He needed financing (that basic ingredient that makes all mail-order wheels go around) to launch his publication. But he was unable to find any backers.

So, after trying in vain to get his current employers and various others to underwrite or sponsor his publication, DeWitt Wallace and his fiancee, Lila Bell Acheson, decided to publish the magazine themselves. With the help of a loan from Lila's older brother, Barclay Acheson, they put together a mailing announcing their publication plans and inviting friends to subscribe. They mailed this letter out to a small list—1 believe it was 5000 or so names. Barclay once told me that the three of them—Wally, Lila, and Barclay—inserted the letters by hand into the outer envelopes, on his kitchen table, over a pane of glass, which they used so that the letters would be clean and neatly folded.

Then Barclay (an ordained minister) performed the marriage ceremony for Lila and DeWitt, and they went off on a honeymoon. When they returned, they found that they were in business.

For a while, they published the *Digest* from their apartment in Greenwich Village. Then they came to the attention of a public relations consultant named Pendleton Dudley, who offered them an apartment over his garage in Pleasantville, New York, a rural community not far from New York City, and they utilized the garage apartment as their publishing office.

The magazine staggered along, without any great success. Wally was a natural born, if untrained, mail-order man; he had the instincts that made for good mail-order copy. Some of the mailings that he put out in those early days would serve as great models even today. But capital was limited, and although Wally went up and down the streets of Pleasantville, offering banks and others who had money an opportunity to purchase shares of the *Digest*, he got no takers. He lacked the money to make big mailings. The *Digest* reached some 20,000 circulation, and stuck there.

Then Mr. Wallace thought of newsstand sales. At the time, one distributing company—the American News Company—had a monopoly on the national distribution and newsstand sale of all magazines. Mr. Wallace went to see the president of the News Company, who promptly told him that his "little magazine" was too small for newsstand distribution, had no potential for growth, and therefore he wanted nothing to do with it.

Meanwhile, a hugely successful young ad salesman named Albert Cole had become president of the Popular Science Company, and he fretted over the antiquated, inefficient sales methods that the American News Company used in distributing his publications, *Popular Science* and *Outdoor Life*. The News Company was particularly infuriating to magazine publishers because it refused to do any real promotional work, kept demanding increases in commissions, and—because it was a monopoly—conducted all its dealings with its captive magazines on an "our way-or else" basis.

So Al Cole persuaded the publishers of *McCall's* to join the Popular Science Publishing Company to form the S.M. News Company ("Science-McCalls")—an independent national distributor in competition with American News—and to set up a network of independent local wholesalers throughout the country. Ultimately, the wholesalers all became millionaires, and they put the American News Company out of business.

Along the way, Mr. Cole saw a copy of the *Digest*, recognized its potential, and inquired after its newsstand sale. It had none, so he sent the president of the S.M. News Company to see Mr. Wallace and solicit his business.

Wally was so overwhelmed by this overture—after his rude dismissal from the American News president's office—that he gave the *Digest's* newsstand distribution to the S.M. News Company on the spot. And thus the *Digest* acquired the second force which led to its success—Albert L. Cole.

Popular Science and *Outdoor Life* were basically mail-order magazines, and Al Cole—the ad salesman—was fascinated by the intricacies of mail-order sales. Al told me once how he tried to sell Bob Beatty, who did the space buying for the Schwab and Beatty mail-order advertising agency, ads for one of their mail-order clients. Bob had pulled out record books, showing the relative cost-per-order of ads in different publications—and how *Popular Science* and *Outdoor Life* failed to measure up. This introduction to scientific, tested, measurable advertising was a revelation to Al, and, typically, he set out to learn the business.

Another client Al called on was Frank Herbert, who was a partner in another small mail-order agency—Thwing and Herbert. Al got Frank Herbert's permission to visit Thwing and Herbert regularly, after hours, and go over the results of the scientific ads that Frank was running. He also made similar arrangements with Bob Beatty. And Al learned the mail-order business.

When Al became president of Popular Science Publishing Company, he realized that he needed a mail-order expert to promote his magazines, so he induced Frank Herbert to join the Popular Science Publishing Company as its circulation manager. Frank was, ultimately, the third major force in the *Reader's Digest* success.

Al recognized the *Digest* as a potentially great mail-order product. The *Digest* wrapped up everyman's needs, hopes, and ambitions, and offered helpful advice on how to achieve those objectives. The *Digest's* editorial format—"31 articles of lasting interest every month, *condensed* for quick and easy reading"—made self-improvement a pleasure. So, once the *Digest* was in the S.M. stable, Al (a man of prodigious energy) started making suggestions for its mail-order sales. Mr. Wallace gradually succumbed to Al's forceful coaching. He invited Al to serve the *Digest* as a consultant, Al rang Frank Herbert in as the mail-order copywriter, and the *Digest* was off and running. The arrangement was soon formalized with Al installed as the *Digest's* general manager and Frank the circulation manager.

All this took place during the 1930s, before World War II. With Wally creating a quintessential mail-order product, Al engineering and masterminding its promotion, and Frank Herbert producing mail-order masterpieces, the *Digest's* sales jumped. By the time the United States entered World War II, domestic sales of the *Digest* had reached 2 million copies a month.

Meanwhile, the *Digest* had (under Al) started a number of foreign editions: English, French, Latin American, Spanish. When the war engulfed America, the *Digest's* propaganda value as an overseas "Voice of America" was recognized by the U.S. State Department. The *Digest* was encouraged to start new overseas editions. Paper for these editions, as well as the domestic edition, was made available.

One of the new editions was the Arabic edition. A very young emissary of the *Reader's Digest*, Fred Thompson, went to Saudi Arabia and brought that edition into being.

The wartime newsstand sales of the *Digest* were phenomenal. With little else to read besides comic books, soldiers, sailors, marines—everyone in the armed services—read the *Digest*. Newsstand circulation shot up to 2 million net paid sales per issue. The *Digest's* overall sales went up to 5 million. As a mail-order entity, the *Digest* had arrived.

Then, after the war, newsstand sales collapsed. When I joined the *Digest*, newsstand sales were down from 2 million to 700,000 copies a month. Subscription sales were suffering, too. Mailings that had pulled 6.5 percent dropped to 5 percent, to 4.5 percent, to 2.5 percent. It became necessary to put out bigger and bigger mailings just to stay even. And bigger mailings cost more. Although most magazines would have considered a 2.5 percent response on a 20 million mailing pretty exciting stuff, the *Digest* was accustomed to 6.5 percent. And without advertising revenue, the *Digest* was wholly dependent on subscription revenue for its continued existence.

Mailings in those days cost a mere $50 per 1000—including postage. The *Digest's* subscription offer was "8 months for $1.00." A 2.5 percent response—25 orders per 1000—brought in $25 against a $50 cost. That way the *Digest* seemed doomed to early extinction, and this was perhaps why Al Cole and Frank Herbert decided to beef up their subscription promotion department by hiring a new mail-order copywriter. And of course, the new mail-order copywriter turned out to be me.

4

Creating Mail-Order Copy that Sells Your Product

The Basic Techniques and How Reader's Digest Applied Them

My personal education in the fundamentals of writing mail-order copy took place over a period of 12 years at *Reader's Digest*. Since this book is intended to spell out, by example, the techniques that make the difference between success and failure in the unforgiving business of creating mail-order promotions, I believe the *Reader's Digest* approach to these problems is a good introduction to basic mail-order copy principles. So in the following pages I'll tell you how *Reader's Digest applied* some of the *techniques* that make the *principles* of mail-order work.

When I joined *Reader's Digest*, 80 percent of its circulation was mail-sold subscriptions, and the *Digest's* sophisticated mail-order techniques did much to explain the *Digest's* superior success compared with other, lesser magazines like *LIFE* and *The Saturday Evening Post*. Frank Herbert, the Digest's Circulation Manager, had simply applied a couple of the basic principles of mail order, which the circulation managers of other magazines didn't believe in or understand.

These principles seem so obvious that it is hard to see how Frank's competitors could have overlooked them. Yet even today, I encounter circulation managers and other mail-order practitioners who pooh-pooh these principles and fail to use them—because they fail to recognize their importance.

Incidentally, the mail-order techniques utilized by *Reader's Digest* to sell magazines are equally applicable to whatever you are trying to sell by mail—whether your product is a magazine, a book club, a contribution to a worthy cause, an expensive holiday gift package of steaks or grapefruit, subscription to a series of collectibles (porcelain figurines or model trains), or grandfather clock construction kits.

The first of these principles is to get action (that is, orders) by offering prospective customers a special introductory bargain. The offer must really be "special"—that is, not generally available elsewhere or every day of the year. The first mistake most magazines make is the flaunting of this cardinal rule.

The *Digest* sent out just one mailing a year, making a special introductory offer to new subscribers. The offer was available for a limited time only. To take advantage of the offer, it was necessary to act at once. The "introductory bargain" was not open to people who already subscribed.

The offer was made only by mail—a single letter, once a year. The offer was made only to new subscribers.

In contrast to this simple and perfectly obvious bit of salesmanship, *LIFE*, *The Saturday Evening Post*, and *Look* (not to mention *TIME*, *Newsweek*, and lesser lights in the magazine field) flooded the market, their newsstand buyers, and even their regular customers with offers, throughout the year. They customarily put bound-in cards (two, three or even four!) in every issue of the magazine, offering cut-rate subscriptions. The magazines made "introductory half-price offers" available to field selling sources— door-to-door salesmen—on a year-round basis. These crews of high-powered "crips and gimps," as they were familiarly known in the trade, did much to convince the general public that nobody should ever pay full price for a magazine. They destroyed the value of the magazine's so-called introductory offers. The public knew that it could pass up the offer received today—because the same offer, or perhaps a better one, would be around tomorrow.

Yet the operators who conducted such magazine circulation promotion could not understand *why* they were getting a mere 1/2 to 1½ percent response on their mailings (that is, between five and fifteen orders for every 1000 letters they sent out). They would never have believed it if I had told them that, helped by Frank Herbert's first principle, when I took over at *Reader's Digest* I ended up getting 9 percent response—90 orders for every 1000 letters I mailed out—on a 20 million mailing: 1.8 million new subscribers from a single letter!

Even today, if you doubt that this basic principle of making a *genuine, restricted, limited-time* special offer is still not understood by most magazine circulation directors—watch your mail box, and see how many identical letters you get in the course of a year, offering you a cut-price subscription to a popular magazine. Shake the current issue of any magazine you have in your hands—then count the "introductory bind-ins and blow-ins" that fall out!

The *Digest* did not, in those days, have bind-ins or blow-ins. It did *not* utilize the services of field selling organizations or of the direct mail magazine agencies like Publisher's Clearing House. All the others did—and the difference was directly reflected in the low percentage of returns they got on their mailings.

Incidentally, the principle of the "special offer" wasn't invented by *Reader's Digest*—it's used by intelligent merchandisers in every field of marketing as an action device to get sales. Again, consult your Sunday newspaper; you'll find it crammed with ads for special retail sales, for everything from rugs to automobiles to videorecorders. Retailers, who have their fingers on the public's buying pulse, know the effectiveness of *genuine* special offers, and use them.

A second, and again perfectly obvious principle that Frank Herbert developed and refined was the "action device" or "hot potato." Frank didn't just offer you a half-price subscription to *Reader's Digest*—he mailed you a $1.00 discount certificate, which you could use to secure a subscription for half-price. If you used it, it was worth a dollar to you. If you threw it away, in effect, you had lost a dollar. It was a "hot potato" you *had* to do something with, one way or another. The difference between a *physical, tangi-*

ble valuable *object* and a vaguely worded *offer* was all-important.

Before the dollar discount and the half-price offer, however, Frank used another *action* device—the offer of a *premium* book. Subscribe to *Reader's Digest*, said Frank, and you will receive— absolutely FREE—a copy of *"Getting the Most Out of Life,"* a book of *Digest* article reprints.

Again, "hot potatoes" and "premiums" were neither a *Digest* invention nor exclusively a mail order idea. Retail stores fill the Sunday supplements with "cents off" coupons—which are simply another form of the "hot potato." And they use premiums on every conceivable kind of product: "Buy one product get another free" is a universally-used offer. Once the principle is grasped, it is easy enough—or at least it becomes easier—to apply it for any product you may be selling.

From what Frank told me, eventually the premium book offer wore out, and he then went to an ingenious $1 offer. The *Digest* at that time sold for 25¢ a copy on the newsstand and $3 for a one-year subscription (same per-copy price, single copy, or subscription). Frank's offer was *eight months* of the *Digest* (a regular $2 value) for only $1. This made it both a half-price offer and a $1 bargain. Just pop a dollar in the mail, and you receive eight months of the *Digest*, at half price.

But there was more to Frank's offer than met the eye. About six months after you subscribed, you received a second friendly letter from Frank (or from Carolyn Davis, as he called himself in the circulation letters he signed). "When we invited you to enter a trial subscription to the *Digest* for only $1," said Carolyn-Frank, "it was not our intention to give your money back later on. But because you've been so nice to us—putting up your dollar, sight-unseen for a magazine you didn't know—we'd like to show our appreciation for your confidence in us—and return the favor. So here's your dollar back: a one-dollar discount certificate which will enable you to *renew* your subscription to *Reader's Digest*—regular price $3—for only $2."

This was called the "short-term renewal effort." It walked new subscribers up from $1 to $2 and it was only at the end of 18 months that the "regular renewal" offer of a subscription for $3 arrived in the subscriber's mail box. By that time, of course, the subscriber had had 18 months to form "the *Digest* habit"—and better than 80 percent would renew.

This simple technique explained why the *Digest's* renewal rate ran over 80 percent, while the most sophisticated popular magazines were greatly pleased when they got a 60 percent renewal.

But the *Digest's* subscription-getting technique went even further. The outside mailing went out in January, and subscriptions started with the February issue. Thus, they expired with the October issue. So in September of the second year, the *Digest* made a Christmas mailing—offering an opportunity to enter gift subscriptions at a special gift rate—and to renew your own subscription at the same time, at this same special gift rate.

When I joined the *Digest*, I was astonished to discover that only one-third of its subscriptions were regular, full-price sales. An additional one-third were introductory, cut-price subs (first eight months $1, or second year $1 off)—and one-third were Christmas gift rate subs!

By these devious techniques—making just one offer a year, offering a premium or a dollar discount, "giving back" the original dollar to secure renewals, and offering Christmas gift rates to pump up renewals even further, Frank turned a 20,000 circulation magazine into a 5 million circulation magazine, back in the days when the *Saturday Evening Post's* 3 million was considered big stuff.

THE BASIC DIFFERENCES BETWEEN GENERAL ADVERTISING COPY AND MAIL-ORDER COPY

It should be borne in mind that Frank Herbert was working in an advertising medium which has special rules. To begin with, mail-order copy is a curious kind of advertising, quite different from general advertising copy, and its principles are almost never used in general advertising. General advertising tends to try to create a favorable impression of a product which, it is hoped, will lead indirectly to warm feelings, and ultimately, a receptive mood for a purchase. Mail order generally tries to convey the immediate, tangible *benefits* of a product ("MAKE *BIG MONEY* IN RADIO") and calls for an immediate response. The two approaches are at opposite poles of the marketing spectrum.

A good example of the difference in concept—and the difficulty in getting good advertising people to write good mail order copy—was demonstrated to me, month after month, after I joined the *Digest*, when I was put in charge of the newsstand promotion, and I tried, every month, to get the top copywriters of one of Madison Avenue's biggest and best agencies to write mail-order copy for me.

We had decided, with the help of John Caples—the advertising agency genius who wrote "They Laughed When I Sat Down at the Piano", whose mail order advertisements and books about the science of mail order advertising have made him justly famous—to run a series of little newspaper "reader" ads each month, promoting newsstand sales. I would give the agency copy supervisor brief descriptions of the articles we wanted to feature (the articles were selected by an "advance ad" technique that John Caples invented).

For example, one of the articles might have announced that *Reader's Digest* had discovered that eating carrots was good for your eyesight, and the article might have said that carotene, contained in carrots, was the cure of night blindness. Sure enough, the agency copy department would hand in an ad that said something like this:

READER'S DIGEST SAYS
EATING CARROTS
HELPS EYESIGHT

The current issue of *Reader's Digest* contains an article, "Night Blindness Can Be Prevented," which states that carrots contain a substance known as carotene, which scientists have found actually improves normal eyesight and enables people to see better in the dark. A common ailment called "night blindness" can be overcome by eating plenty of carrots, says the *Digest*.

Of course, after reading such an ad, it wasn't necessary for readers to dash out and buy the *Reader's Digest*. They already had—for free—the gist of what the *Digest* was selling, and needed only to dash out and buy some carrots.

I tried, every month, to explain to those high-priced Madison Avenue creative people the simple shift in emphasis that was necessary to create *action-producing* (i.e., mail order) ads:

**AMAZING SECRET OF BETTER EYESIGHT
ANNOUNCED IN *READER'S DIGEST***

An article in the current issue of *Reader's Digest*, "Night Blindness Can Be Prevented," tells the amazing "secret" food which, scientists have discovered, you can eat to improve your eyesight—so that you can see "even in the dark!" It's an ordinary vegetable (and it tastes good!) and it's on sale in your grocery store. For the full story on how you can help your eyes see better, even in the dark, get the current issue of *Reader's Digest* on sale today!

The first ad, obviously, doesn't *offer an advantage which can be served by purchasing the advertised product*. The second ad offers such an advantage—which can be satisfied only by purchasing the product. It's a very simple principle.

Naturally, you, the copywriter, must light on a credible advantage, as well as one that people will really want. If, for example, I had run an ad promoting a *Digest* article on family finance with a headline that said "Reader's Digest Tells How to Get Rich in the Stock Market," the claim would have been unbelievable, and only the most credulous would have responded. In the long run, such exaggerated, unbelievable advertising is bound to damage the product's image.

At one time in Baltimore I taught a night course in advertising copywriting. Each week we gave the class a copy assignment, to be handed in the following week. One of the students, who was an example of the teaching problems I encountered, was an enthusiastic student who took copious notes on everything. One week the copy assignment was to write a headline for an electric dishwasher sales brochure, with copy that should show a *positive* advantage, a benefit that people would really want. Next week the student proudly handed in this headline:

INCREASES THE PLEASURE OF DISHWASHING!

This was, indeed, a positive advantage. As you can see, it's not always altogether easy to isolate the "positive advantage" that a product offers. How for example, would *you* headline a mail order brochure for a lowly dishwasher—a headline that would bring customers clamoring into the store that offered the dishwashers for sale?

I won't attempt to give you instructional dishwasher headlines,[1] but here's a real-life copy problem which The Weintz Company encountered in launching a new product—you might like to try your hand at putting together some trial headlines before you look at the successful solution, which I'll explain later in this book.

A TYPICAL MAIL ORDER COPY PROBLEM

At one time Meredith Publishing Company called in The Weintz Company (which then consisted of my son, Todd Weintz, and me), and announced that they were planning to start *The Better Homes and Gardens* Crafts Club.

This club would offer members books telling them how to make beautiful, valuable, expensive hand-crafted products: knitted sweaters, leather belts, decoupage and macrame objects, wall decorations, handbags, even furniture.

How would you headline the announcement mailing inviting readers to become members of such a club? Both the successful approach (created by Todd Weintz) and the approach that failed (created by me) appear on the next two pages. I give a Monday-morning explanation for success on the one hand and failure on the other, in the last Chapter of the book.

There is another important difference between space, radio and TV advertising, and advertising by direct mail, which governs the techniques you apply—a difference which I have found difficult to impress upon the advertising agencies I've worked with. In magazine or newspaper advertising, the agency usually has not more than a single page to tell their story. The advertising message must be brief. On network TV, where a few seconds of time may cost $100,000 or more, every second-consuming word is expensive. Again, brevity is the watchword.

BETTER HOMES AND GARDENS *CRAFTS CLUB "JUST IMAGINE"*
An envelope that didn't work.

Reproduced with permission of the Meredith Corporation.

In contrast, the U.S. Post Office charges postage on mailings by the ounce—and (currently, in 1987) the allowable weight limit for a third class mailing is 3.3 ounces. An annoying amount of paper can be crammed into 3.3 ounces: for example, a 9 × 12" envelope; a 4-page 11 × 17" letter; a 6 × 9" "lift" letter; a "bedsheet" circular, size 22 × 34"; an order form; a plastic card; a business reply envelope.

In one such mailing, thousands of words can be printed and dozens of four-color pictures can be included. The Post Office charges, currently, about 12¢ postage for such a mailing. But the Post Office charges the same 12¢ for a mailing that consists only of a double postcard, in which only 50 or 100 words, in small, 8-point type, can be reproduced. Obviously, a full-scale mailing gets

BETTER HOMES AND GARDENS *CRAFTS CLUB "YOURS FOR $1.00"*
MAILING
And the "motivated" envelope that won.

YOURS FOR ONLY $1⁰⁰
this big $7⁹⁵ volume
your introduction to membership in the
exciting Better Homes and Gardens
CRAFTS CLUB

Better Homes and Gardens
CRAFTS CLUB
1716 Locust Street
Des Moines, Iowa 50336

BULK RATE
U.S. POSTAGE
PAID
Meredith
Corporation

30N65
JEANETTE GOODWIN
73411 SANTA ROSA WAY
PALM DESERT CA 92260

Reproduced with permission of the Meredith Corporation.

the mail order company more mileage for its money than does a
postcard.

But a question that always comes up, when a mail order practitioner attempts to explain his peculiar way of doing things, is
"Wouldn't a postcard be more effective?"

And usually the observation is added, "Personally, I never read
all that junk I get in third-class mailings. Really now, why do you
have to write 4-page letters? Wouldn't a one-page letter do just as
well, or even better?"

The answer is, a 4-page letter will generally pull twice as many
orders as a one-page letter, provided that the copywriter has
something to say, and says it with some skill. This isn't just an
opinion: it has been proved over and over, by *tests*—where a
skeptical client has prepared a one-page letter, in finest prose, and
tested it against a long-winded 4-pager.

In fact, Meredith Publishing Company (publishers of *Better Homes and Gardens* and *Modern Living* magazines, as well as numerous books and clubs) generally prefers a *six-page* letter—because their tests have proved that a good 6-pager pulls even better than a 4-pager!

The other criticism leveled against direct mail, which I might as well dispose of right now is, "Nobody reads it." And if you prod the person who loftily puts forward this view, you'll generally get a supplementary statement: "I *never* buy anything by mail."

My usual response to this comment is a question: "Do you subscribe to any magazines? Are you a member of any book or record club? Did you ever purchase a Christmas gift—steaks, or pecans, or fruit—from a mail order advertiser?"

The fact is, just about everybody in the United States (at least, everybody with money) buys products by mail. And with the increasing complexity of modern life—the many difficulties of personal shopping, in crowded shopping malls or department stores staffed by untrained and hostile personnel—mail order has become an increasingly popular alternative.

Mail order, I should say, is here to stay. It may end up incorporating home computer terminals, and it is already incorporating telemarketing, but in one form or another the U.S. mails will probably continue to be a major marketing vehicle.

---

[1] Actually, "increases the pleasure of dishwashing" is not far from the mark as a good headline. Before the advent of dishwashers, dishwashing—by hand—was at best a time-consuming, unpleasant daily chore. By a slight change this headline explains why dishwashers today are a universal convenience of the affluent society: "It Actually Turns Dishwashing Into A PLEASURE!"

Today—where dishwashers are an accepted part of the American scene—a different kind of headline would be called for: probably one which touts the superior qualities of the brand and model of the dishwasher under promotion. Maytag's symbolic theme of the lonely Maytag serviceman—he never gets to fix anything because nothing ever goes wrong with Maytag appliances—may not be mail order but it is good "product benefit" copy.

5

A Short Chapter on How to Get a Job—and Get Promoted—as a Mail Order Copywriter

Occasionally I am invited to give talks on mail-order to student groups, and one of the questions I am most frequently asked is, "How do I get a job in mail-order? How do I get started?" And then, "Now that I've got my foot on the bottom rung of the ladder, what do I do next to get ahead?"

My own experiences, starting at the bottom at *Reader's Digest* and moving up, are certainly not typical, yet they do illustrate how the application of basic mail-order principles is useful in selling any product—even yourself! So, before going on to more general applications of the rules of mail-order, at this point I'll interject a brief illustrative biographical note.

In 1947 I was 32 years old, working as copy chief and creative director of a small but excellent Baltimore advertising agency named Van Sant, Dugdale and Company, which was strong on mail-order advertising. They had accounts like the Calvert School, a mail-order school for globe-trotters' children, and the National Radio Institute of Washington, DC ("I will train you at home in your spare time to *MAKE BIG MONEY IN RADIO*"—J.E. Smith, President). I was happy and secure, basking in the good life for which Baltimore is famous, and I never intended to go back to New York City or even New York State again.

Then an ad in *Printer's Ink*, the advertising trade journal, caught my eye. It seemed that the *Reader's Digest* was looking for a mail-order copywriter to work in Pleasantville, New York, promoting the magazine with the world's largest circulation (5 million in the United States, 13 million overseas).

The *Digest* was, in those days, a mail-order operator's idea of heaven. It was known (according to *The New Yorker*) as "The Little Wonder"—an incredible mail-order success that defied understanding. Rational people (like *New Yorker* editors) just couldn't believe a magazine like that, filled with Pollyannaish platitudes and celebrating and promoting middle-class values, could achieve such phenomenal circulation when (after all), *"Nobody I know* ever reads it."

In those days 5 million circulation was indeed formidable, far outstripping such publications as *The Saturday Evening Post* and *Life*. The *Digest's* extraordinary growth was one of the great success stories of the mail-order business. Naturally, I wanted that job. And I was pretty well prepared for it.

From 1938 to 1940, before Van Sant, Dugdale, I had worked for Schwab and Beatty, starting as a copy cub and working up, in three years and slow stages, to the full-fledged title of *copywriter*. I worked on Doubleday's trade book promotions, their Blue Ribbon Book and Triangle Book Catalogs, Walter Black's Classics Club, Charles Atlas ("The World's Most Perfectly Developed Man"), the Cortina Academy of Languages, sports and games books for David McKay, mail-order promotions for Simon and Schuster, circulation promotion for the *New York Journal* newspaper. I worked on Book-of-the-Month Club. My contributions were small, but my education was great. Schwab and Beatty was the great mail-order advertising agency of its day, and Vic Schwab, its president and copy chief, was considered one of the greatest mail-order copywriters of all time, and it was Vic who trained me to write mail-order copy.

However, it is important to emphasize that my pre-*Digest* experience was in mail-order *advertising*—not direct mail; and there is a world of difference between mail-order space or TV advertising, and direct mail promotion where you have 3.3 ounces of foolscap to work with.

In any case, when I answered the *Reader's Digest* help-wanted ad, I was already familiar with basic mail-order concepts. I knew the difference between general advertising promotion and the kind of direct result promotion that was necessary to sell *Reader's Digest*. I also knew, from my experience at Schwab and Beatty, where I worked with editors and authors, that hard-sell copy, for a literary product, had to be disguised as low-pressure sell: What I called "mail-order with kid gloves on." So I had to convince the *Digest* that I knew mail-order *and* its literary limitations. And I knew that one of the most effective devices in mail-order selling was the *testimonial*.

In my last days at Schwab and Beatty, I had done a series of ads for Booth Tarkington's last novel, "The Heritage of Hatcher Ide." Tarkington liked the ads so much he wrote the Doubleday editor about them, and the letter was passed on to me. So *my* letter to *Reader's Digest* started out:

Dear Sir:

When Booth Tarkington published his last novel, "The Heritage of Hatcher Ide," I wrote the ads that helped make it a best-seller. Here's what Booth Tarkington said:

"Thanks for the sample advertisement for "Hatcher Ide." The tone of it is just right and, I think, should be kept throughout. I couldn't have phrased it so well, myself, and I much appreciate the thought given to it."

This—my letter of application to *Reader's Digest* continued—was an example of my understanding of the problem of selling a magazine like *Reader's Digest*: To create "mail-order with kid gloves on," which would not only sell magazines (and magazine subscriptions) but would also set just the right tone, so that readers *and* editors *and* authors would all feel comfortable with the magazine's promotion. I told *Reader's Digest* that I understood all this—*and would be glad to show them some samples.*

I thought it was a pretty good letter. I sent it out shortly after my 32nd birthday, in April of 1947, and waited confidently for an answer. Weeks went by and none came. I forgot all about *Reader's Digest*, and prepared to spend the rest of my life in Baltimore.

Then, one Friday morning in August, I received a night telegram. "Be in New York Saturday morning at 9 A.M. for an interview." I got on a night Pullman train (the accepted mode of transportation in those pre-shuttle days) and was interviewed by a young man of about my own age, named Fred Thompson. He explained that the *Digest* needed someone to write promotional letters, to get readers and subscriptions. I asked him what prospects the job had for the future, and he explained that the circulation manager, a Mr. Frank Herbert, was nearing retirement age, and the *Digest* needed someone to some day replace him. It sounded awfully good to me, and Fred said he would get in touch with me shortly.

I went back to Baltimore and more weeks went by.

In September, I received another summons. Come to Pleasantville. There I met Frank Herbert, the circulation manager, who was a good friend and admirer of Vic Schwab's—and that broke the ice. One of Frank Herbert's many strong points was his ability to set people at their ease; he genuinely liked and was interested in everybody he met. He soon had me telling him the story of my life.

In the midst of this pleasant discussion, a connecting door in Frank's office popped open, and a second man entered. Frank introduced him as Al Cole, the *Digest's* general manager. Al was considerably more intimidating (remember, I was then 32 years old) than Frank was.

His first words were:

"What political party do you belong to?"
"I'm a Republican."
Al bustled out. Frank and I continued to talk, Al returned.
"What's your favorite book?"
"Bunker Bean."

I assumed Al had never heard of the book, but he broke into laughter. *Bunker Bean* is a rags-to-riches novel about a young man who discovered the Power of Positive Thinking, some years before Norman Vincent Peale explained it in his book and in the *Digest* condensation that helped make his book a best-seller. Al knew exactly what I was talking about. He bustled out again.

Throughout the morning, Al would reappear with a fresh question.

"Do you drink?"
"Yes."
"How much?"
"Moderately."
"What's moderately?"
"It doesn't interfere with my work."
"How are your nerves? Can you stand pressure?"
"I was in the South Pacific for two years and I never had any problems that I know of."
"What's your religion?"
"Protestant."

The questioning—with Al, it was more like a cross-examination—continued. At the end of the day, Frank Herbert put me in a limousine for New York, and said he'd let me know. Another month went by.

Again—it was now late October—I was summoned to Pleasantville, this time to see DeWitt Wallace. Frank Herbert briefed me for the meeting for half an hour, warning me not to be nervous, which of course made me exceedingly jumpy, and Al led me into Mr. Wallace's office and left me.

Mr. Wallace impressed me as a quiet, pleasant, diffident man, who appeared to be even more ill at ease than I was.

"I understand that you would like to work for the *Reader's Digest*," he began.

I assured him that I would indeed.

"Of course, we don't know if you would work out, so I have a suggestion. Would you be willing to go back to Baltimore and your present job there, and let us give you some assignments over the next five or six months, so that we could see what you can do? We'd pay you, of course."

I chose the words for my answer very carefully.

"I'll do better than that. As you know, I have a good job with a good future in the Baltimore agency I work for. It wouldn't be fair to them for me to stay on their payroll while I did moonlight assignments for you. So I'll give up that good job and come to work here with no committments whatsoever on your part. If I don't work out, the *Digest* can fire me in a week, or a day, without any further obligation. I'm willing to take the risk."

"I guess you do want to work for the *Digest*," Wally said. "I'll tell them to hire you."

What are the lessons (if any) for a beginner to learn from my experiences in getting a job with *Reader's Digest*? To begin with, I simply thought about the *Digest* and its problems—and offered a product advantage: I could help them do "mail-order selling with kid gloves on." I didn't talk about how good I was, I talked about how I understood their problem.

Most beginners' applications that I see nowadays have a standard resume which has obviously been mass produced and mass mailed. The resume leaves it up to me to figure out how the applicant—the product—can solve my problem. A little research and some intelligent thought put into a *personal* letter would go a lot further toward getting an interview.

Second, I *demonstrated* my understanding of the prospect's needs by turning my application itself into a mail-order letter, which began with an instantly-recognizable mail-order device: The *testimonial* from a recognized literary figure, Booth Tarkington. When Frank Herbert got that letter (even though he took months to respond) he instantly recognized that he was being subjected to a professional mail-order pitch, and he liked it.

Third, when I had my interviews with Frank and Al Cole, I tried to present my product (me) *honestly*. And fourth, I did not fall into Mr. Wallace's trap of taking on six months of test assignments. I "closed the sale" by putting *him* in a position where he either had to "take it or leave it." Perhaps unconsciously, I had subjected him to a "hot potato" mail-order offer. If he didn't hire me, then and there, obviously he, not I, would be the loser.

Now as to getting ahead, once a job is landed. At *Reader's Digest*, I was working for a very promotable product, where the application of sound mail-order techniques paid off in big dividends, and I was fortunate in getting the assignment of creating the promotion. Even more important, however, were the men I worked for, Al Cole and Frank Herbert, and the training I received from them. I was lucky in having the world's best instructors to guide me.

There are, I believe, three lessons to learn here. My first advice to any aspiring beginner is that you should set your sights high when you go job hunting. It's just as easy to get a job with a *good* organization as it is to get a job with a second-rate outfit, working on a second-rate product. And, most anything you do for a *good* outfit is bound to make you look good: Most anything you do for a low-grade employer will probably come out making you, too, look like a second-rater.

My second lesson is that you should be equally choosy in your choice of employers. Ask any 10 successful business executives how they got to the top of their profession; maybe not all of them, but most will tell you they got there with the help of the senior executives who trained them. It's a fact of American business that good management people make it their prime responsibility to train and upgrade the people who work under them.

So, in job hunting, it's important that you remember you are not only seeking employment, you are seeking employers who can help or hinder your career!

My third rule for success, drawn from my own limited experience (a one-person survey I've conducted) is that you should accept the opportunity for training that your boss (or bosses) offer you, if they are the right kind of bosses (or change jobs if they're not). In my case, Frank Herbert was planning to retire. He had a lifetime of knowledge and experience he *wanted* to pass on. I was very grateful for the opportunity to sit at his feet and learn the lessons he was eager to impart. Rather naturally, when he retired, I got the job.

* * * * * * * * * * * * * * * *

In November, I went to work for the *Digest*, as one of Frank Herbert's circulation assistants. Frank's promotion team consisted of a subscription promotion manager; a public relations manager (who also did newsstand promotion in his spare time); an agent sales manager, who also managed *Reader's Digest* School Edition (which had a sale of about 250,000 copies a month)—and now me, making the Circulation Department executive staff, counting Frank, total five.

In addition we had two assistants, one who took care of reprints and newsstand promotion ads, and one who set the monthly print orders and helped Frank do the circulation promotion dollars-and-cents forecasts. This was the complete Circulation Department of *Reader's Digest*. This staff planned, created, and executed all the promotion which had made the *Digest* the world's biggest selling magazine.

We worked directly for Al Cole, who had Fred Thompson as his assistant general manager, and that was the *Digest* Promotion Department.

Al Cole also presided over the Production Department, which consisted of Kent Rhodes, and the Fulfillment Department, where the Fulfillment Manager, Suzanne Quarenghi, supervised between 200 and 800 fulfillment people (depending upon the time of year and the work load), and managed a bank of Speed-0-Matic machines and some 3.5 to 4 million metal Address-O-Graph plates, each bearing a subscriber's name and address, which were used to address the labels for the subscription copies each month.

And that was the *Digest* Business Department.

Once you get a job with a future in a good mail-order company, the rest is up to you, so I won't bore the reader with a lecture on industry, loyalty, and other characteristics worth cultivating if you want to get ahead. However, I will tell a story out of my own experience which does illustrate another characteristic that's worth having. It is a trait which employers do not always feature on their list of desirable employee characteristics.

After I had been at *Reader's Digest* for some time, and had racked up a number of fairly tangible successes, I naturally expected that I would succeed Frank Herbert as circulation manager. After all, I'd been hired with this in mind.

Then Al Cole called me into his office one day in 1955, and remarked that he'd heard I was making a trip to Washington the following day on some Post Office matter.

"Good," said Al. "I've got to see the President. We'll go down together on the shuttle."

Next day Al's limousine picked me up, and together he and I boarded the Eastern shuttle. Al was in a genial mood, and we talked of this and that until the plane started circling for the Washington landing.

"By the way," Al remarked casually, "you know Frank's retiring, of course."

"Oh, sure," I said. I knew this was bound to happen in the next few years, although no definite date for Frank's departure had been set.

"Next week," said Al. "And I've decided that nobody will replace him. I'm going to take over Frank's job, and each of you people in the circulation department will report directly to me. It's all in an announcement I'm going to make in a day or so. I wanted you to know in advance."

"But I thought . . ." I began to sputter.

"Please fasten your seatbelts for our landing," said the loudspeaker.

"I'm going to have to run for my meeting at the White House," said Al. "Let's meet at the shuttle gate at 4:20 and we can catch the 5:00 back."

I decided that I couldn't throw a scene on the airplane, although I was boiling. But, I told myself, keep cool. You have all day to think this thing through. When you get back on the plane, Al will be strapped in the seat next to you, and he'll have to listen. If you explode now you'll simply get Al mad and you won't accomplish a thing.

So I marched off the plane, and I tried to sort out my thoughts.

I was supposed to be the next circulation manager. Al was obviously trying to avoid the unpleasantness that can arise when a department head pulls out and one of his assistants has to be selected to replace him; in which case the other assistants who are probably equally as well qualified, if not better, have their noses put out of joint. On the other hand, it wasn't like Al to dodge a fight. So perhaps—very likely—he simply didn't think I deserved the job.

It was a good thing that I didn't have the opportunity to talk the problem over with him just then, as I was pretty worked up. But I got my Post Office business done very shortly, and spent the rest of the day in Washington, getting ready to have a cool, rational discussion with Al, explaining to him why his scheme wouldn't work.

We met at the shuttle gates at 4:20.

"If we hustle, we can just catch the second section of the 4:00," said Al. We did—we were among the last passengers to board—and of course, Al got a seat at the front of the plane, and I took the last seat at the back of the plane, 20 rows away.

When we landed, I rushed after Al and caught up with him at the parking lot.

"Look, Al," I said, "I've got to talk to you. This plan of yours won't work . . ."

"There's my car now," said Al. Evidently he hadn't heard me. "I'll be home in Greenwich in time for dinner. See you tomorrow, Walt!"

And he jumped into the limousine. The car departed, leaving me standing in a swirl of dust.

I made my way home, and the more I thought about his plan to abolish the post of circulation manager, the madder I got. I decided I had no alternative but to quit. I decided that the time to quit was now. Right now! At 11:00 that night I called Al on the phone.

"Look, Al," I said. "This idea of yours is no good. So I'm quitting."

"What do you mean," Al said, "calling me up and waking me up at 11:00 at night? I'm trying to get some sleep."

"Well, you fixed it so I'm not getting any sleep, so I don't mind if I'm spoiling yours," I said. "Your idea is no good and I quit."

"I can't hear what you're saying," Al said. "And besides, whatever it is can wait till morning. Now I've got to get some sleep. Good night!"

And he hung up.

By morning I had lost some of my hot rage, but as far as I was concerned my resignation was a *fait accomplis*. I had only to confirm it with Al, and then start packing.

The *Digest* office opened at 8:00, and I was there. At 8:01 my phone buzzed. "Come down to my office" said Al.

"Come in here and shut the door," he greeted me. "Now look— before you say something we'll both regret and put me in a position where I'll have to do something I don't want to do, you're the new circulation manager. I'll make the announcement next week that Frank's leaving and you're replacing him. Meanwhile, I don't want you to talk about it. Do you know anything about newsstand sales?"

I sputtered out my thanks, and admitted complete ignorance of newsstand circulation.

"Then you'd better start learning," said Al. "Why don't you get on the road and go visit some big wholesalers all over the country. Congratulations on your new job."

We shook hands and I went back to my office to lay out an itinerary.

I took off the next day on a trip that carried me to 20 or so cities where I met with the leading regional magazine wholesalers and got a quick education in newsstand selling. I visited Philadelphia and Atlanta, New Orleans, Beaumont, Amarillo and Lubbock, Texas, Los Angeles, and Topeka, Kansas.

I was in Beaumont, Texas, when a telegram from Al reached me. "FRANK HERBERT'S RETIREMENT AS READER'S DIGEST CIRCULATION MANAGER HAS BEEN ANNOUNCED TODAY AND YOU HAVE BEEN NAMED AS HIS SUCCESSOR. CONGRATULATIONS. SIGNED A.L. COLE."

Some weeks later Al and I were having a meeting alone in his office. Apropos of nothing, Al remarked:.

"It's always interesting to watch how a man reacts to the crises he meets in business. You never really know what somebody is like until you see him tackle a serious problem, where the chips are down and he's got to make a tough decision on his own."

Evidently I had reacted to his satisfaction. I made no comment, and the topic didn't arise again.

And the moral of that story, I believe, is that, if you are an employee in a big organization, you must believe in yourself—and have the confidence that such a belief brings!

6

How to Write a Direct Mail Letter That Pulls

The Case History of a Successful Mail-Order Campaign, From Start to Finish

When I arrived on the scene at *Reader's Digest*, the standard subscription promotion mailing was a thing called "the Persian Poet effort." Frank Herbert had commissioned Leo McGivena, the promotion guru of the *New York Daily News*, to write some purple-passage copy for a test letter for the *Digest*; he had Vic Schwab put together a hard-sell mail-order offer, and he had wedded the two efforts into one of the best mail-order efforts of all time . . . a good example of "mail order with kid gloves on."

The mailing package consisted of a plain white "baronial"—that is, small 5½" × 7"—outside envelope, a fairly short letter, printed on two sheets of baronial letterhead (6" × 9"), a simple order form, and a business reply envelope. There was no circular, and there were no graphics, except that the *size* of the outside envelope was somewhat unusual, and therefore attention-getting; it *looked* different.

The letter said:

Dear Reader:

An ancient Persian Poet said, "If thou hast two pennies, spend one for bread. With the other, buy hyacinths for thy soul."

The letter went on to say: To buy hyacinths for thy soul, to increase your enjoyment of life, make yourself a more interesting and interested person, needn't be a task. One little publication will bring you—every month—31 articles of lasting interest that will help you expand your soul, fill your life with new meaning.

And so on!

But, said the letter, you don't know the *Reader's Digest*, so we'll be happy to send you a copy—FREE.

Or, if you wish, you can enter an introductory, short-term, 8-month trial subscription now for half price: $1.00 (regular price $3.00 for 12 issues).

The letter was signed *Carolyn Davis*.

The order card said:

Check one:

_____Please send me a free sample copy of *Reader's Digest*.

_____I enclose $1.00. Please enter an 8-month subscription to *Reader's Digest* in my name.

This mailing, during the World War II years and a couple of years thereafter, had gone out by the millions, with spectacular results. Results had averaged a 6 percent return—60 orders for every 1000 letters mailed out. In an industry where a 2 percent return is considered *good*, 6 percent was phenomenal. This mailing was the backbone of the *Digest's* growth.

But by the time I got there, the old Persian Poet was getting tired. Results were down substantially to about 2½ or 3 percent. Frank Herbert suggested that I write a new mailing to beat the Poet and get returns back up to a satisfactory level.

He said the way to accomplish this rebirth was to do a number of different tests, and then cross-breed and line-breed the most successful (just as he had done with Leo McGivena's and Vic Schwab's mailings).

So I began by getting out and retesting every major mailing the *Digest* had made since 1922, starting with Mr. Wallace's original

READER'S DIGEST "PERSIAN POET" MAILING
The letter that built the Reader's Digest.

READER'S DIGEST
The Reader's Digest Association, Pleasantville, N.Y.

Dear Reader:

An ancient Persian poet said: "If thou hast two pennies, spend one for bread. With the other, buy hyacinths for thy soul."

Poetry, perhaps; but hard sense as well.

. . .

To buy hyacinths for the soul, to become informed, alert, interesting in what you say to others, is just as important as progress in your business or social life.

And it needn't be a chore ! One compact little magazine -- 12 times a year -- can stave off mental stagnation, give you something worthwhile to think about and talk about, keep you from being bored -- and boring !

Reprinted by permission of *Reader's Digest*.

effort. I wanted to see how the current *Digest* effort compared with previous efforts. I mailed out 10,000 of each effort, to *identical* cross sections of the rented mail-order lists we were using, and counted returns.

The returns indicated that from 1922 to 1948 (when I made the tests) results improved in a steady, even progression. The poorest effort on my retest was Mr. Wallace's original mailing. The best was the current Persian Poet effort.

I puzzled over these results. In part, the steady improvement in returns from one year's effort to the next could be attributed to refinements—what Frank called "line-breeding and cross-breeding." The offer was improved a bit, wording was made more interesting; a phrase was inserted here or there that added life to the letter. But these minor changes hardly explained the difference in results. As I recall it, Wally's letter pulled less than 1 percent on my retest, while the latest Persian Poet pulled around 3 percent— at least three times as well as the effort that launched the *Digest*.

My conclusion at the time—and one which experience has confirmed over the years—was that there is a subtle change, from year to year, in the public's tastes and interests. What appealed to a more naive audience in 1922 failed to move the more sophisticated audience of 1948.

It follows that almost any successful last year's mailing can be beaten this year by a new mailing which merely incorporates the copywriter's subtle, slight, even unconscious and subliminal current-year feelings of what's the right way and what's the wrong way to write copy.

Mailings that evoked tons of orders in the 1920s are more likely to evoke laughter than orders in the 1980s. A perfect illustration from the annals of mail-order *advertising* is John Caples' famous ad for the U.S. School of Music: "They laughed when I sat down at the piano . . . but when I started to play!" This was one of the most effective mail-order ads ever written. Today, it wouldn't sell.

The changes in public taste are perhaps imperceptible from year to year, but over a period of time tastes certainly do change, dramatically. A good mail-order copywriter must somehow sense this subtle change, and let it guide him or her in writing.

A second proof of this curious "aging" of mail-order copy came to me several years after I joined the *Digest*. By this time I had become extremely test conscious, guided by my private assessment of my own uncertain creativity. I was *trying* to instil some of the accountant's ice water into my own veins. So I set up a "Monthly Index Test."

Each month I sent out 100,000 identical letters to an identical, updated cross-section of names from the telephone book. The object was to discover, scientifically, the best month to make a mailing.

These were fresh names, freshly selected each month, from the latest phone books available. Over the course of a year, the 1.2 million letters I sent out created a beautiful chart of the best—and worst—times to make a mailing.

The chart confirmed, incidentally, what mail-order people had known since the first Egyptian or Etruscan letter-writer sent out a batch of papyrus or graven-stone letters: The best month to make a mailing is January.

Nobody knows why this is so; at least I don't. There are all kinds of explanations. Back when Frank Herbert was starting out, the accepted explanation, he told me, was that in January, farmers (the big mail-order buyers) are snowed in and they have more time to look at their mail. But of course, farmers no longer get snowed in, and from 60 percent of the nation's population, they've dwindled to less than 5 percent.

In my own early days, it was argued that January was a time when people had Christmas bonuses to spend, and because everybody now worked for a big corporation that paid Christmas bonuses, the time to sell things to them was in January.

Then it was argued that January 1st is the day when well-intentioned men and women make New Year's resolutions, so they are vulnerable at that time to mailings offering them a chance to improve themselves, make more money, be happier, and so on.

This thesis has been somewhat disproved by the fact that January is a good mailing time for luxury foods, which have nothing to do with good resolutions (although they are perhaps related to a euphoria or a sense of well-being that may attend the birth of a new year).

However the whole "January Mailing" theory is gradually being wrecked by the competition among mailers for "First Place in the Mail Box." An astute mailer decided, some years ago, to mail December 31st, and thus make sure his mailing would be the first letter in the annual January mail-order avalanche to arrive. Someone else decided to beat him by mailing December 24th, and it worked. (The cynical theory here is that the U.S. mailmen don't do any work or deliver any mail between Christmas and New Years anyway, so December 24th mail won't be delivered until January 2nd.)

Then someone decided to beat the December 24th mailers, and put out his "January" mailing December 15th.

Successfully!

At any rate, there is still a substantial seasonal variation in almost all mail-order returns, which applies to most nonseasonal products like books, magazines, and records. (One exception is the field of charitable organizations, like the National Tuberculosis and Respiratory Diseases Association—they do best in the pre-Holiday season. Another, quite naturally, is gardening products organizations, like Spring Hill Nurseries which have seasons of their own.) My "Monthly Index" in 1948 showed:

January	110 orders
February	104
March	90
April	85
May	75
June	60
July	80
August	90
September	95
October	100
November	75
December	70

In other words, there were two "humps" in returns—Spring and Fall—and the four best months were (in that order) January, February, October, and September.

These figures, incidentally, *do* change from year to year. The Fall "hump" keeps moving forward in the calendar: It now appears to peak in July–August. The January mailing date has definitely moved up into December. And of course seed catalogs, Christmas gift catalogs, financial services, and other seasonal items do have different seasonal laws of their own.

At any rate, I was quite pleased at the end of my first year's Monthly Index Test, so I repeated it the following year. Imagine my astonishment when I discovered that the identical mailing, mailed to an identical, updated cross section of the same telephone list, pulled exactly the same monthly index pattern—but every month was down by approximately 10 percent!

I checked and rechecked. The list was fresh, the selection was the same, there were no variables that I could uncover, except seasonal—and the 10 percent difference in pull between one year and its successor.

So I ran the test a third year. The identical seasonal pattern emerged—but at a level 10 percent lower than the second year.

I gave up. Apparently my mailing hadn't changed, but the public had—the mailing, somehow, seemed "dated," and it was in a terminal decline.

Which leads me to another of the truisms I have used in some of my after-luncheon speeches: The mail-order business reminds me of the words an Irish New York cop said to a drunk he found hanging onto a street corner lamp post: "If yez want to stay here, yez got to keep moving!"

So it is with the mail-order business. And this is why, today, I am pretty confident that I can beat any mailing, written by anybody—if the other mailing was written last year.

And when people tell me that they have been running the same mailing for years, but have never been able to beat it, I am skeptical!

In any event, there are four bits of useful information that I gleaned from my multiple previous-years'-mailings test.

1. The *offer* makes a tremendous difference.
2. The *lists* are *extremely* important.
3. The *appearance* of a mailing seems to make a lot of difference.
4. The introduction of some action device (what we at the *Digest* dubbed a "hot potato") increases returns.

As to offers, I knew that the easier you made it for a customer to order—the fewer roadblocks you put in the way—the more returns you would get. And the *Digest's* basic "Persian Poet" mailing violated that cardinal rule—*by asking for cash with order*. Even though the cash required was only a dollar, it was still money that someone had to fork out (reluctantly) and put into an envelope. That, I reasoned, slowed down the sale.

Frank Herbert was immensely proud of the flood of one-dollar bills his mailings brought in every January. From a 20 million mailing, he took in up to 3 percent—that is, 600,000 orders—and 600,000 one-dollar bills. The *Digest* was literally afloat in dollar bills on the second Monday in January!

But I knew, without even testing (from previous experience with other mail-order clients), that a "bill me later" offer would increase returns by about 50 percent—and that 96 percent of those who ordered would pay!

And 96 percent of 150 orders is 144 net paid orders compared with the 100 net paid orders I would get from the standard "cash with order" effort.

Ask any mail-order person today about my basic premise—that 96 percent of those who ordered on credit would faithfully cough up one dollar—and you'll be treated to a raucous horse-laugh. As everyone knows today, the "bad-pay" rate on mailings normally runs between 20 percent and 40 percent—or worse! In fact, it is often as high as 50 percent, when you add bad-debtors to free-loaders who bother to cancel after they get their first issue. But in those days people felt obligated to pay their bills. Then, 96 percent payment was normal. Today, 60 percent is probably the comparable index of morality. And, quite probably, this is a situation which mail order operators have brought on themselves, with excessive use of "no-obligation" offers that leave the logical impression that there *is* no obligation!

But in those days things were different. So to make a long story short, I decided to send out 20 million "bill-me-later" efforts—and I knew I could then go home and sleep the sleep of the just.

The second element in the evolution of the *Digest's* mailings, which I helped bring about, and which did help increase those returns, was a change in mailing *lists*. The *Digest* was in the habit of mailing its subscription offers to rented mailing lists: lists of people who had subscribed to other magazines, or who had ordered some other product (books, gifts, seeds, etc.) by *mail*. These were "mail order lists"—lists of people who *bought things by mail*.

To mail out 20 million subscription solicitations, it was necessary to rent some 400 to 500 such mailing lists. The lists averaged 40,000 or 50,000 names apiece.

In reviewing my keyed returns from my initial tests, I noted that some keys (lists) pulled much better than others, even when each list had received an identical quantity of identical mailings. Obviously, some lists were much better—much more productive—than others.

A further discovery about lists was born in upon me by sarcastic complaints about my activities which reached me from the fulfillment department. Here I was, said Suzanne Quarenghi, the fulfillment department head, mailing introductory offers to thousands of people who already subscribed to the *Digest*: So, instead of renewing at the regular price, they renewed at the much lower *introductory* price. Thousands of knowledgeable subscribers, she said, were taking advantage of this opportunity, even though I firmly stated in my mailings that the introductory offer was "for new subscribers only." Naturally, Suzanne had to fulfill their orders at the cut price.

The cause of this problem was simply my inability to screen the lists I rented, to remove existing *Digest* subscribers. This was in pre-computer days. There was no practical way to eliminate 3 or 4 million *Digest* subscriber names from mailings to 400 different lists with a total of 20 million names.

Some regular subscribers reacted even more negatively when they accidentally received one of my introductory mailings. They wrote me (by this time I was Carolyn Davis) letters denouncing me for offering strangers a better price than old friends, like themselves, were getting—and therefore they cancelled their subscriptions and asked for their money back.

In addition, it came to my attention that when you mail to every name on every one of 400 mail-order lists, you encounter duplication *between* lists, as well as duplication with existing customers. The same name may appear on two lists—or three or four. The more habitual a mail-order buyer, the more likely duplication would occur; and I got letters from these people too—complaining about the number of mailings they'd received, and how wasteful this practice of sending out multiple mailings could be. And how foolish Carolyn Davis was.

Not only did they write to me, however—they also wrote to Mr. Wallace. One indignant writer was the president of IBM, who received 16 identical introductory letters from the *Digest* in his mail box in a single day. And he was already a subscriber, as well as a friend of Wally's! He was pretty sarcastic with Mr. Wallace, who in turn was sarcastic with Mr. Cole, who simply gave me hell and told me this sort of foolishness would have to stop.

Accordingly, out of desperation, I made what I believe was the first "merge–purge" list study in mail-order history. And I did it without the help of a computer (which would have made a small, routine job of such a matter).

Today, indeed, such "merge-purge" list cleanings are a routine thing on most mailings, but in those days they were unheard of. I purchased the entire mailing list segment for the State of Maryland from my 400 or so list owners. This represented perhaps a 5 percent sample of the 20 million national total of these lists—about a million names. And I set down a dozen or so *Digest* fulfillment department people at long tables, with little individual "Dick Strips" for these million names, and I had them sort out the names, in geo-alpha order, and then count the "dupes." Against these net names, I laid out the *Digest*'s subscriber list for the State of Maryland, and counted those dupes too. And I discovered some astonishing things!

First, the *Digest* then had the biggest subscriber list of any magazine—and all the subs were mail sold, secured by mailings to those 400 lists. Therefore the duplication between subscribers and names on some of the lists was appalling—as high as 40 percent! And overall, it easily averaged 5 percent! So, by mailing 20 million unsorted names, I was actually mailing to a million *Digest* subscribers, making some of them very angry, irritating them all, inducing some to cancel, giving others an opportunity to get their subscriptions renewed at a reduced price, and educating some others to the idea that the *Digest* was no better than any other magazine—it really *did* give better prices to strangers than it did to faithful regular subscribers.

The odd thing (but perfectly logical when I stopped to think about it) was that the better the mail-order list I was renting, the greater the duplication with *Digest* subscribers; and the greater the saturation of *Digest* subscribers on any list, of course, the poorer the list pulled, in spite of its basic high quality.

Thus, lists which had at one time pulled 6 percent or more were now down to 1 percent or 2 percent—and I was sure that this was due to saturation. I was simply mailing to *fewer* net nonsubscriber names.

The other startling fact that emerged from my "merge-purge" test was the extent of duplication between the lists I was using— the same name occuring on two or more lists; and *that* sometimes ran as high as 50 percent. In effect, when I mailed out 20 million letters thinking I was mailing to 20 million individuals, I was actually mailing to perhaps 15 million individuals. A lot of them were getting two or three identical letters, and one million of these individuals were *already Digest* subscribers!

Obviously, something had to be done. Even before my arrival, and my education in the pitfalls of list rentals, Frank Herbert had set a rescue operation in motion.

Frank introduced me to Mr. O. E. MacIntyre, a mail-order list salesman who understood our duplication problem—and offered a simple solution.

"Give me the *Digest* subscriber names," he said, "and I will run them off by hand against the national telephone subscriber lists, scratching out all *Digest* subscribers' names. Then you'll have an absolutely clean list of some 60 million telephone names to mail to. And when you mail 20 million names, you'll have 20 million prospects. Not 15 million. In fact, you don't have to mail 20 million— you can mail 15 million and get the same results, at a lot less cost than 20 million."

A contract was drawn up, and Mac set up shop in a rented quonset hut in Great Neck, Long Island. He introduced a money-saving invention into his list compilation procedure; the home typist. In the quonset, operators with blue pencils searched the phone books and checked them against a dick-strip list of *Digest* subscribers. The subscribers' names were eliminated, the phone book pages were given out to home typists, and these typists typed up labels.

I put out a million telephone name test, and it worked as well as the mail order list names. In fact, much better!

It immediately became obvious to us that there was an extra, hidden advantage to using the giant telephone list. By mailing 20 million telephone names in the eastern half of the USA one year, and 20 million in the western half the following year, I was able to give each half of the telephone list a rest, which improved results even further. Thus the lists didn't wear out as fast as they would have if I had mailed every year.

In subsequent years, at cocktail parties, I was often amused by knowledgeable suburbanites who informed me that they *never* renewed their *Digest* subscriptions at full price—they simply waited for an introductory offer just as they did for other magazines, and subscribed year after year at half price. In fact, this was impossible. I eliminated all *Digest expires* from my telephone book mailings. So, counting the 2-year interval between introductory mailings, with an extra year of expire elimination, an expired subscriber didn't get a new introductory offer for at least three years.

I now had a new and better offer: *"bill-me-later"* instead of *"cash-with-order,"* and I had a new and better list to mail my offer to . . . a list of 60 million individual telephone subscribers from which existing *Digest* names had been eliminated. There were, however, two additional elements that helped me secure a 500,000 overall increase in returns on my mailings.

The third element affecting results, that I had noted in examining previous *Digest* mailings was what I would call "dramatization." The *Digest's* mailings were all rather plain and simple. Still, the "Persian Poet" effort *looked* different and the presentation of the offer in its wedding-invitation baronial format had a certain simple drama to it. I concluded that it was not enough to make a good offer; it was necessary to present the offer in a dramatic *package* to get attention. So I looked about for ways to make the mailing look important and different.

In those days direct mail generally consisted of a plain white envelope—after all, it was said, the purpose of an envelope was simply to convey a mailing into the hands of the intended recipient. It was considered bad form to put any message on the outside of an envelope—a blank envelope, it was argued, would arouse curiosity, and the recipient would open it to find out what went on inside. At best, some daring practitioners wrote "IMPORTANT" or "DATED MATERIAL ENCLOSED" or "FIRST CLASS MAIL" or some similar, earth-shaking attention-getting message on the outside.

But it was apparent to me that the envelope was the first thing the intended customer saw—and as such, it played a far more important role than that of a mere "package." The envelope was, I decided, the equivalent of the upper half of a full-page magazine advertisement: It was the direct mail equivalent of a headline and an illustration. And if you left it blank, you were doing the equivalent of leaving the top half of an advertising page blank, occupied by mere white space.

In fact, I decided, envelopes were tremendously important in direct mail—perhaps the most important element in the entire package!

The Persian Poet envelope, with its baronial format was not just a package; it conveyed a subtle hint that a *personal* message was inside. I needed an envelope that would convey this message, but not quite so subtly. I needed something that would look *important*.

There existed, at the time, two kinds of direct mail envelopes that *did* stand out in any mail box—and *did* look important. These were government checks and electric power company bills. Both came in brown Kraft envelopes. Oddly enough, when I looked around, I saw no one else using this kind of envelope. So I decided to clothe the Persian Poet in Kraft, rather than a baronial enclosure. Not much of a change—but at the time, it was considered exceedingly daring. It immediately made my mailing stand out and look important. There was a Pavlovian "conditioned reflex" reaction on the part of the recipients. They knew that important mail came in Kraft envelopes. Therefore, this mailing had to be important.

Then there was a further element that I felt my mailing needed: a way to *dramatize* my offer, to present the offer with some kind of action-inducing device, what Frank and I called "a hot potato."

Now, what made *my* offer different from previous *Digest* mailings was the fact that it was "bill-me-later." And, as this was a *billed* approach, I reasoned that there was no need for a business reply envelope, which had been provided in previous mailings so that the customer could mail back a dollar. So, instead, I designed a reply *card*—actually making it *difficult* for the customer to mail back money, but making it much *easier* to send in a bill-me-later order.

At that time, first class postage on a postcard cost one cent—$10 per 1000 postcards.

As a fairly new member of the *Digest* promotion team, I was still in the process of learning what makes people respond to mailings, and what doesn't. Ideas came, of course, from other members of the department; we had a veritable factory for turning out new promotion ideas. Les Dawson, the Circulation Promotion Manager, was using all kinds of ingenious devices to renew subscribers and to get gift subscriptions from them. One device which he used, with great effect, was the enclosure of a postage stamp for the customer to paste on the reply envelope and mail back the renewal. This little action-getting device vastly increased returns.

In looking over competitive direct mail, I saw one other mail-order outfit which was pioneering brilliant, different looking and sounding direct mail. This was Time Inc. Their mailings often had a distinctive touch. I was particularly impressed by a *LIFE* billing effort which—like Les Dawson's renewals—enclosed a stamp. The accompanying letter said something like "Jones of Binghamton— he pays the freight!" and went on to explain that this was the slogan of a successful furniture manufacturer who did business by freight and paid the delivery charges. And "since *LIFE* knows you want to pay the enclosed bill promptly, here's the 'freight' prepaid in anticipation of your payment—a postage stamp, to convey your payment back to *LIFE*." The letter was signed by Roy Larsen, *LIFE's* circulation manager.

The stamp was a "hot potato"—a physical action-getting device.

As far as my bill-me-later *Digest* mailing went, the applicability of a 1¢ stamp was obvious. I was mailing out an order card;

instead of making it a postage-paid *business* reply card, I made it a plain reply card, and enclosed a 1¢ stamp for the customer to paste on the card, to get attention and get action.

Naturally, I tested everything: the offer, the list, the action device format. Everything clicked, and returns immediately went up from about 3½ percent to 7½ percent. The following January (this was 1950) I mailed out 20 million letters and slept soundly, knowing that results would be sensational.

We had projected a 5 percent response—one million subscriptions—which was the most that we could possibly have gotten on a cash-with-order offer. Instead, 1.5 million orders came in. And I knew that 1,440,000 of those customer would pay for their subscriptions.

I had increased response, from a previous 3½ percent, to 7½ percent. I had turned the downward tide of *Digest* mailing returns. And I was a hero! This was, indeed, the turning point at which the *Digest* was able to move up from 5 million readers to 10 million, 12 million and before I left, to 13.5 million. It was also the turning point which enabled the *Reader's Digest* to expand from a business with a worldwide sale of $18 million, to one with a worldwide sale of well over $1 billion.

But also, while I was celebrating, there arrived a letter from the Postmaster in St. Louis.

"The Book," he said—referring to the Post Office Manual—"specifies (in Section 131.217) that, according to the rules effective January 1, 1943, a first class postcard must have a maximum size of 3⁹/₁₆ × 5⁹/₁₆." I have measured the *Digest* order card and it is 3½ × 5¹⁰/₁₆." Therefore it is oversize by one-sixteenth of an inch in one dimension and is therefore illegal. Accordingly, the Post Office at Pleasantville must charge one cent *extra* for oversized mail, plus one cent postage due, a total of two cents on each *Digest* reply card they receive."

On 1.5 million cards, this amounted to $30,000. I had made a mistake—a very sizable mistake—on my very first major subscriber mailing for the *Digest*. This official size restriction of the Post Office, on penny postcards, was all news to me. As a matter of fact, I was ignorant of the very existence of the Post Office

Manual—"the Book." I had ordered a card that fitted the standard outside envelope, and nobody told me a postmaster in St. Louis would take the trouble to measure the card.

The Pleasantville postmaster informed me, with due regret, that there was no way out of my difficulty. The St. Louis postmaster had sent a copy of his letter to the Washington Post Office's Department of Classifications, and they would insist on compliance.

I did not mention my problem to Mr. Herbert or Mr. Cole. Instead, I got on an airplane and headed for Washington. I made my way to the office of Ed Riley, the head of the Post Office Department of Classifications, and I told him my tale of woe.

"I am a young man," I said, "and this is my first, big outside mailing for the *Digest*. I didn't know there was any size restriction on postcards, down to the sixteenth of an inch. I thought I was complying. Thirty thousand dollars is a lot of money to the *Digest*, and I will lose my job for this mistake. Isn't there anything you can do?"

Ed Riley expressed regrets. He got out the big, black Post Office Manual and read me the applicable rule. "There's nothing we can do about it," he said. "We can't make exceptions to the rules. You should have been more careful."

"Well, there goes my job," I said.

Riley reflected. Then he said: "Tell you what. Mr. Wenzel used to be head of the Department of Classifications, before me. He retired several years ago, after 50 years or so of service, and the Post Office has kept him on as a consultant. In the past 50 years, he has solved every Post Office mailing classification problem that ever came up. We can ask him if he sees any way out of your dilemma."

So he summoned Mr. Wenzel—a pleasant, little, white-haired man with a handsome white moustache. I shall never forget Mr. Wenzel.

"This young man has made a stupid mistake that is going to cost him his job," Ed said. "He sent out 20 million of these first class postcards without checking their size against Post Office classification regulations. The card is oversize. Now the *Digest* has to pay $30,000 in oversize postage due because of this stupid mistake. But the Book is specific about sizes, and I don't see anything we can do about it, do you?"

Mr. Wenzel took the sample card that Ed Riley handed him, glanced at it and shrugged.

"I don't see anything wrong with it," he said. "We simply reclassify the card as a third class postcard instead of a first class postcard. Third class can be bigger, and rides for one cent. The Book says third class must not have any personal messages on it— no handwriting. This card has only the customer's address printed on it—no personal messages, the customer doesn't even have to sign it, so it's third class mail and it rides for a penny."

"I guess your troubles are over," said Riley.

"Oh thank you, thank you, Mr. Wenzel," I said. "But would you mind putting that in writing so that I can show it to the postmaster in Pleasantville?"

"No, I don't think so," said Mr. Wenzel. "No need to clutter up your files. You just go back to Pleasantville and tell the postmaster I said it's all right, your card is third class and rides for one cent. If he raises any objections, tell him to call me. But if he does, tell him he should bill *Reader's Digest* for the cost of the phone call!"

I went back to Pleasantville to bask in the plaudits of my superiors for a job well-done. And I didn't mention my little first class/ third class contretemps to Mr. Herbert or Mr. Cole.

However, my troubles with that first promotional mailing were still far from over. I got in the 1.5 million orders and, as expected, I got 1.44 million payments. True, I had 60,000 "bad debts" to write off, but I'd already anticipated this. I sent these 60,000 people pleasant, low-key collection letters with results no better than expected. I was satisfied that 60,000 bad debts was a small price to pay for 440,000 extra paid subs, secured at no extra cost.

But, somehow, these bad debts came to Mr. Wallace's attention—and drew down his fury. Before me, of course, there had never been any problems with bad payments or bad debts, since everything had been on a cash-with-order basis.

"You mean to say we have 60,000 people who didn't pay us for their subscriptions?" Wally demanded of Mr. Cole. "Sixty thousand! That's outrageous. Something should be done about it!"

"Do something!" Mr. Cole said to me.

So I did something. I wrote the toughest series of collection letters that ever came out of a copywriter's typewriter.

I began, casually enough, with Letter No. 1, which merely asked, politely, for payment. It was signed with my alias, Carolyn Davis. Then I sent out Letter No. 2—a Friendly Reminder—from the Head of the Subscription Department. Next came Letter No. 3, from the Accounting Department—slightly puzzled, a little hurt, but businesslike, firm. Letter No. 4 came from the Treasurer, a huffy financial fellow, who took off the gloves, and demanded immediate payment or suitable action would be taken. Letter No. 5 was the Last Chance: Pay up, or else we'll do something dreadful. I inferred our lawyers would get into the act. Indeed, this came from the corporate lawyer.

Letter No. 6 got more specific. A dollar is a small sum, I said, but your credit is at stake. If you don't pay up, I'll expose you as a bad debt. I'll put your name on a list of "deadbeats" and make that list available to other mail-order companies from whom you might try to buy things on credit. In effect, I'll ruin your credit standing.

This series was sent out at one-month intervals. It was effective, particularly the last letter. I got lots of squawks, but lots of payments, too. Evidently, people were afraid of being exposed as deadbeats. And I was able to report to Mr. Wallace that the nonpayment rate on credit subs had taken a drastic downturn. Things seemed to have quieted down.

Then, one day, I received a call from the receptionist.

"Mr. Weintz," she said, "there's a man here who wants to see you. He has a little leather wallet with a big silver star attached to it, and he says he's an Inspector from the Post Office."

"Send him up," I said. As one of the Post Office's biggest customers, I wasn't afraid of Postal Inspectors.

We introduced ourselves, and the Inspector opened fire.

"Mr. Weintz, do you know the legal definition of extortion?"

"No," I said. "What is it?"

"To obtain money from somebody by threat of exposure. It doesn't matter if the exposure you threaten happens to be for a wrong-doing. Extortion is threatening to expose if you don't get paid. Do you realize that you are guilty of extortion with these collection letters you have been sending out?"

And he laid a copy of Letter No. 6 on my desk.

"Also," he said, "you have been using the U.S. Mails for extortion; and that is a Federal offense. The Post Office takes a very serious view of extortion. Extortionists usually end up in Leavenworth."

"Good gosh," I said. "I didn't know. What can I do about it?"

"Well, for one thing, stop sending out these letters. They could get you in deep trouble. And tell me in writing that you are not going to send out any more letters, so that I can report back to Washington."

"Sir," I said, "I will certainly do that. And thank you very much."

"By the way," he added. "We're having a convention of Postal Inspectors in Albany next month. Would the *Reader's Digest* be interested in running a complimentary ad in our Convention Program? We'd certainly like to have you on our list of friends."

"How much would such an ad cost?"

"Five hundred dollars."

"You sit right there," I said. "I'll be right back. How do you want the check made out?"

I scuttled into the Treasurer's office.

"Give me a check for $500 quick," I said. "Make it out to 'Post Office Convention Program,' and don't ask any questions."

I took the check back to the Inspector, we shook hands, and I didn't go to Leavenworth. But thereafter I tried (although not always successfully) to comply with the rules in "the Book."

I have one more footnote on that troublesome first *Digest* promotion mailing of mine. Some years before I put the mailing out, Mr. and Mrs. Wallace (with the help of Al and Frank) had become so successful and well-to-do that they had moved their offices from Pen Dudley's garage apartment in Pleasantville to a magnificent new Georgian brick building which they had constructed in a nearby town with the unpronounceable, unspellable, name of Chappaqua.

However, recognizing that "Pleasantville" was a much more

suitable mailing address for *Reader's Digest*, management had elected to keep the Pleasantville address—which was all right with the Pleasantville Post Office. There remained the problem of picking up the mail, so arrangements were made with a local farmer, who owned a pick-up truck, to meet the trains, pick up the bags of *Digest* mail, and deliver them to our fulfillment department. All well and good, the system worked for a time . . . but then, one year, when a big January mailing went out, complaints started trickling in.

"I sent you a dollar for my subscription," the complaint letters said. "Where's my subscription?"

The complaints swelled to a chorus; something was obviously amiss. The *Digest* notified the Post Office, who put an Inspector on a train. He watched the farmer pick up two bags of *Digest* mail—and deliver only one bag at the *Digest* Receiving Department.

In the farmer's back yard, the Inspector found remnants of half-burned post office mail bags, and charred remnants of many, many *Digest* new subscription orders. And, although they found no dollar bills, the farmer went off for a stay in Leavenworth, and the *Digest* got its own delivery van to pick up and deliver the mail.

It appears that the farmer was then confined in a cell in Leavenworth which he shared with a very professional hood from New York City. They exchanged experiences, as cellmates do.

"If you really want to make it big," said the farmer, "after you get out, go stick up the *Digest* delivery truck on Monday of the second week in January. You'll find it loaded with one million dollars or so in nontraceable one dollar bills. A single heist will set you up for a million bucks!"

The professional eventually got out of jail. He enlisted a couple of friends. They cased the *Reader's Digest* delivery system carefully and timed their hold-up to perfection. With faces covered by Halloween masks, they stepped out of a patch of woods beside the *Digest's* private drive one Monday morning in January, stopped the van, shot and killed the driver, tied up his companion, drove the van to a rendevous with their getaway car, and hurried back to an apartment in New York City, where they gleefully opened the heavy sacks of mail.

But of course, there were no dollar bills, and no million dollars. In fact, there was nothing except thousands of orange order cards, which said "Please enter my subscription to *Reader's Digest* for six months and bill me for one dollar." They were examining my first returns on my first big "bill-me-later" mailing.

The New York State Police spent months investigating the case and tracking down the perpetrators. Eventually they caught them and hauled them into court accused of murder.

The bit of evidence that tied the knot in their conviction was a small triangle of orange paper—a fragment of the order form from my mailing. It had been found lodged in the lining of an empty suitcase in one of the criminal's closets. The card had a few type characters on it—part of my sales message. The printer testified that this type could only have come from the particular mailing I'd put out. I was unaware, until then, of the fact that linotype printing is like human fingerprints—no two lines of type set by linotype are spread and aligned exactly alike—and under the microscope this piece of paper convincingly identified itself as part of my order form.

One of the criminals was let off with a life sentence, for turning state's evidence. The other two were electrocuted. This was in 1950. They were the last criminals, up to the time of this writing, to be executed in New York State.

I've told the story of my first big *Reader's Digest* mailing in considerable detail here because it illustrates just about every principle and every technique that's involved in making a successful mail order mailing. These elements are as follows:

1. A good mail order *product* with wide consumer appeal (*Reader's Digest*).
2. A very large mailing list (60 million names) of likely prospects.
3. A dramatic, appealing *offer*: 8 months for a *dollar* . . . half price . . . and (most importantly) "bill me later".
4. An attention-getting *envelope* (the Kraft envelope *looked* important).
5. An action-getting "hot potato" device: the one cent postage

stamp (worth only a penny if you don't use it—but worth a dollar if you use it to mail back the order card).

6. An easy-to-order form. No need to make any choices. No need even to sign your name. Just stamp and mail it back.

7. The "rule of three"—one-third of your product price goes for product cost, one-third goes for promotional cost (your mailings), and one-third goes for overhead and profits—was clearly violated by the early *Digest* mailings. The product price was $1; the cost-per-sale, on a mailing that cost $50 per thousand letters and brought in 75 $1 orders, was 66¢ per order (two-thirds the product price, instead of one-third); and the product cost—15¢ per copy, times 8 issues, or $1.20—would appear to have been substantially out of line. We got away with it because our "product" was actually not an eight-month subscription, but (with reselling renewals and gifts) in effect, over a period of five years (and particularly after we started selling books and records) more like a $25 or $30 sale.

7

Putting it All Together

*How the National Republican Party's Winning
Fund-Raising Program was Built*

Once the basic principles and techniques of mail-order promotion
are understood, they can be applied in the most unlikely places,
and for unexpected products. Although my own initial mail-order
experience happened to do with magazines and books, the same
rules would have applied had I been working on a correspon-
dence course in accounting, the mail-order sale of Christmas hams
or Chesapeake crabmeat, securing leads for Ford cars, or, indeed,
getting political candidates elected or fund raising for a political
organization like the Republican National Committee.

As it happens, I discovered through personal experience how
effectively mail-order procedures can be applied to politics. So, in
this chapter I'll go through the story of the development of the
National Republican Party's elective and fund raising program,
which I helped develop and execute. I believe that the procedures
we set up for the Republicans can be applied to any good mail-
order product. What amazes and amuses me is that, with the

Republicans' mail-order success story right under their noses—a success story which began in 1950—the Democrats still (in 1987) haven't really applied the same principles to raise money and elect their candidates.

To the best of my knowledge, the Republicans started using direct mail on a scientific, mass basis back in 1950. At that time, Senator Robert Taft was running in a desperate race for re-election.

The big unions had announced that they had earmarked a war chest of several million dollars for a campaign in Ohio to defeat Taft, because he was coauthor of the Taft–Hartley Act, which gives the Federal Government the power to halt strikes that hurt the interests of the nation. At the time, the Taft–Hartley Act was a tremendous political issue. The big unions considered the Act an outright attempt to kill unionism in America, and Robert Taft their mortal enemy. They believed they had to get rid of him!

In those days, *Reader's Digest* had well-established conservative leanings, and the *Digest* had published articles on certain conservative issues by Senator Taft. Senator Taft was a friend of DeWitt Wallace and Al Cole.

So the *Digest* volunteered my services to do a direct mail campaign to help get Senator Taft re-elected.

Senator Taft was convinced that he should take his stand on the Taft–Hartley Law, and, of course, we tried to talk him out of that, because we knew that blue collar workers would be against him on the basis of the Taft–Hartley Act.

But Senator Taft argued that the big issue of his campaign was, obviously, the Taft–Hartley Act—and therefore he had to stand or fall on the merits of that Act. So we had to do a mailing, he said, built around the benefits of the Act for the ordinary working man.

Fortunately, in direct mail you are able to test almost anything, including political appeals. We mailed out, as I recall, several different letters, each one putting forward a different central idea on why the recipient of the letter should support Senator Taft.

We needed some way to measure the effect of our different appeals, so in each mailing we included a "contribution card," keyed to the letter it went with. That is, we put an inconspicuous letter of the alphabet in a corner of each card: A, B, C, and so on—depending upon which letter the card originally went out with. In each case we said "Send us some money to help re-elect

Senator Taft." When contributions came in—each with a keyed card—we were able to count returns from each letter and tell which pulled the best.

We sent out about 20,000 copies of each letter. I was astounded when the letter (written by Senator Taft), which was built around a positive presentation of the Taft–Hartley Act, was far and away the most successful.

We subsequently mailed hundreds of thousands of Taft–Hartley letters into the blue collar worker sections of the industrial cities of Ohio: Cincinnati, Cleveland, Akron, and so on. The blue collar workers responded by voting overwhelmingly for Taft against the urging, advice, and $3 million campaign fund of their union leaders.

In addition, much to our surprise, we received a substantial number of small contributions, which helped us finance the direct mail campaign. Indeed, the campaign paid for itself!

Subsequently, in 1952, when Taft and Eisenhower were rivals for the Presidential nomination, I was a Taft partisan because of my previous experience working for Senator Taft. I was very disappointed when Eisenhower got the nomination.

A few days later, Mr. Cole called me into his office and said, "How would you like to take a leave of absence and run the direct mail campaign for Citizens for Eisenhower–Nixon?"

"I wouldn't like that," I said.

"Good, I knew you would," Mr. Cole answered. "I told them you'd be down there this afternoon."

So in 1952 I went to work for the Citizens for Eisenhower–Nixon, and I might add, I quickly became an enthusiastic supporter of General Eisenhower.

We decided that the experience we had had on the Taft campaign gave us a beautiful model for doing direct mail on behalf of Eisenhower and Nixon.

At the start of Eisenhower's campaign, he didn't have a clear-cut political theme, and he was burdened with all kinds of conflicting advice from well-meaning, self-appointed experts.

The politicians who surrounded him implored him not to say anything, it being their philosophy that campaigns are won by not taking a stand on anything. They suggested his theme should simply be, "It's time for a change."

Others were incensed over the "deep freeze" and "fur coat" scandals which had plagued the Truman Administration. In the latter days of President Truman's Administration, various accusations about political graft involving some prominent Democrats had surfaced, and our Republican political advisors suggested that a simple, dignified phrase like, "Throw the rascals out" would make a good mail-order theme that would hit home.

And, of course, the war in Korea was much on everybody's mind.

Al Cole asked me to write 10 letters, each based on a different campaign appeal.

With these letters, we reasoned, we could test different campaign appeals and find out exactly what issues really did arouse the voters. Were they really upset over corruption in Washington? Was it inflation and the high cost of living that troubled them most, or government regulation (a favorite Republican issue, even in those days)? We would ask for money, just as we had in the Taft campaign, to check the relative effectiveness of various appeals. We would then mail millions of letters, using the most successful appeals, and the mailing would be at least partially self-financing, because it would pull for contributions.

The letters, besides making money, would reach millions of people, with strong arguments in favor of Eisenhower and Nixon. Most importantly, we would then have hundreds of thousands of small contributors who had "bet on a horse"—given small sums ranging from a dollar up to $25 or so to support Eisenhower's campaign.

We reasoned that anyone who contributed money for a candidate would be much more likely to go out and vote for that candidate on election day.

We sent out an initial test of 10,000 of each of 10 letters, and in each case we said, "If you would like to see Eisenhower elected President, please send back the enclosed contribution card, together with your contribution and your name and address."

The cards were keyed, so we were able to count results.

Here are samples of the first pages of five of the letters, with some comments on each, which will help to explain why we did what we did, and why we did it that way.

LETTER NO. 1

WILL *YOU* VOTE FOR MORE WASTE AND CONFUSION IN WASHINGTON?

Dear VOTER:

Before the Democrats took over, *you* were helping to pay for almost 600,000 Federal employees. *Today YOU are taxed to meet a payroll of 2,600,000 Federal "workers."* (The payroll is TEN BILLION DOLLARS in 1952!)

That's costing *you* money in direct payroll deductions for taxes—and in hidden taxes on everything *you* buy. (151 hidden taxes on a single loaf of bread, 116 taxes on a man's suit, 100 taxes on an EGG, 206 taxes on a car, 11½¢ taxes on one pack of cigarettes!)

But the big ten billion payroll is just a start—because waste and confusion are costing *you* as a taxpayer, *tens of billions of dollars a year.*

YOU helped pay for the latest scandal to come out of Washington—the $455 million which was mostly WASTED in N. Africa building air bases that collapsed as soon as they were built! ("Mass loafing and drunkenness" blamed.)

YOU helped pay for the confusion caused by Truman's seizure of the nationwide steel industry, without Constitutional power, without Congressional law—on the assumption that HE has the power to do whatever he likes to *our* lives, *our property, our jobs!* The extension of the steel strike by Truman's illegal operation is estimated to have set America's war production back *ONE FULL YEAR.*

SURPLUS DEALS have cost us *more billions.* For instance, WAA sold 5,443 planes

(*continued*)

for $2,780,000. The buyer then discovered
he had 5,481 planes—the WAA had forgotten to count them! So—the WAA let him
keep the extras as a "premium!"

(More waste!)

Then, the buyer discovered 3 million
gallons of aviation gas in the planes—
which WAA again let him keep. The gift of
the gas alone was worth $500,000!

(Confusion!)

In 1949 the Commodity Credit Corporation *lost* $366,643,129. After trying for a
while to find it (under Congressional prod-
ding), the CCC finally simply "deducted" it to
bring their books in balance! To this day,
nobody knows what became of the money!

(Government inefficiency!)

This same CCC in twenty months paid
storage charges *in excess of* $382,000 for
grain storage IN GOVERNMENT buildings—
which were leased by a private company
from another branch of the government for
only $11,270! (Profit to the private com-
pany: $370,000 on $11,270 invested!) . . .

The letter went on to say: "Help elect Eisenhower and Nixon,
and all this waste, which is hitting you in your pocketbook, will be
curtailed. You have a *personal* reason to help elect Eisenhower. Get
him elected, and you'll gain a very real advantage: lower government costs will translate into lower taxes for *you*. So help us elect
Eisenhower President. Send back the enclosed contribution card
together with $1.00, $5.00, $10.00 . . . whatever you can spare!"

THE THEORY BEHIND LETTER #1

Damning the politicians who have their hands in the public's
pocket has always been a favorite hobby of the American public.

CITIZENS FOR EISENHOWER–NIXON TEST

Testing political themes with mail-order letters—Test No. 1: "Waste and Confusion" letter.

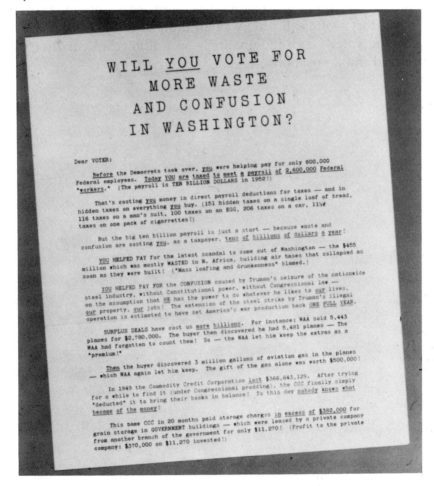

And one of the dictums of political campaigning is that people vote *against* issues rather than *for* them. Give the voter an issue he or she can get riled up about, and you've got a winner!

So in this letter on the issue of "Waste and Corruption," I tried to translate Washington venality into personal symbols the voter could relate to: taxes on a loaf of bread, the cost of a man's suit. I cited some actual examples of huge Federal waste and inefficiency, and I tried to relate these examples to the *personal* interests of the voter.

In theory, this "Waste and Corruption" approach embodied a good, strong, political appeal. The copy was intended to be inflammatory—after all, this was an indignant letter, intended to arouse the voter's own indignation—so I didn't particularly try to soft-pedal my accusations.

LETTER NO. 2

(Another negative
headline, which relates
more directly to the
voter's pocketbook.)

**WILL *YOU* VOTE FOR *HIGHER LIVING
COSTS* FOR *YOUR FAMILY*?**

Dear VOTER:

(A specific example
showing how *your
interests* were hurt by the
Truman administration.)

A basket of groceries that *you* paid $10
for in 1939 costs you $24.29 today—
according to the Government's own statistics!

(Strong language—
intended to arouse voter
ire!)

But that's *just a sample* of what the
Truman gang and their crown prince Adlai
Stevenson plan for you if they're elected!
Here are a few additional samples of "Democratic prosperity"—which will give you an
idea of what's to come if the Truman gang
stays in office!

(Specific examples of the
way the Democrats are
hurting you.)

The Washington Bureaucrats don't publicize it, but *their own figures* show that
people ate *LESS* butter, potatoes, fresh fruit
and bread, consumed LESS milk and high
protein foods in 1951 than in 1932. *YOUR
OWN POCKETBOOK* tells you the reason.
(How many times a week do *YOU* eat
steak?)

(Another *example*, calling
attention to a common
problem.)

The gang that supports Stevenson boasts
that a million new homes will be built this
year. They don't mention that if it weren't
for their postwar inflation, we could build
1,760,000 homes this year for what it now
costs to build a million. (Could *YOU* afford a
new house at today's inflated prices?)

(Specific examples of how
high government costs
were hurting the voter.)

The Democrats don't mention the loss
YOU and other citizens have taken on the
value of *YOUR* life insurance, *your bonds,
your savings, your* social security benefits
. . . the values of which have all been *cut in
half* by inflation under the Democrats!

(continued)

The Democrats *do* talk about the fact that people today have more washing machines, refrigerators, radios, and television sets than they did before the Democrats (as if the Democrats were responsible for this steadily-rising production of private American enterprise)! The Democrats *DON'T* mention that—because of their inflation—nobody can really afford *to pay for* these household necessities today and *individuals owed $20,640,000 million* on such purchases in 1951!

(Bringing the issues down to a personal level!)

Why does everything cost *YOU* so much today?

It's because the dollar is worth *only 52¢* instead of the "$1" that's printed on it. Inflation—caused by crazy government spending, tragic waste, and incredibly high taxes—is turning *YOUR* dollars into *dimes*. And as long as the Democrats are in office, you can be sure that this trend will continue. Stevenson has *promised* to continue Truman's programs, and that means *MORE* high *taxes*, more high living costs for *you* . . .

COMMENTS ON LETTER #2

This letter was another attempt to turn government spending into *personal* disadvantages the voter allegedly suffered under Truman—disadvantages which would continue under Eisenhower's Democratic opponent, Adlai Stevenson. The letter spelled out the familiar Republican anti-big-government theme—and tried to make the voter recognize that the Democratic "big government" hit the voter where it hurt the most—in the pocketbook.

I thought this appeal was one the voter could relate to. It reminded the voter that his or her self-interest was being *hurt* by big government spending. I thought the letter had a good chance of winning.

CITIZENS FOR EISENHOWER–NIXON TEST

Test No. 2: "Higher living costs," which sounded like a sure winner, before we tested it!

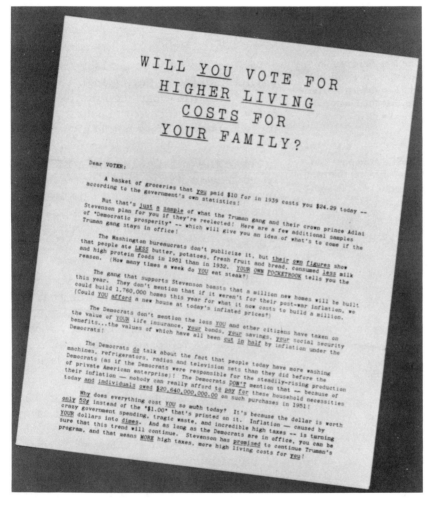

WILL <u>YOU</u> VOTE FOR <u>HIGHER LIVING</u> <u>COSTS</u> FOR <u>YOUR</u> FAMILY?

Dear VOTER:

A basket of groceries that <u>you</u> paid $10 for in 1939 costs you $24.29 today -- according to the government's own statistics!

But that's <u>just a sample</u> of what the Truman gang and their crown prince Adlai Stevenson plan for you if they're reelected! Here are a few additional samples of "Democratic prosperity" -- which will give you an idea of what's to come if the Truman gang stays in office!

The Washington bureaucrats don't publicize it, but <u>their own figures</u> show that people ate <u>LESS</u> butter, potatoes, fresh fruit and bread, consumed <u>less</u> milk and high protein foods in 1951 than in 1932. <u>YOUR OWN POCKETBOOK</u> tells you the reason. (How many times a week do <u>YOU</u> eat steak?)

The gang that supports Stevenson boasts that a million new homes will be built this year. They don't mention that if it weren't for their post-war inflation, we could build 1,760,000 homes this year for what it now costs to build a million. (Could <u>YOU</u> afford a new house at today's inflated prices?)

The Democrats don't mention the loss <u>YOU</u> and other citizens have taken on the value of <u>YOUR</u> life insurance, <u>your</u> bonds, <u>your</u> savings, <u>your</u> social security benefits...the values of which have all been <u>cut in half</u> by inflation under the Democrats!

The Democrats <u>do</u> talk about the fact that people today have more washing machines, refrigerators, radios and television sets than they did before the Democrats (as if the Democrats were responsible for the steadily-rising production of private American enterprise)! The Democrats <u>DON'T</u> mention that -- because of their inflation -- nobody can really afford to <u>pay for</u> these household necessities today <u>and individuals owed $20,640,000,000.00</u> on such purchases in 1951!

Why does everything cost <u>YOU</u> so much today? It's because the dollar is worth only 52¢ instead of the "$1.00" that's printed on it. Inflation -- caused by crazy government spending, tragic waste, and incredible high taxes -- is turning <u>YOUR</u> dollars into <u>dimes</u>. And as long as the Democrats are in office, you can be sure that this trend will continue. Stevenson has <u>promised</u> to continue Truman's program, and that means <u>MORE</u> high taxes, more high living costs for <u>you</u>!

LETTER NO. 3

(An appeal to self-interest—tied to a prevailing widespread impression that Washington politicians were stealing money from *you*!)

(The idea here was to capitalize on a widely held Republican impression that the Democrats were venal.)

(Specific examples intended to get the reader aroused to take action!)

WILL *YOU* VOTE TO HAVE MORE OF *YOUR MONEY* STOLEN BY THE CORRUPT GANG IN WASHINGTON?

Dear Fellow VOTER:

YOU are doing your part for America— paying high taxes, paying high prices, and seeing *your* American men drafted. Isn't every decent family in the country carrying its fair share of these burdens?

Yet in the midst of these sacrifices, *corruption in Washington has reached the proportions of an epidemic!* The cronies and crooks in high government jobs have been feathering their nests—with *your* money! To cite *just a few examples*—

—White House Stenographer, Mrs. Merl Young, received a $9,540 mink coat "gift." White House General Harry Vaughan and White House aide Matt Connelly received $390 and $520 deep freeze "gifts" from favor-getters and influence-peddlers . . .

—166 Tax Collectors were fired in 1951 after Congressional investigation revealed nation-wide hook-up between big-time crooks and grafting collectors. Revenue Commissioner Dan Bolich living on $62,000 more income than he reported; Commissioner Noonan exposed $176,000 unexplained income; Commissioner Finnegan, Collector Malone, Collector Delaney, Collector Schofield, Collector Downing, Collector Smyth, Chief Counsel Oliphant, Asst. Attorney General T. Lamar Caudle, Collector Herslee, Collector Marcelle, Collectors Johnson, Schoeneman, Olson, "Clean-Up" Chief Newbold Morris, and Attorney General McGrath all resign ("for

ill health"), are fired, or indicted, or
convicted!

—$455 *MILLION* was mostly wasted
through "large-scale loafing, drunkenness,"
plus "widespread frauds" in North African
air bases that collapsed as soon as built!

Kefauver (the only Democrat who fought
for honesty in government) uncovered a
national hook-up between crime syndicate
and government. Kefauver was rewarded by
being "ganged" by the big city bosses, and
defeated at the Democratic convention
(while O'Dwyer, when a grand jury became
interested in questioning him about his
connection with Moran and Costello, was
rewarded by an Ambassadorship to Mexico!)
. . .

COMMENTS ON LETTER #3

The Republican professionals were all convinced that the public
felt strongly about certain alleged Democratic scandals that were
getting a certain amount of publicity at the time. Their "scandals"
involved some embarrassing gifts, of fur coats and deep freezes,
which were unwisely accepted by some of President Truman's
staff; the gifts came from interested parties who needed Federal
help to feather their own nests, and were willing to pay for such
help. I was told that "corruption in government" was a burning
issue, so in this letter I tried to make it a burning issue.

The letter concluded, as did the others, with an appeal for a
contribution to help elect Eisenhower and Nixon. The phraseology
of this appeal was identical in all 10 of the letters.

CITIZENS FOR EISENHOWER–NIXON TEST

Test No. 3: "Corruption in government"—a favorite political theme for the out-of-power party.

WILL <u>YOU</u> VOTE TO HAVE
MORE OF <u>YOUR</u> <u>MONEY</u>
STOLEN
BY THE CORRUPT GANG
IN WASHINGTON?

Dear Fellow VOTER:

<u>YOU</u> are doing your part for America -- paying high taxes, paying high prices, and seeing <u>your</u> American men drafted. Isn't every decent family in the country carrying its fair share of these burdens?

Yet in the midst of these sacrifices, <u>corruption in Washington has reached the proportions of an epidemic</u>! The cronies and crooks in high government jobs have been feathering their nests -- with <u>your</u> money! To cite <u>just a few</u> examples --

-- White House Stenographer Mrs. Merl Young received a $9,540 mink coat "gift," White House General Harry Vaughan, White House aide Matt Connelly, received $390 to $520 deep freeze "gifts" from favor-getters and influence peddlers...

166 Tax Collectors were fired in 1951 after Congressional investigation revealed nation-wide hook-up between big-time crooks and grafting collectors. Revenue Commissioner Dan Bolich living on $62,000 more income than he reported; Commissioner Nunan exposed for $176,000 unexplained income; Commissioner Finnegan, Collector Malone, Collector Delaney, Collector Schofield, Collector Downing, Collector Smyth, Chief Counsel Oliphant, Asst. Attorney General T. Lamar Caudle, Collector Herslee, Collector Marcelle, Collectors Johnson, Schoeneman, and Olson, "Clean-Up" Chief Newbold Morris, and Attny. General McGrath all resign ("for ill health") or are fired or indicted or convicted!

-- $455 <u>MILLION</u> was mostly wasted through "large-scale loafing, drunkenness," plus "widespread frauds" in N. African air bases that collapsed as soon as built!

Kefauver (the only Democrat who fought for honesty in government) uncovered national hook-up between crime syndicate and government. Kefauver was rewarded by being "ganged" by the big city bosses, and defeated at the Democratic convention (while O'Dwyer, when a grand jury became interested in questioning him about his connections with Moran and Costello, was rewarded by an Ambassadorship to Mexico)!

LETTER NO. 4

(continued)

(The classic political flag-waver!)

IT'S TIME FOR A CHANGE! WILL YOU VOTE FOR "ONE NEW FACE"—OR A TOP-TO-BOTTOM HOUSE CLEANING?

Dear Fellow VOTER:

(An attempt to "show an advantage" with a call for action.)

When the political gang in Washington rakes off $30.00 out of every $100 earned by every person in this country—working men, farmers, and office workers (and *that* includes *YOU*)—THE PEOPLE KNOW IT'S TIME FOR A CHANGE!

(Bringing the argument down to a *personal* level.)

(Perhaps you didn't realize it, but *YOU* "pay off" the present administration through hidden taxes on everything you buy, through direct payroll deductions and other forms of income taxes, to the tune of $300 out of every $1,000 you earn. Couldn't YOU use that $300?)

(Specific examples of *Democratic* venality—aimed at arousing Republican indignation.)

When that same political gang conspires with gamblers, gangsters, and big-time crooks to help them avoid their taxes and leave *YOU* to pay their rightful share—THE PEOPLE KNOW IT'S TIME FOR A CHANGE!

(You know that 166 collectors of internal revenue recently "resigned" or were fired, while six others were caught and indicted for taking bribes and cheating the government out of hundreds of thousands of dollars in taxes. Is it possible that these "little" chislers and crooks who finally got caught could have gotten away with such wholesale stealing so long without their bosses knowing? And yet Truman says "he knows of no mess in his administration!")

When America wins the greatest war in history—and then for seven long years is pushed around by a second-rate nation of Communists . . .

(continued)

> When over 116,000 American men (*your*
> friends, *your* neighbors, *your* sons) pay with
> their blood for the stupid blunders that created
> Korea . . . THE PEOPLE KNOW IT'S TIME
> FOR A CHANGE! . . .

COMMENTS ON LETTER #4

I personally didn't have much confidence in the appeal I tried to
set forth in this letter. But it was an appeal that all the professionals were very fond of. "Don't promise anything—just keep ham-
mering away on the theme of "throw the rascals out!" So went the
prevailing philosophy among politicians who were supposed to
know. So we tested it in a letter, which did its best to relate
political chicanery (imputed to the Democrats) with resulting in-
conveniences and problems suffered by ordinary citizens.

CITIZENS FOR EISENHOWER–NIXON TEST

Test No. 4: The classic political theme: "It's time for a change—throw the rascals out!"

IT'S TIME FOR
A CHANGE!

WILL YOU VOTE FOR
"ONE NEW FACE"--
OR A TOP-TO-BOTTOM
HOUSE CLEANING?

Dear Fellow VOTER:

When the political gang in Washington rakes off $30.00 out of every $100 earned by every person in this country -- working men, farmers and office workers (and that includes YOU) -- THE PEOPLE KNOW IT'S TIME FOR A CHANGE!

(Perhaps you didn't realize it, but YOU "pay off" the present administration, through hidden taxes on everything you buy, through direct payroll deductions and other forms of income taxes, to the tune of $300 out of every $1000 you earn. Couldn't YOU use that $300?)

When that same political gang conspires with gamblers, gangsters and big-time crooks to help them avoid their taxes and leave YOU to pay their rightful share -- THE PEOPLE KNOW IT'S TIME FOR A CHANGE!

(You know that 166 collectors of internal revenue recently "resigned" or were fired, while 6 others were caught and indicted for taking bribes and cheating the government out of hundreds of thousands of dollars in taxes. Is it possible that these "little" chiselers and crooks who finally got caught could have gotten away with such wholesale stealing so long without their bosses' knowledge? And yet Truman says "he knows of no mess in his administration!")

When America wins the greatest war in history -- and then for seven long years is pushed around by a second-rate nation of Communists...

...When over 116,000 American men (your friends, your neighbors, your sons) pay with their blood for the stupid blunders that created Korea...THE PEOPLE KNOW IT'S TIME FOR A CHANGE!

LETTER NO. 5

(The "Personal Advantage" is not strongly presented in this headliner—but the *issue* is.)

(America was deeply involved in the war in Korea—and the public was getting pretty upset over "coddling the Russians.")

WILL YOU VOTE TO *CONTINUE CODDLING THE RUSSIANS?*

Dear VOTER:

Adlai E. Stevenson says:

"The BIG ISSUE of this election is FOREIGN POLICY."

This big issue will be put up to *YOU* November 4th. Which way *YOU* vote will help decide how your government deals with the Russians for the next four years. (And don't forget, what your government does will probably determine whether or not Stalin's bombs blast *your* home town— with *OUR* stolen atom bomb!)

SO LET'S TAKE A CLOSE, CAREFUL LOOK AT THE PROGRAMS OFFERED BY EACH SIDE!

The first words Stevenson spoke when the big city bosses and the Truman gang hand-picked him as "crown prince" were:

"I ACCEPT YOUR NOMINATION—AND YOUR *PROGRAM*."

Stevenson has backed up his pledge by coming out flatly in favor of *continuing Acheson's foreign policy.* He has defended Acheson, attacked Eisenhower's program.

All right, then—what *IS* the policy Stevenson "accepts?"

Seven brief years ago America emerged victorious and unchallenged from World War II—the greatest power in history.

Then our President's secret deal with Russia gave the Communists Poland (nobody asked the Poles how they'd like that) and led to Russia's quick capture of Rumania, Czechoslovakia, East Austria, and East Germany. Half of Europe was thrown to the bear—AS A MATTER OF POLICY . . .

CITIZENS FOR EISENHOWER–NIXON TEST

Test No. 5: "Coddling the Russians" (the winning letter in the Eisenhower–Nixon campaign.)

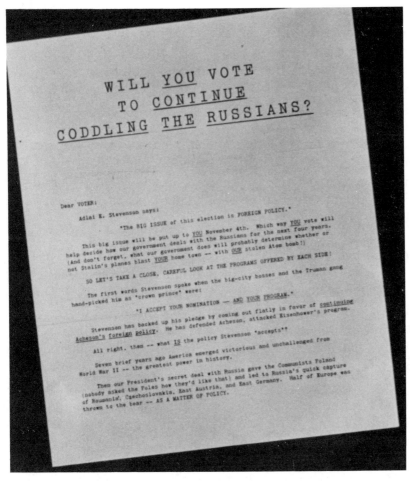

COMMENTS ON LETTER #5

This letter—which concentrated on foreign policy—would seem, on the face of it, to relate less directly to the voters' strong personal interests and problems than did some of the other letters. They concentrated on high taxes, inflation, big government interfering with the little voter's rights and privileges, and government waste dipping into the voter's pocketbook. In reviewing the 10 letters we put out, I did not particularly expect this letter to be the big winner. But that's what testing is all about; it replaces guesses with *facts*!

Nine out of the 10 letters pulled almost exactly the same. The tenth letter, "Coddling the Russians," which talked about Korea, and the seemingly never-ending war in which America had gotten embroiled, pulled about 2½ times as well as any of the other letters.

It was a striking, clear-cut proof that the war in Korea outweighed every other political appeal Eisenhower could make.

The results were so conclusive that we put together a report, and Walter Williams, Chairman of the Citizens for Eisenhower–Nixon Committee, got on a plane and hurried out west, where Eisenhower was campaigning, and showed him these results. A few days later, Eisenhower made his famous "I shall go to Korea" speech, and suddenly his campaign was off and running.

I can't say that it was the direct mail results alone which convinced Eisenhower that Korea was the important issue, but Walter Williams told me that it was decisive in helping Eisenhower make up his mind. Certainly, the tests proved overwhelmingly that the war in Korea was the most important issue in the public's mind.

Sidney Weinberg was the financial manager of the Citizens for the Eisenhower–Nixon campaign, and when I told him that a big mailing would pull the same percentage of returns as did the original test, he was full of suspicion. Sidney was a Vice President and partner of Goldman, Sachs, and he was accustomed to financial projections that were based on 100-page business analyses—not a skimpy page of mailing test results. The whole thing smelled like Madison Avenue flim-flam to Sidney. Very reluctantly, he gave his permission to roll out with a huge, major mailing, but Sidney was prepared for the worst.

Fortunately, the big mailing pulled exactly as the test mailing projected that it would.

We mailed out some 10 million letters based on the Korean issue. And the interesting thing is that, in addition to getting 10 million messages out to voters, we were able to get some 300,000 voters to send us a contribution. These were 300,000 votes that we could pretty well count on.

The contributions were small. They averaged only $5.00 or so. But the $1.5 million that they represented easily paid the cost of our 10 million campaign. Thus, we had harnessed a powerful self-financing force.

And equally important, we had that most precious of all mail order and political properties—a *list* of Eisenhower supporters— people who had voted for Eisenhower with their pocketbooks. We had their names and addresses. We could go back to them again for future contributions, for campaign activities, for vote-getting and voting.

As it turned out, the mailing not only paid for itself, but brought in thousands of dollars over its actual cost. Sidney Weinberg then declared that this raised a moral issue. We had asked for contributions to help elect Eisenhower. Now he was elected, and we had money left over. Therefore we were obligated to refund the excess contributions.

For some time after the election, therefore, Sidney's staff was busy figuring out a *pro rata* refund on every contribution, and making out thousands of refund checks which were sent to our innumerable small contributors. Everyone got a refund, even if it was a check for only 69¢!

This isn't the end of the story, however. Years later, when I came back to working for the Republican Party after a considerable absence, the Party was still getting contributions from those original 1952 contributors! And this was a "secret weapon" which the Republicans had in subsequent elections that the Democrats didn't possess.

The names of our 1952 Citizens for Eisenhower-Nixon contributors were put in a "bank" for future use. In 1956, when Eisenhower and Nixon ran again, we wrote to these same people and asked for additional contributions, and they gave generously.

The contributions were small, and the contributors were certainly not "fat cats." On the contrary, they reminded me of the slogan that is posted in the children's zoo in the Bronx, over the guinea pig colony, "We are small, but we are many."

Together, these small contributors represented a very important part of the Republican fund raising in 1956.

Again in 1960, Spencer Olin, who was then the Finance Chairman of the Republican Party, turned to direct mail to solve his Party's financial problems. In the spring of 1960, the Party was almost literally broke.

Mr. Olin asked me to "put out a letter and raise a million dollars." We still had several hundred thousand contributor names from the original Citizens for Eisenhower mailing. I could have written to these partisans and simply asked for money, and I was sure that such a mailing would pull some contributions. But I decided that the appeal needed some mail order "hooks." So this is the letter that I wrote:

SPENCER T. OLIN
1625 Eye Street N.W.
Washington, D.C.

Chairman

Republican National Finance Committee

Dear Fellow American:

(This is a fund-raising letter. But this first paragraph lowers the reader's guard with news of an interesting upcoming event.)

On January 20th President Eisenhower will complete his seventh year as President of the United States—seven wonderful years of Peace and Prosperity. And on January 27th thousands of grateful Americans will gather for "Dinner with Ike" at some 75 to 100 appreciation dinners to be held across the country from New York to California and from Maine to Texas. The dinners will be linked together through television. The purpose will be two-fold—to pay tribute to a great leader and to provide funds so that we may build for a great Republican victory in 1960.

First, I want to urge you to attend the "Dinner with Ike" if one is held in your area. It will be part of the largest and most inspiring political event in history and the special television program will be one that you will never forget.

However, if you cannot attend one of the dinners, we know that you would like to join in saying "Thank you, Mr. President." To give you this opportunity I am writing you now. Here's how you can participate personally in this great event.

(Personal involvement—through a "hot potato" offer—and an emotional appeal.)

A beautiful "Thank you, Mr. President" book is being prepared for presentation to President Eisenhower. We would like to inscribe your name in this appreciation book as your means of saying "Thank you, Mr. President." Just complete the enclosed

(continued)

card and mail it to me with your contribution. Be sure to print your name clearly so that it may be properly inscribed in the book.

We are also having a specially designed "Eisenhower Appreciation" medal issued in commemoration of the seven wonderful years of Peace and Prosperity. The original, cast in gold, will be presented to President Eisenhower. Replicas of the medal in bronze will be available to be given free as souvenirs to those who attend the "Dinners with Ike" and those whose names are inscribed in the "Thank you, Mr. President" book.

The medals cannot be purchased—and as a memento of one of the greatest events in the history of the Republican Party they will become prized keepsakes. If you would like to have one of these souvenir medals as a participant in the tribute to President Eisenhower just indicate on the enclosed contribution card and we will be glad to send you one free.

(*Not* "Please send us a contribution"—but "here's how to participate in this heartwarming salute to President Eisenhower!")

This will be your last opportunity to join in a nationwide tribute of this kind to President Eisenhower. In January, 1961, a new President of the United States will be inaugurated. We must prepare now for a Republican victory. So complete and mail the enclosed card today. Join with millions of your fellow Americans in saying, "thank you, Mr. President." Do not delay—let us inscribe your name in the "Thank you, Mr. President" book and send you one of the gift souvenir Eisenhower Appreciation medals before the supply is exhausted.

SINCERELY,
S/ SPENCER T. OLIN

The enclosed reply card said:

Mr. Spencer T. Olin, Chairman
Republican National Finance Committee
1625 Eye Street, N.W., Washington 6, D.C.

Please inscribe my name in the "Thank you, Mr. President" book to
be presented to President Eisenhower, and send me my FREE
Eisenhower Peace and Prosperity Commemoration Medal. I enclose
my contribution for the amount checked below.

$10 ...... $15 ...... $20 ...... $25 ...... Other $ ......
Name (please print) ....
Address .... Zone ....
City .... State .... Country ....

Checks should be individual, not corporate, and made payable to
the Republican National Finance Committee. An official receipt will
be sent to you.

We mailed approximately one million letters, and we cleared the
million dollars that Mr. Olin asked for. We were able to do this
because we had amassed a *list* of dependable contributors to
whom we could turn in our hour of need, and because we were
able to make an *emotional* appeal on a very personal basis, which
offered the reader an *opportunity to do something nice and be somebody
important*!

Unfortunately, Spence Olin's tenure as Chairman of the Republican National Committee presently came to an end, and he was
replaced by a new "expert."

This man came from the old "fat cat" school of fund raisers. His
first act on assuming office was to call his staff together and
deliver a challenge.

"The only way to raise money is eyeball-to-eyeball solicitations
of large sums from big donors," he announced. "Direct mail is
wasteful and expensive and only brings in piddling little contributions that are not worth fooling with. If anybody here thinks I'm
wrong and he's right, speak up. No takers? OK—from here on, no
more direct mail."

And that, for the time being, terminated my active relationship as a fund-raiser with the Republican Party.

The following year, I was told, the National Party's expenses exceeded its income by a million dollars. Evidently the fat cats didn't respond properly to eyeball-to-eyeball solicitations.

After 1960, for a number of years I wasn't directly associated with the Republican fund raising. When Goldwater ran for President, Richard Viguerie induced him to execute a massive direct mail campaign which was highly successful. Viguerie secured hundreds of thousands of small contributors, and these names went into a Republican National Finance Committee contributor file. So the idea of continuing Republican financing through small contributors, secured by direct mail, did not perish after my departure.

Then, in 1969, when Jeremiah Milbank, Jr., became Chariman of the Republican Finance Committee, he invited my son Todd Weintz and me—the Weintz Company—to come in and help him set up a systematic procedure for soliciting contributions from previous contributors, and to help him secure new contributors. And this began a new chapter in Republican Party fund-raising.

SUMMING UP: WHAT WE LEARNED FROM THE EARLY REPUBLICAN DIRECT MAIL EFFORTS

There were several important lessons to be learned from our experiences with the tests and mailings for Senator Taft, for General Eisenhower, and for the Republican Party itself in the years while Eisenhower was President.

1. We proved that political *appeals* can be *tested*—just like sales appeals for any other product. And we substituted test results for opinions, in the cases of both Senator Taft and General Eisenhower.

2. We discovered that we could make such tests, and subsequent rollout mailings, self-financing.

3. We had found a way (in the guise of fund-raising) to influence millions of voters, through *self-financing* mail order appeals;

and we had evolved a method of getting many voters to "bet on a horse"—that is, contribute money to a candidate—which made it much more likely that those voters would indeed get out and *vote* for the candidate of their choice.

4. And, finally, we'd established a way to secure the names of hundreds of thousands of supporters—people who could be counted upon to contribute to our cause in response to future appeals. We had that most precious of all mail order possessions: a list of customers!

The final Eisenhower letter, which I wrote, put all these elements together, and produced the desired effect: $1 million in contributions. With established mail order basics at our service, raising that $1 million was a simple matter. It took only one letter!

8

Choosing the Right Lists

The Case of Ruby Red Grapefruit versus Registered Republicans

At the invitation of the new Republican Finance Chairman, Jerry Milbank, in 1969 Todd and I went down to Washington to interview the subordinate who had been running the financial affairs of the Republican National Committee. We found this individual sitting in a little room with a pile of envelopes and a letter opener. He was slitting open the letters by hand, and extracting checks.

He informed us that he had some 60,000 contributors, left over from the original Eisenhower and Goldwater direct mail campaigns. Once a year he wrote these contributors a simple letter and asked for a contribution, and they sent him $1 million. The average contribution was about $16.

We asked him what he was doing to secure new contributors, and he said, "Nothing." With $1 million floating in every year, practically without effort, there was no need to solicit new contributors.

We asked him how he acknowledged these contributions, and he said he didn't—acknowledgments would cost money, and as he didn't acknowledge contributions, contributors would naturally understand that the Republican Party was too frugal to waste good money on acknowledgment letters.

Under the direction of Mr. Milbank, we began to institute a few changes.

The first and most drastic step was to change our promotion mailing from a *contribution solicitation* to an *annual membership dues* notification.

Instead of saying "Please give us some money," we said, "You are a *member* of the National Republican Party, and here is a statement for your 1969 Membership *dues.*"

Then, we took an obvious "hot potato" step and *dramatized* the offer by enclosing a plastic Membership Card. And—since the days of computerized mailings had finally arrived—we *personalized* the mailing, with the contributor's name on both the card and the letter. On the plastic Membership Card, the name was embossed in raised gold lettering.

We followed this procedure throughout Jerry Milbank's tenure. Here's a sample of a typical mailing:

> REPUBLICAN NATIONAL FINANCE COMMITTEE
> DWIGHT D. EISENHOWER REPUBLICAN CENTER
> 310 FIRST STREET S.E.
> WASHINGTON, DC 20003

YOUR CONTRIBUTION LAST YEAR WAS $99.99

SUGGESTED 1973 CONTRIBUTION $100.00

Dear Mr. Weintz:

Your 1973 Sustaining Membership Card enclosed—which I hope you will detach and place in your wallet now—is a two-way message. First, it is a reminder of our gratitude here at National Headquarters for the generous support you gave to our campaign last year.

Without the support of Sustaining Members like yourself, who provide the financial backbone of the Republican Party, we would not have been able to wage the successful campaign which has returned President Nixon to the White House for four more years.

I want you to know that you have the heartfelt thanks of this Administration.

Secondly, your 1973 Sustaining Member Card is a reminder of the important job ahead in 1973 for us, for you and all of the President's supporters. We've sent you the card in advance, because we know . . .

And so on. The original mailing we prepared established the pattern of sending a letter accompanied by a plastic Sustaining Membership Card, with a computerized reply/contribution form. On this form, we offered the Member the option of increasing his/her contribution from $15 to $25, or from $25 to $50, or from $50 to $100. By this procedure, we were able to raise the average contribution from $16 to approximately $25.

And we started testing mail-order lists, to bring *new* contributors into the fold.

I have already listed "lists" as one of the important ingredients of a successful mailing. Given a good product, most mail-order operators would probably list "good lists" as *the* most important ingredient in any mailing. The most skillfully prepared mailing in all the world will fall on its face if sent to a poor list. A weak, limping, routine mailing will pull in orders, contributions, and money if it goes to a good list.

Also, the closer your product's relationship with the people whose names are on the list you are writing to, the better returns will be. At *Reader's Digest*, for example, when I started selling books to *Reader's Digest* subscribers, I got returns of 5 to 10 percent on each book offer I made. *Digest* subscribers would buy anything the *Digest* offered to sell them, because they trusted the *Digest*. The same offers, to outside lists, would probably have pulled 1 or 2 percent.

There are certain obvious characteristics by which you can prejudge the likelihood of getting a good response from any given mail-order list.

First, a list of *mail-order buyers* is more likely to be responsive to a mail-offer than a list of *non*-mail-order buyers. For instance, on a *compiled* list such as a list of names from a telephone book, all you know about the individuals on the list is that they each have a

REPUBLICAN PARTY "PLASTIC CARD" MEMBERSHIP MAILING

Plastic membership cards—the breakthrough that brings the Republican party an extra $20 million in contributions each year.

REPUBLICAN NATIONAL FINANCE COMMITTEE
1973 Sustaining Membership

DWIGHT D. EISENHOWER REPUBLICAN CENTER
310 FIRST ST. S. E. • WASHINGTON, D. C. 20003

**1973
Republican
Party
Sustaining
Member**

☐ YES, I wish to support the 1973 Sustaining Membership Program of the **REPUBLICAN NATIONAL FINANCE COMMITTEE**. Enclosed is my personal check.

* If your contribution is for $25 or more, you also receive MONDAY, the weekly Newsletter of the Republican Party.

10783567

MR WALTER H WEINTZ
DWIGHT D. EISENHOWER REPUBLICAN CENTER
310 First Street SE Washington DC 20003

MR WALTER H WEINTZ
HIGH RIDGE RD
POUND RIDGE, NY 10576

MAKE CHECKS PAYABLE TO: *REPUBLICAN NATIONAL FINANCE COMMITTEE*
10783567   (Note: Corporate checks prohibited by law.)   000022/000022 15A
First remove your 1973 Membership Card. Then return top portion of this letter in accompanying reply envelope with your contribution. No postage required.

YOUR CONTRIBUTION LAST YEAR WAS $99.99
SUGGESTED 1973 CONTRIBUTION $100.00

JANUARY 15, 1973

DEAR MR WEINTZ

YOUR 1973 SUSTAINING MEMBERSHIP CARD ABOVE -- WHICH I HOPE YOU WILL DETACH AND PLACE IN YOUR WALLET NOW -- IS A TWO-WAY MESSAGE. FIRST, IT IS A REMINDER OF OUR GRATITUDE HERE AT NATIONAL HEADQUARTERS FOR THE GENEROUS SUPPORT YOU GAVE TO OUR CAMPAIGN LAST YEAR.

WITHOUT THE SUPPORT OF SUSTAINING MEMBERS LIKE YOURSELF, WHO PROVIDE THE FINANCIAL BACKBONE OF THE REPUBLICAN PARTY, WE WOULD NOT HAVE BEEN ABLE TO WAGE THE SUCCESSFUL CAMPAIGN WHICH HAS RETURNED PRESIDENT NIXON TO THE WHITE HOUSE FOR FOUR MORE YEARS. I WANT YOU TO KNOW THAT YOU HAVE THE HEART-FELT THANKS OF THIS ADMINISTRATION.

SECONDLY, YOUR 1973 SUSTAINING MEMBERSHIP CARD IS A REMINDER OF THE IMPORTANT JOB AHEAD IN 1973 FOR US, FOR YOU, AND ALL OF THE PRESIDENT'S SUPPORTERS. WE'VE SENT YOU THE CARD IN ADVANCE, BECAUSE WE KNOW YOU WILL WANT TO CONTINUE AS A SUSTAINING MEMBER IN 1973, TO HELP KEEP OUR COMMITTEE STRONG AND ACTIVE, AND TO STRENGTHEN OUR POSITION TO BUILD ON PRESIDENT NIXON'S VICTORY DURING THE COMING MONTHS.

WE MUST MAINTAIN OUR VITALITY AS AN ORGANIZATION IN OFF-ELECTION YEARS IF WE ARE TO HAVE THE CAPACITY AND RESOURCES TO WIN FUTURE ELECTIONS. KEEPING THE REPUBLICAN PARTY STRONG REQUIRES GOOD FINANCING, AND FOR THIS WE MUST DEPEND UPON DEDICATED, LOYAL REPUBLICANS LIKE YOURSELF.

OFFICE OF THE CHAIRMAN • REPUBLICAN NATIONAL FINANCE COMMITTEE telephone. They may or may not be mail-responsive; some of them will, some won't. But on a mail-order buyers list, you at least know right at the start that you're dealing with a *responsive* list.

Secondly, in compiling lists to test for any mailing you propose to make, you should try to find lists of prospects who have *interests* or *characteristics* that relate to your product. For instance, if you're doing a fund-raising mailing for a worthy cause (such as the Republican Party) you'll probably do better on a list of *well-to-do* individuals—people who have bought *expensive* items by mail. You'd also *probably* do better on a Republican mailing to lists of people who have previously contributed money to conservative causes, although we found, by testing, that conservatives were *not* always good prospects for our mailings.

In our efforts to secure new contributors to the Republican Party, Todd and I tested all kinds of lists—lists of mail-order buyers, contributor lists, and Republican Party member-voter registration lists.

Interestingly enough, we found that the *best* lists were not (as might have been expected) "contributors to worthy conservative causes" or even "registered Republicans." Instead, they were lists of mail-order buyers of luxury items. Such lists as Ruby Red Grapefruit and Pfalzer Steaks actually pulled best! And registered Republican Party members were the poorest lists of any we tested!

I can usually explain, Monday morning, *why* something happened on a Friday afternoon test. In this case, we were after (1) wealthy people—at least, people with money, (2) those who had previously responded to direct mail, thereby identifying themselves as mail-order responsive individuals, and (3) people who were Republicans. The mail-order buyers of luxury items fulfilled the first two criteria—obviously, they were well-to-do, and they responded to direct mail; and such lists would have their fair share of Republicans.

The registered Republican lists, on the other hand, included *all* Republicans—rich and poor; some could have been direct mail responsive, but many were not. The lists bombed because, basically, they weren't mail-order lists, or lists of well-to-do people who could afford to give money to the Party. Finally, the contributors to worthy causes were presumably wealthy, but they tended to be *ultra-conservatives* — and ultra conservatives, more often than not, were as much against Republicans as they were against Democrats!

By 1972 (the year of the Nixon–McGovern race), we had increased our basic contributor list from 60,000 to 350,000, and our annual income from $1 to $8 million.

Naturally, we wrote to everyone who sent in a contribution (i.e., everyone who paid their membership dues) and thanked them profusely. And we suggested that, if they wished to make an additional contribution, it would be most kindly received.

At this point, in 1972, Maurice Stans, the Secretary of Commerce, became the head of the Finance Committee to Reelect the President. It's important to note that first qualifying word: the *Finance* Committee (not the *Committee* to Reelect the President, which the press fondly dubbed "CREEP").

It was Maurice Stans' job, pure and simple, to raise money as needed, on call, for the Reelection Committee—and nothing more. He had no responsibility for the disposition of this money.

This *Finance* Reelection Committee was also separate and independent from the Republican National Finance Committee, which Jerry Milbank headed, and which continued its own fund-raising efforts.

Maurice Stans was an impressive, high-powered, eyeball-to-eyeball fund-raiser. However, he was also very intelligent, and Jerry Milbank and Al Cole convinced Maurie that direct mail could and would supplement his personal fund raising, so the Weintz organization was retained to work for *both* these organizations as two separate accounts: the Finance Committee to Reelect the President, and the Republican National Committee.

Early in the year of 1972, Hugh Sloan, Maurie's young assistant treasurer, gave me a hand-scribbled check, over his signature on behalf of FCRP, for one million dollars—an advance against my estimate of the sum that would be needed to get our mail order campaign rolling. When I deposited the check at the little branch office of our local bank, the manager was more than a little doubtful about accepting it—he suspected it wasn't real. Several days later, after the check had cleared, he called me aside and presented me with a silver-plated strawberry spoon, as a token of the bank's appreciation for getting this account. In the months that followed, a great deal more money rolled through that account. Incidentally, this silver-plated spoon was the one and only gift or gratuity, or payment, other than our established fees, that The Weintz Company received while working for the Republicans!

At Maurice Stans' first meeting with Todd and me, he asked us how we proposed to spend our million dollars. We explained that we would begin by testing several different copy approaches, and testing a great number of mailing lists.

"But you don't need to test lists," Maurie said. "All you need is a national list of registered Republican voters."

I told Mr. Stans that this was probably the worst list we could use, because it was non-mail order, and had no built-in prosperity index. He was somewhat doubtful, and asked me, then, just what I would consider a good list.

I told him, "Ruby Red Grapefruit"—because anybody who could afford to pay $110 for a supply of grapefruit ordered by mail on the strength of a promotion letter, had to be both well-to-do and *very* mail-order susceptible. Maurie thought this was pretty funny.

We subsequently tested some 400 lists. Ruby Red Grapefruit came out among the top winners, and registered Republicans came out last.

Maurie Stans was both surprised and amused by this lesson in list responsiveness. But he had a logical question. "If you knew Republicans would be weakest of 400 lists, why did you test it in the first place?"

The answer was—and is—we *thought* we knew, but this was only an opinion, and mail order is full of surprises. We dealt in *facts*, not opinions, and the test was necessary to be *sure*.

Incidentally, the registered Republican lists today are much better than they were in 1972, because today it is possible to vastly refine such lists, by overlapping demographic characteristics on your basic list, and then mailing only selected *segments* of the list.

For example, you could take the registered Republicans list for the State of New York, and match it to a U.S. Government census tract neighborhood analysis, which gives the *average* age, income, and family status of people who live in a given tract. Then you could mail only to Republicans who live in the more *prosperous* tracts. And you could further refine the list by then superimposing a "mail-responsive" compilation (such as is available through the big telephone and auto list companies) on your list of *prosperous* Republicans. Then, theoretically, you'd have the ideal Republican fund-raising list: registered Republicans who are both prosperous and mail responsive.

In the course of a year, with fund-raising letters using assorted appeals and the best names on our 400 lists, we raised about $22 million for the Republican National Finance Committee and over $10 million for Mr. Stans' Finance Committee to Reelect the President. In addition to the money we raised, our millions of letters undoubtedly influenced many voters.

We kept scrupulous records of every penny expended and every penny received. When Watergate erupted, the IRS sent an investigator from Washington to examine The Weintz Company books, and he spent some time in our office. He returned to Washington empty-handed—and was told to go back and investigate us again. He made another visit to our office, and disallowed part of my expenses on a company car, which he declared I used personally on weekends. Otherwise, he found our books in order, and this was our only Watergate-related experience.

During this period I was astounded one night when I saw, on a CBS TV newscast, Mike Wallace following Maurice Stans about at a Republican convention, needling him: "You mean to say you raised all that money and you don't know how it was spent? You want us to believe that you raised millions of dollars and had nothing to say about how it was spent? Explain that!"

Of course Maurie did not have anything to say about how the money he raised actually got spent, except that it was to be turned over to the Reelection Committee to spend toward Nixon's reelection, in whatever way the Reelection Committee deemed best— and naturally it was assumed that whatever they did would be legal. The smear campaign and the public persecution that Maurice Stans underwent provided a sorry commentary on the way that the entire Watergate witch-hunt got conducted.

The basic letter that we used for FCRP, which went out over Maurice Stans' signature, read as follows:

Dear Fellow American:

As you know, we are now in the final stages of an historic
Presidential election campaign—which will surely determine how
you and your family live for many years to come!

Whether you are an Independent, a Democrat, or a Republican,
your whole way of life is at stake. I believe that you, like millions
of other concerned Americans, are anxious to help save our Country from the radical programs that George McGovern has put
forward. This is why—regardless of your Party affiliation—I am
appealing to you for help in reelecting President Nixon.

Specifically, I ask you to contribute $15 ... $25 ... $50 ... $100
..., or more if you can ... to help carry President Nixon's campaign to the people.

As a token of appreciation for your support—and a lasting
symbol of your active participation in the historic 1972 Presidential Campaign—I will be happy to send you a unique and priceless
keepsake: a special limited edition of our bronze *Official 1972
Presidential Campaign Medal* struck by renowned Franklin Mint.

This limited bronze edition medal is being struck only for those
who make a contribution of $15 or more at this time. It is literally
priceless, since it is not for sale *at any* price—and is being
awarded only to those who participate in the final stages of this
great Presidential Campaign.

Your 1972 Presidential Campaign Medal will be a keepsake
which you will proudly display at home or in your office as evidence of the important role you played in this critical and historic
campaign—a family heirloom which your children and their
children will be thankful you acquired and saved for them ...

Enclosed (taking a page from the Spencer Olin letter that we
mailed out years before) was a flyer depicting "The Official 1972
Presidential Campaign Medal of the Republican National
Committee—A Priceless Memento of your Participation."

The order card said:

FINANCE COMMITTEE TO RE-ELECT THE PRESIDENT
1701 PENNSYLVANIA AVENUE, N.W.
WASHINGTON, DC 20006

Membership Application

I want to help in President Nixon's campaign for reelection.

Please accept my contribution, enroll me as a Member of the Finance Committee to Reelect the President, and send me my Bronze
Limited Edition Nixon Campaign Medal.

The odd thing about all this was the Democrats' failure to emulate the Republicans. While the Republicans built a huge constituency of "Members" who *paid dues* (we ended the year with a total, between the two Committees, of well over a million contributors, and the current Republican National Committee total, in 1987, is over 1.5 million), the Democrats persisted for many years in their dependency upon the "Political Action Committees" of big unions, and the generosity of other big contributors—which are known in the trade as "fat cats." The Democrats have only recently begun to discover that there are, indeed, other members of the Democratic Party besides the "fat cats."

One amusing aspect of the whole Nixon reelection campaign revolved around this question of campaign funding. George McGovern did a lot of complaining about the so-called fat cats who contributed to the Republican Party. The inference, widely accepted by the press, was that the Republican Party got all its money from big contributors. The Democrats, of course, were the Party of the Little People.

As a matter of fact, the Republican National Finance Committee was basically depending upon hundreds of thousands of *small* contributors—the average contribution was about $25—for the funds to keep it in business. Something like 80 percent of the Republican National Finance Committee budget in 1972 was provided by donations secured through direct mail, and most of those donations came from "members" we had secured—some of them going all the way back to the Citizens for Eisenhower–Nixon in 1952.

And a major part of the Finance Committee to Reelect the President funds also came from small, mail-secured contributors.

In 1972, we followed the same principles that we laid down in 1950 and 1952. We tested different pieces of copy on a small scale, and then mailed millions of letters built around the most successful theme.

We asked for a contribution because (1) this helped finance the dissemination of our sales letters, (2) every contributor "bet on a horse" and was therefore much more likely to get out and vote, and (3) every contributor that we secured in 1972 would help us keep the Republican Party going in 1973, 1974, 1975, 1987, and years to follow.

After the 1972 elections—and Watergate—the Finance Committee to Reelect the President closed down. And, ultimately, Jerry Milbank departed from the Republican National Finance Committee. For some years, The Weintz Company lingered on as consultants to this Committee; ultimately the Committee grew its own in-house creative and administrative staff, and we went on to other things.

However, the basic fund-raising structure of the Committee, as The Weintz Company set it up under Jerry Milbank, is a juggernaut that rolls on, still using the basic mail-order principles that we set in place—membership, membership cards, annual dues, and above all, recognition for the *members' participation*.

And I'd swap 1.5 million Republican small contributors ($25 average) any time for the far fewer Democrat fat cats!

WHAT'S TO BE LEARNED FROM THE REPUBLICAN EXPERIENCE THAT YOU CAN PUT TO WORK ON YOUR OWN PRODUCT?

In writing this chapter, I've tried to emphasize, as I went along, the elements that made our mailings for the Republicans successful. I will emphasize again that these are universal elements that you can and should apply to any product you are promoting. So it won't hurt to review those elements here:

1. *Testing* is the key to successful mailings. With tests, you make your mistakes on a small scale, and go forward confidently with "roll outs" on only the most successful tests.

2. *Lists* are fundamental. The *relevancy* of a list to the product you're selling is of primary importance. *Lists* form the backbone of any testing program.

3. Offer the recipient of your mailing a *reason* to buy your product: a *personal* advantage which can be secured by contributing to your cause or buying your product. In the case of the Republicans, we offered *recognition*, the plastic card; we offered *participation* in accomplishing a desired political objective. If you're selling a product, your first problem is always to isolate *what that product will do for me*; what personal advantage does it offer?

4. Try to dramatize your offer with a *tangible device*: the plastic card, the offer of a bronze medal, or, if you're selling a product, a *discount*, a limited edition, a special membership privilege, a *free* 10-day trial, a *free* premium, a chance to win a million dollars in a sweepstakes.

With these applications of basic mail-order techniques in mind, you've got a good start toward making successful mailings!

9

Mining Your Customer List

How to Double Your Profits with Subsidiary Sales

In the last chapter we were talking about mailing lists in general; there is, of course, one list which is always better than any other. That is *your own customer list*. In this chapter I'll demonstrate, from my own experience, how to get extra mileage and extra profits from mining your own customer list.

It should be self-evident that once you have established a friendly relationship with a customer, once you have demonstrated your integrity and your dedication to the quality of a product, once you have won your customers' trust, the next sale is easy.

If you uphold your reputation for quality, your list becomes more and more valuable with each passing year. It is no exaggeration to say that the most valuable asset any mail-order company can possess is its own list of loyal customers.

Indeed, most successful mail-order companies depend upon *subsidiary sales* as their main source of profits. An obvious example of the continuing value of a customer list is Book-of-the-Month

Club. At one time, when I was doing consulting work for Book-of-the-Month, their management was willing to pay $25 to secure a new member, whose only obligation was to purchase four books during the coming year. But a very large percentage of *new* members normally purchased at least five books that first year, at least three or four books the second year, and more books each year thereafter. Thus the *value* of a new customer to Book-of-the-Month was at least $25, and if you had attempted to purchase the Book-of-the-Month Club, the value of its million or so members *alone*, at that time, would have been at least $25 million. Of course, you couldn't buy Book-of-the-Month Club for anything like $25 million, because, besides its list, the Club has an invaluable name and reputation, an astute management, promotion savvy, and advertising space franchises. But with all these assets, the Club would be in deep trouble if it somehow lost its list of customers.

Before I joined *Reader's Digest* I had had a fair amount of experience with the sale of books and records and, from experience with Book-of-the-Month Club and other mail-order clients, I knew a little something about the value of subsidiary sales. But at the *Digest* I got my first real experience in the business of *mining* a customer list.

The story of this experience is a good demonstration of how it's done.

In 1948, shortly after I arrived at the *Digest*, Al Cole called a meeting in his office with Fred Thompson, Frank Herbert, and me.

"Last year," said Al, "the *Digest* had gross sales, domestic and overseas, of $18 million, and we made a $1 million profit. This year we'll have a sale of $18 million and we'll break even. Next year, if costs of printing, paper, and promotion continue to rise, we'll have an $18 million dollar sale and we'll lose $1 million. The year after that, if we keep on the present track, we'll go out of business."

This was the giant, successful, mail-order organization to which I had committed myself!

"So we've got to do something fast," said Al. "Of course, if the *Digest* took advertising, all our problems would be over. But Mr. Wallace is concerned that if we take advertising it will be impossible for the *Digest* to secure the reprint rights for articles from other magazines that the *Digest* depends on.

"So, Fred, you go up to Canada and we'll break off the Canadian circulation." (The *Digest's* Canadian circulation, at the time, was served by the U.S. edition.) "You'll start a Canadian edition, and you'll take advertising, just as we take advertising in our Foreign Editions. And if it succeeds in Canada and there aren't too many complications, we'll persuade Wally to let us take advertising in the U.S. edition and our troubles will be over.

"Meanwhile," he said, addressing me, "Walt, you're the new boy, and you haven't got much to do. Some years ago, in 1941, Fred had the idea for a *Digest* book. It was a collection of *Digest* book condensation reprints. He called it *'Reader's Digest Books.'* It sold 170,000 copies, at $1 a copy, and made the Digest $56,000 net profit. And Mr. Wallace was so pleased (at the time he'd probably never seen a lump sum like that) he split the $56,000 into bonuses and handed it all out to the employees.[1] So why don't you publish a new *Reader's Digest Books*, and see if you can sell 170,000 copies and make us another $50,000 or $60,000 to help tide us over."

Of course, selling books was the one thing that I already knew something about from my Schwab and Beatty education. And I knew that the *Digest's* huge subscription list—some 3.5 million or more loyal subscribers at that time—all mail-order sold and all mail-order receptive, was one of the most valuable and responsive mail-order properties in the world. Those loyal readers, I knew, would buy *anything* the *Digest* offered them!

I had been given a secretary, Florence Travis, and together we put together, tested, and published the desired book, utilizing basic mail-order testing principles.

HOW TO MAKE A MAIL ORDER TEST: THE PROCEDURES TO FOLLOW TO ASSURE RELIABLE ANSWERS TO YOUR QUESTIONS

Here I'll interrupt this account of my own mail-order testing to briefly review the steps and procedures involved in a proper test. As already discussed, you can test almost anything by direct mail—from a product to a price to an offer to a copy appeal. We did it for Eisenhower on political appeals. In this case of my first experience of selling books to the *Digest* list, I needed to test *everything*.

Tests are intended to answer questions both scientifically and reliably. Some of the questions I needed answering, on this *Digest* Book project, were:

1. Will *Digest* readers buy another *Digest* book? How many will buy? What will be the cost-per-sale, and what margin will be available for profits if we make a major mailing to the entire *Digest* list?
2. What should be the product's concept? Its contents? What name should I use?
3. What price will attract the most customers at the highest level of profit? Should it be $1.00? $1.50? $1.69? $1.89?

To begin with, the laws of probability say that you need a response of about 300 orders *on each key you mail* in order to get a statistically reliable result. The first rule of testing is that the test quantity must be adequate to bring you a *reliable* test result.

So if you mail 10,000 of test key "A," and 10,000 of test key "B," and secure a 1 percent response—100 on each key—your tests are unreliable. And if one test pulls, say, 90 orders, while the second key pulls 120, a re-test could very well reverse these results.

On the other hand, if you mailed two tests of 10,000 each, and got a 10 percent response overall, but one test pulled 900 and the other 1200, the *difference* would be big enough to be statistically significant. The whole point here is simply that a test must be *big enough* to be reliable, and if you are expecting a return of 1 percent or thereabouts, you probably need to mail closer to 100,000 on each key, rather than 10,000 each key, to get results you can live with.

(In fact, on insurance accounts I've worked with, where results normally run around 1 percent on a key, statistically minded insurance actuaries usually call for a 100,000 quantity on each key. If they are testing 10 different elements, as they often do, this means the overall test might run to one million names!)

So you begin by deciding how many questions you want your test to answer and how big a test will be necessary to give reliable answers to your questions. Then you make sure you are getting a reliable cross section of your available mailing universe in your testing sample.

Test samples can be woefully biased and misleading. For example, if I had tested only *new, trial* subscribers, on my first *Digest* book test, I'd have gotten quite a different answer than if I had tested only *old* (i.e., at least second or third year renewal) subscribers.

Again, on almost any list, California names tend to pull better than New York names, and certain states are notoriously "bad pay."

Sometimes, when a mailer *rents* the use of another company's list, the owner has been known to provide new, *active* names for the test, which are quite unrepresentative of the entire list, as the testing company later finds out to its sorrow.

In short, there are a lot of pitfalls hidden away in mailing lists!

So it is necessary to select test names very carefully to assure a fair demographic, geographic, and statistical cross section of the master list.

One simple way to do this (now that the age of computers is here) is by asking for "*N*th name selection." If you want to test 10,000 "As" and 10,000 "Bs" on a one million list, for instance, you'd ask for and expect to get a selection of every 100th name for each key. This way you'd presumably hit small towns and big cities, rich and poor, old and young—whatever variations lie inside a list.

The procedure is then to *key* two sets of order cards, an equal quantity on each key, and to *address* one set of cards to one test group, the other set to the second test group.

I've reproduced three typical sample keyed test order cards on the next page. Note that the "keys" on the three cards are different; by counting the "*keyed* returns" the mailer knows which offer will pull best on a big mailing.

Incidentally, which offer do *you* think outpulled the others?[2]

One final footnote on testing. There are two basic types of tests you can make. One is a "package" test, where *all* the elements of

"COIN WORLD" 3-WAY OFFER TEST

One of these tests pulled 4 percent and one pulled 2 percent. The difference was in the offer.

=========== RESERVATION CARD ===========

YES! Please send me the next three issues of COIN WORLD free and reserve an introductory subscription in my name. If I like COIN WORLD, my price is just $12.97 for 26 additional issues (making a total of 29 issues.) If I'm not absolutely delighted I'll return your subscription bill marked "cancel" and owe nothing. Whatever I decide, the first three issues are mine to keep free.

☐ 6 FREE ISSUES. I'm already sold. I've enclosed my check for $12.97. Send me six free issues and enter my introductory subscription. I'll receive 32 issues in all!

Mail to: COIN WORLD, P. O. Box 150, Sidney, OH 45365

520082

Box 150   Sidney, OH 45365

☑ Here's my $1.00 for 12 weekly issues of COIN WORLD.

I understand my $1 will be applied to the regular $23.95 per year subscription rate. I'll get a bill for just $22.95 for 52 additional weekly issues — 64 issues in all!

NO RISK: If I like it, I'll honor your bill. If not, I'll write "cancel" on it, return it and owe nothing.

NOTE: Your $1.00
must be enclosed.

OFFER IS LIMITED
ACT BY

This offer is limited to new subscribers only.

CW57-2

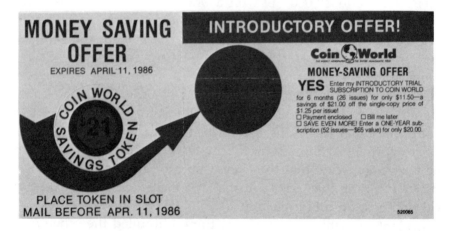

Reprinted with permission of Amos Press, Inc.

126

two different tests may be different. The offers may differ, the selling copy may differ, and the envelopes may differ. And when results are in, you will obviously not be able to tell which specific *elements* of the winning mailing were most responsible for its success.

A second approach is to test different elements in individual tests. You have a basic control, incorporating offer, price, copy, and format.

In a second test, you offer a different price, which is the *only* variable in the second test. A third test package might add a "lift letter," a fourth might have a differently illustrated envelope, and so on. In each "element" test you are testing only *one* variable, so you can find out what effort, if any, includes a variable that will justify a big, roll-out mailing.

This element-by-element testing strategy is perhaps more accurate in the answers it gives you. But often it is impossible to test one element at a time. For example, if one test offers a *free cookbook* as a premium, and a second test does *not* offer a premium, you're obviously not testing the potential *power* of a premium unless you feature it with a picture on the envelope, a special flyer, and so on. We'll have more on this subject when we come to a later chapter discussing a mailing I made which featured 100 million premiums.

With this brief lesson in the science of testing completed, we'll go on to my own experience.

First, I tested titles. I knew I was going to publish a collection of "*Reader's Digest* Book Condensations" (the *Digest* published one such Book Condensation in the back pages of each issue). I sent out a letter to a couple of thousand *Digest* subscribers explaining that we planned to publish a collection of book "reprints" and asking them to choose the ones they'd like to see in the book. I enclosed a list of about 50 titles, with brief, 30-word descriptions; these were outstanding book condensations the *Digest* had published over the years, including such titles as "How to Win Friends and Influence People," by Dale Carnegie, "Peace of Mind" by Dr. Joshua Liebman, and "On Being a Real Person" by Harry Emerson Fosdick.

The customers voted and there wasn't any doubt about which titles to pick. We named our volume *"14 Reader's Digest Books."*

Then I tested offers: a price of $1.00 versus a price of $1.50, versus a price of $1.69. At the same time, I tested *response*. Would the entire *Digest* subscriber list respond to the offer? Which level of price would they be willing to pay? What overall returns, at what price, could I get? I got the answers through a series of simple tests by mailing out a few thousand letters on each offer and counting the responses.

This was the *Reader's Digest* subscriber list I was mailing to—my *own customer list*—and it was virgin ground which hadn't been worked for years. The upshot was that I didn't sell the books for $1.00—I sold them for $1.69 (cash or C.O.D.!)—because it turned out that price was no consideration to our readers; just as many responded to the $1.69 offer as did to the $1.00 offer. And I didn't sell 100,000, I sold a total of 600,000 copies on the initial mailing, and ended up (with follow-up mailings) selling a total of almost a million books in 1948 and 1949, on a single book title. And I didn't make a $50,000 profit, I brought in $500,000, over and above expenses. Florence Travis and I did it pretty much by ourselves with only a bit of guidance and encouragement from Frank Herbert.

The big mailing went out early in 1948, and the follow-up in January 1949.

Thus, within a little over a year after I joined the *Digest*, I brought in approximately half as much profit, on a single book, as the entire *Digest* (Domestic and International) had made in the year before I joined the Association.

Naturally, the word got around that I was a mail-order whiz, and naturally, I did nothing to dissuade people of the idea. The project was Al Cole's, based on Fred Thompson's previous success and executed under Frank Herbert's supervision, with mailings that offered a *Digest* book to the most responsive list of *readers* in the world, the *Reader's* Digest subscribers.

Still, I *did* execute the project. I wrote the copy, laid out the lists, counted the returns, and entered them laboriously, by hand, on a sheet of paper the accounting department loaned me. My secretary sent out the checks (small checks because these were reprints of reprints) to the lucky copyright owners. I set the print order. The printer shipped the books out and the money rolled in.

As Mark Twain said in his *Autobiography*, concerning his birth in Florida, Missouri, a village containing a hundred people, "I increased the population by 1 percent. It may not be modest for me to refer to, but this is true."

I feel the same way about my accomplishment with the first mailing I made for *Reader's Digest*.

SUMMING UP

The case of *14 Reader's Digest Books* is a classic example of what can be done when you own a good mail-order list and can *mine* that list with a related product (in this case, the offer of a *Reader's Digest* book to *Reader's Digest* subscribers).

The test results also demonstrate the surprises that tests can uncover. Who would have thought, before the test, that a $1.69 price would pull just as well as $1.00?

We *tested* our master list's responsiveness so we were able to go ahead with a huge, multimillion mailing with great confidence. We tested price, offer, and copy. We substituted scientific, *tested* answers for hunches or opinions.

Most importantly, we discovered a rich field for subsidiary sales to our own subscribers which we immediately started to mine.

---

[1]In 1941 the *Digest* mailed 1,700,000 circulars and secured a 10 percent response on "Reader's Digest Books." The *Digest* later sold 162,000 copies through newsstand sales, inserts in the magazine, and expire mailings, and earned an additional profit of $37,000.

[2] Key 520065 pulled 2 percent

Key CN 57-2 pulled 3.8 percent

Key 520082 pulled 4.0 percent

10

Further Lessons in List Mining

How the World's Largest Mail-Order Book Club Was Born

Our initial success with *14 Reader's Digest Books* convinced the *Digest* business department that we could reap tremendous *extra* income and *extra* profits by subsidiary sales to the *Digest* subscriber list.

This "discovery"—or rather, this rediscovery of one of the basic tenets of mail-order marketing—is worthy of another brief aside. Simply put, the most valuable asset of any mail-order company is its list of customers. If you have customers—a list of folks who have previously purchased something from you, and who have been satisfied by a good product and fair treatment—you have a list of friends who are likely to purchase additional products from you if you offer them something that can be perceived as fulfilling a want or need. These customers are like money in the bank.

Of course, aside from Sears, Roebuck, and Montgomery Ward, the *Digest* had one of the biggest mail-order lists in existence in 1950—about 3½ million subscriber names. The *Digest* cover at that time carried the proud line, "Over Five Million Copies Printed."

This was true. It was also true that this print order was divided up betweeen 3½ million paying subscribers, perhaps ¾ of a million newsstand buyers, and another ¾ of a million of unsold newsstand copies—"returns"—plus assorted complimentary subs and giveaways. But the *Digest* still had one of the largest lists of loyal mail-order customers in existence.

"SYNDICATIONS" AND THE DIFFERENCE IN PULL BETWEEN RENTED LISTS AND HOUSE LISTS

I have since seen good start-up mail-order products perish for want of a "house list." I have also seen, in a thing called "syndications," the difference in results between a mailing signed by a stranger and the same mailing signed by a familiar supplier. "Syndications" are arrangements that two mail-order companies make with each other when one company has a product and the other company has a list. The company with the *list* writes to its customers: "We have made arrangements to make a good product, produced by another company, available to you at a good price. We think it's a product you'll want, and we guarantee it."

This endorsement will normally increase returns by as much as 100 percent over the results that would have been received by the company that *owns* the product had that company merely *rented* the other company's list and mailed the list over its own signature. In other words, a house list is apt to be as much as twice as responsive to an offer from the list owner as it is to a solicitation from a stranger.

In "syndication" selling, the two companies make arrangements to split the costs and split the profits on some equitable basis. Many mail-order companies actually have a complete syndication *department* which does nothing but arrange syndications of its products by other mail-order list owners. Some mail-order companies make *all* their annual profits from syndications and rentals of their lists.

One example was the publication of the Abrams Company's *Medical Encyclopedia* by World Book Encyclopedia, Inc. With inexpensive billing inserts and solo mailings, Frank Shaffer, Vice President of World Book, told me that World Book sold over 6,000,000 4-volume *sets* of Medical Encyclopedias at some $20 per volume. A $48 million sale made possible because World Book had loyal *customers*!

But let's go back to *14 Reader's Digest Books*. The test was successful, and the initial big mailing pulled around 10 percent—some 600,000 orders. One of the unwritten rules of mail-order is that a follow-up mailing will generally pull 50 to 60 percent as well as the initial mailing. I did a follow-up mailing on *14 Books* and got 320,000 additional orders, pushing total sales up close to a million. This was a case of "mining your own list" with a vengeance!

And, immediately, before the dust had settled, Al Cole instructed me to put out another book.

In those days a great feature of the *Digest* was the "Fillers"—the dozens of short, amusing, human interest pieces that appeared in the *Digest*: "Humor in Uniform," "Life in These United States," "My Most Unforgettable Character," and so on. From reader surveys and reader mail, we knew that these were among the most popular *Digest* features (over a million volunteer jokes and anecdotes were submitted to the *Digest* every year by readers). So a *Digest* book of humor was a logical sequel to *"14 Books."*

We called the new book *"Fun Fare"* (and a lawyer on Long Island threatened to sue us for use of a title he claimed he had copyrighted for a book he had never published. We ignored him and he never sued). Two junior *Digest* editors who edited the *Digest's* short features—humor and human interest—selected the material for the book, and Florence Travis, my secretary, and I handled the business details of putting the book together. Again, Florence sent out dozens of $5 and $10 checks as payment for the fillers we planned to reprint. Florence and I shared a single office and I'll never forget her stunned reaction to a telephone call she received one day. She listened with horror on her face, and when she hung up she said, "Well! I never heard such language in all my life as that man used to me!"

"Who was it?" I asked.

"He said his name was James Thurber. I sent him a check for $10 to pay him for reprinting a little article he wrote about a dam,

READER'S DIGEST "FUN FARE" MAILING ENVELOPE

The birth of "pictorial envelopes." One of the first **Reader's Digest** *book mailings.*

Reprinted by permission of *Reader's Digest.*

that was condensed in the *Digest* and you wanted to use in *Fun Fare.* He didn't seem to think $10 dollars was enough!"

Not only did James Thurber vent his spleen on Florence, but he called Wally, and again, my free-wheeling activities came under fire. The editor in charge of reprints sent Thurber a check—money seemed to soothe Thurber—and we did include his short piece.

Again, we had a huge success on our hands. *Fun Fare* sold for a higher price than *14 Books*—$1.89 instead of $1.69. And I had the courage to make the book easier to buy—I no longer demanded cash with order or C.O.D. I gave the customer a bill-me-later option which of course kicked up returns because the offer made it *easier* for the customer to *pay.* We mailed out a total of six million circulars on *Fun Fare* in 1949 and that year we had a profit of

$230,000 on *Fun Fare* alone. The total profit from books in 1949 was $418,979.72, and the total book sale that year was 794,691 copies of *14 Books* and *Fun Fare* combined.

Following these two "one-shot" successes, we continued to sell single volumes. In 1951, I proposed a *"30th Anniversary Reader's Digest Reader"*—"a selection of memorable articles published in the *Reader's Digest* in the past 30 years." This contained, in 500 pages, 108 complete articles by just about every celebrity of the day in 1951, starting with Dwight D. Eisenhower.

The book was a good demonstration of *why* the *Digest* itself was such a huge journalistic success. Here are just a few of the 108 articles and their authors:

"An Open Letter to America's Students"—Dwight D. Eisenhower

"Chaplains Courageous"—Quentin Reynolds

"The Most Unforgettable Character I've Met"—Helen Hayes

"The *Titanic* Is Unsinkable"—Hanson W. Baldwin

"I'm Sick of Sex"—Robert Thomas Allen

"Your Second Job"—Albert Schweitzer

"Double-Barreled Hope for Alcoholics"—Paul de Kruif

"Lou Gehrig's Epic of Courage"—Paul Gallico

"We Have With Us Tonight"—Dale Carnegie

"Mother's Bills"—Clarence Day

"Whose Business Was It?"—Fulton Oursler

"Lincoln Goes to Gettysburg"—Carl Sandburg

"Confessions of an Actor"—John Barrymore

"The Enemy's Masterpiece of Espionage"—J. Edgar Hoover

"The American Language"—H.L. Mencken

"Our Four Months on an Ocean Raft"—Thor Heyerdahl

"How to Guess Your Age"—Corey Ford

"The Quest of Our Lives"—I.A.R. Wylie

"Two for a Penny"—John Steinbeck

"How I Made a Crime Wave"—Lincoln Steffens

"Captain Weskon's Men Say Good-bye"—Ernie Pyle

"The Child Who Never Grew"—Pearl S. Buck

"The Size of Living Things"—Julian S. Huxley

"Marriage"—Booth Tarkington

"My Ninety Acres"—Louis Bromfield

"Grand Canyon"—Donald Culross Peattie

"The Best Investment I Ever Made"—A.J. Cronin

"Are You Alive?"—Stuart Chase

"Why The Doctor Was Held Up"—Billy Rose

"Taking America For Granted"—an unsigned editorial from
    Vogue

With titles and authors like these (and, once again, the *Reader's Digest* subscriber list to work with) it was no wonder that the *30th Anniversary Reader* had tremendous sales. I don't have a record of the actual total, but like the two previous *Digest* books, it came to approximately a million copies.

None of these books were sold through book stores or appeared on best-seller lists. A simple letter or two accounted for sales of a million books and a total income of over a million dollars. The only trouble was I feared that I might run out of one-shot books to sell and, perhaps, the *Digest* subscriber list would tire of buying such one-shots.

The solution to *that* problem seemed pretty obvious to me, even as early as 1948, when the success of *14 Reader's Digest Books* showed us the *Digest's* book sale potential. Here I was, beating my brains out selling just *one* book while Book-of-the-Month Club, Literary Guild, and Walter Black's Classics Club all sold their customers whole series of books with a single ad or a single mailing.

Clearly, the cost-per-book-sold would be greatly reduced if you could induce a customer to become a "member of a club," who would agree to purchase a *number* of books instead of just one book. Both the income and profit per customer would be multiplied if you succeeded in making a multiple sale.

What was called for, I reasoned, was a *Reader's Digest Book Club* and I told Al Cole so in a memo I sent him in December 1948, after my initial success with *"14 Reader's Digest Books."*

I still have the original copy of my memo to Al, which he sent to Ralph Henderson, the *Digest's* Condensed Book Editor, with a pencilled note:

> "Ralph—you could be interested in this from one of our newest young men on our promotion staff—Al"

The memo got passed on to Wally who sent the memo back to Al, with the okay for a go-ahead.

Like the previous *Digest* book innovations I'd been working on, this book club idea was most certainly not entirely original with me. Fred Thompson had suggested a book club some years before, but the time had not been right. The idea had been proposed and discussed from time-to-time, but rejected for various reasons. Now, however, we could point to the truly astounding success we were having with *Digest* books, starting, in particular, with *book* condensations.

THE FIRST PRINCIPLE IN MINING YOUR HOUSE LIST: SELL THEM A RELATED PRODUCT

Wally had previously turned thumbs down on other proposals for subsidiary *Digest* activities because he thought we should "stick to our knitting." Periodically, someone would suggest that the Reader's Digest Association start another magazine and Wally had always insisted that such activities were out of character for the Association. A *condensed* book club, however, was "in character." It made use of the *Digest's* strong point—skillful editorial selection and condensation. It was a *related* product. It utilized our most valuable asset—the *Digest* subscriber list. And it was based on Wally's favorite dictum—that busy readers didn't have time to read the complete texts of books and, as was demonstrated by the book condensations at the back of each issue of the *Digest*, they *liked* book condensations.

So we put together a complicated 10-way test mailing announcing the birth of the *Reader's Digest Condensed Book Club*, and mailed this out in January 1950.

THE THREE ALTERNATE APPROACHES TO MAIL-ORDER BOOK SALES (AND TO THE SALE OF OTHER MAIL-ORDER PRODUCTS)

In those days (as in these) there were three ways to make multiple book sales by mail in the United States.

One was by the conventional book club "negative option" process, pioneered by Harry Scherman in his Book-of-the-Month Club. When you joined the Club (and the procedure was definitely *joining*), you received an introductory gift and were then *obligated* to accept a minimum number of books during the following year—usually four volumes.

However, you weren't required to accept *every* "monthly selection" the Club offered you. You received an advance notice of the selection, and you then had a "negative option"—you could say "NO" by mailing back the convenient refusal card which always came with the Club's announcement.

Usually, a Club member could be counted on to purchase at least five books in a year. This compared most favorably with my single-copy one-shot.

A second method was the "continuity program," under which you entered a *subscription* for a series of books, and continued to receive them *automatically*, a book a month, *"until forbid."* Walter Black's Classics Club, on which I had worked at Schwab and Beatty, was such a continuity program, even though it went by the name of a "Club."

What distinguishes continuity programs from ordinary book clubs is the fact that the "continuity" is a *series* of similar or related books, whereas the book clubs sell unrelated works—sometimes a potential fiction best-seller like *"Gone With The Wind,"* and sometimes an outstanding work of non-fiction like *"The Rise and Fall of The Third Reich."*

Walter Black took double advantage of his continuity format by offering the first book for only 10¢ and saying you were under no obligation to take a single additional book. This was the ultimate "soft offer," and it had much impressed me back in the days when I first encountered it at Schwab and Beatty.

The "continuity" approach has been used by a number of mail-order companies other than publishers, notably Franklin Mint, with its many series of "collectibles"—coins, paintings, ceramics, plates, and, of course, "Great Books" in deluxe bindings.

A third approach to mail-order selling favored by mail-sold encyclopedias and other "sets" is the outright *gift* of the first item in the series, sent as an inducement to future purchases. For example, *The International Wild Life Encyclopedia*, which was one of my clients after I left *Reader's Digest*, would send you your first book *free*, accompanied by Volume 2, which you were expected to pay for. If you paid, you received Volume 3 (perhaps both 3 and 4) a month later. Then, if you paid for that, they backed up their truck and delivered the remaining 24 volumes in the series with the explanation that they *knew* you couldn't wait to get your complete set, so here it was, but for their part they would kindly *bill* you on the same generous one-volume-a-month basis.

PUTTING THE PRODUCT CONCEPT TOGETHER: THE WAY WE DID IT: HOW IT IS DONE

The *Digest's* Book Condensation Editor, Ralph Henderson, who was put in editorial charge of the Book Club project, conceived of the Club as offering something half-way between a conventional club and a continuity. It would be a *series* of books—each like the last. Each volume would contain *Digest* "digests" of four or five outstanding new books. This would make it a *related* product which *Digest* readers would probably respond to. And since the *Digest* itself specialized in non-fiction books and articles, it was agreed that *all* the Condensed Book condensations would be works of fiction: novels, mysteries, and adventure stories, to avoid conflict with the *Digest* itself. This approach made the Club a *unique* concept, which (like the *Digest*) answered a human need with a *unique* service. The Club was quite different from any other book club. There was nothing like it on the market.

Because we were trying to sell our books to *magazine* readers (not necessarily *book* readers) it was decided to issue one book every *three* months instead of one every month—a total of four a year—to keep from overloading them. If we'd had an audience of *book* subscribers, rather than magazine subscribers, we'd undoubtedly have offered a book a month.

It seemed logical, with such a concept, for our mail-order selling effort to sit down between two promotional chairs. I put together an offer of "your first book *free*, if you agreed to purchase the next three volumes to be issued during the coming year." This was an "automatic shipment" offer—not "negative option"—no advance notice was mailed out describing upcoming volumes. But it was also a "firm commit." The customer was *committed* to purchase three additional books. Thus the offer partook of both club and continuity characteristics.

The result of the test was alright, but not spectacular. We received a 4 percent overall response. By the time this mailing was made, we had about 5,700,000 *Digest* subscribers, so our big mailing brought in about 230,000 members. I figured these members would buy 731,400 books during the balance of the year, which would yield (at $1.89 plus postage and handling) $1,382,000 gross income. This netted out to $212,000 profit. It was at least a start.

I also tested a variety of other offers. One was a very "soft offer"—"your first book *free*, with no obligation to purchase any additional book." I did this modeled on the Walter Black Classic Club approach.

This offer pulled substantially better than the basic offer. However, I didn't know how the customers would perform. They had no obligation whatsoever to purchase even a single book. So I kept track of the *performance* of both kinds of customers during the following year.

The mail-order business deals with human nature, and human nature is full of surprises. At the end of the year I discovered that my "no obligation" customers purchased just as many books as they would have if they had *signed* a 3-volume purchase agreement. And my "3-book obligation" customers performed no better—they purchased three books if it suited their fancy, or two books, or none. The average purchase on either offer was the same. So much for human nature.

But the *free book* offer pulled 6 percent—nearly twice as many customers as I got when I asked for a commitment up front.

(Incidentally, one other test I made was the offer of the first book for $1.00, with no further commitment, and as might have been expected, this offer *depressed* returns.)

So, at the end of the first year of the Book Club's existence, when I had a track record on those "no-commit" customers, I made a second mailing, with the soft "free book" offer, and I secured some 300,000 new members for the Club. I followed this up the following year with a somewhat refined version of the same offer and got the membership up to three-quarters of a million, at which point the Club became of respectable size.

But my "free" offer was beginning to wear out. I was going back again to the same list, with my same offer, and response was softening. It became evident that I was reaching the end of the road, and the *Digest's* Club was still a poor third to Book-of-the-Month Club and Literary Guild.

I then recalled Walter Black's 10¢ offer, which I had always admired. I reasoned that my *free* offer was not entirely believable. Prospective customers *knew* that there had to be some catch in a "free" offer: No rational commercial organization, not even *Reader's Digest*, would give books away unless they expected to get something in return. So these wary readers avoided the trap and refrained from accepting my free offer.

So I asked myself: "What could be more free than free?" And I answered, "Perhaps if the customer were required to *pay* something—a small, reasonable sum—this would relieve him or her of any obligation to buy or pay for future volumes."

I wasn't sure exactly how much to ask for in a trial order, so I tested a series of offers:

1. Your first book for $1.00
2. Your first book for 50¢
3. Your first book for 25¢

READER'S DIGEST FREE OFFER TEST

A "free" offer that lost to a "cash-with-order" offer.

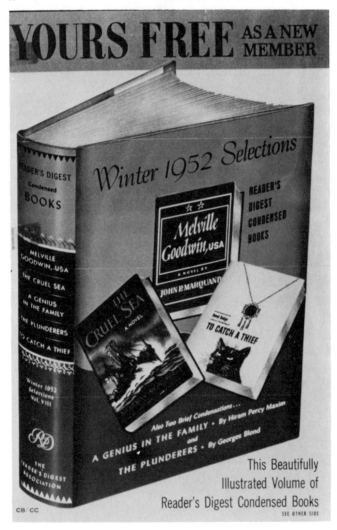

Reprinted by permission of *Reader's Digest.*

READER'S DIGEST 10¢ OFFER TEST

*. . . and a breakthrough "cash-with-order" offer that **won**. (It brought in a million book club members with a single mailing.)*

Reprinted by permission of *Reader's Digest*.

4. Your first book for 10¢
5. Your first book for 5¢
6. Your first book for 1¢
7. Your first book *free*.

As usual, the public surprised me. As could have been expected, the 50¢ offer outpulled the dollar offer substantially. And 25¢ outpulled 50¢. And 10¢ beat the pants off 25¢.

But then 10¢ pulled *better* than 5¢—at least twice as well. And 5¢ pulled better than 1¢, while a penny beat the "free" offer, and "free" had the weakest pull of all!

Evidently 10¢ was the price that my customers put on their conscience—it was big enough to free them from all further sense of obligation!

The only trouble with this test was that the 10¢ offer was so spectacular—it *doubled* returns, pulling better than 10 percent—that I didn't dare make it a full-scale mailing. I could imagine what would happen if I brought in a million or so new club members for 10¢ and none of them purchased any succeeding books! It could be summed up:

1. *Reader's Digest* would lose a million dollars.
2. Al Cole would fire me.

So we made a modest test mailing that brought in, not a million, but 15,000 new members, under the 10¢ offer. And for a year we tracked their performance. We discovered that 80 out of 100 who took Volume 1 for 10¢ accepted and paid for Volume 2 and that the dropoff rate was about 10 percent for the second volume, 5 percent thereafter: 72 took and paid for Volume 3, and about 68 took Volume 4. Thus, in one year, we sold 100 new members a total of 220 books *at the full price*. And these customers continued on into a second year—65 took Volume 5, 60 took Volume 6, 58 took 7, 55 took Volume 8, and so on. We averaged out, eventually, to more than five *paid* (full-price) sales per starting customer.

It was, however, a trying year waiting to see if those 10¢ members stayed with us. Al Cole, who liked figures, would call me up every morning for a "daily count" of payments, and I would call Suzanne Quarenghi, who was managing the Book Club as well as magazine fulfillment, and I'd ask her for a count. And Suzanne would explain to me, every morning, that the mail had not yet been counted, but she'd give me a count when it was complete. Relations became a little strained. Suzanne suggested that we have a *weekly* count on Monday and Friday, instead of a daily count, as a compromise. I worked this out with Suzanne and we gave Al his first Monday count, which kept him quiet—for the day. Tuesday morning he called up and asked for a fresh count.

I reminded him that we had agreed on a twice-weekly count, Monday and Friday.

"Well, okay," said Al. "Just give me the Friday count today."

At the end of the year, I mailed the entire *Digest* live list the 10¢ offer. As expected, we took in a million new Book Club members. Our Club was finally the largest mail-order Book Club in the world.

The fulfillment department had a slight problem. The million new members sent in a million dimes—$100,000 in cash. I had provided the customers with a "coin card" in which to send back their payment. How do you get a million dimes out of a million coin cards? It presented an enormous clerical problem.

The fulfillment department solved this by modifying their Address-O-Graph machines into punch-out machines. All day long the fulfillment department rang to the clanking of dimes falling into tin buckets. Periodically the men from the maintenance department came in with dollies, and collected the heavy buckets full of dimes and hauled them off to the cashier's cage.

A small hitch arose when it was observed that some of the women who minded the Address-O-Graph machines were developing a certain pendulous look during the course of the day—they went home with a forward list. This was duly corrected when Suzanne announced that she would conduct a personal inspection of all fulfillment department personnel on their way out when the Address-O-Graph machines closed down.

We now had nearly two million Club members—one million of them brand new. And once again, I found myself in the role of a not-too-modest hero.

It didn't last very long.

The storm broke when I came to work one morning and encountered one of the editors I knew in the hall.

"Good morning!" I said.

The editor turned his face away and brushed by me without answering.

Further down the hall I met someone from the production department.

"Good morning, good morning!" I said.

This individual actually gave me a look in which horror and disdain were plainly mingled and fled from my company.

Then I met Harry Wilcox, the *Digest's* personnel manager. Harry came up to me with a long face, took my hand in his, and patted it gently.

"I'm so terribly, terribly sorry, Walt," Harry said.

"What's the matter?"

"Have you been down in the stock room?" Harry asked.

"No, I haven't."

"Then maybe you'd better," said Harry.

I went down and found myself confronting about 200,000 returned copies of *Condensed Books*.

We had, of course, anticipated these 200,000 returned books. We had already written them off. In fact, we had included an allowance for refurbishing some of them and sending them out again to late joiners—people whose Book Club order trailed in weeks after the main response. But even that first pile of returned books made a very impressive stack. It *looked* like 200,000 books, even if it had not yet reached that total.

Some public libraries don't even *have* 200,000 books in their stacks!

During the day it became evident that an impression had gotten abroad: A vast flood of unsold books had come back to engulf us, and the *Digest* was going to lose huge sums of money due to my idiocy.

I shared that idiocy, or at least the blame for it, with a young assistant named Tom Knowlton. By this time the Condensed Book Club had become large enough so that it justified my hiring someone to help me out, and Tom had joined up about a year previously as a member of the circulation department who helped me with all my circulation problems, but took particular responsibility for Condensed Books.

I had plucked Tom out of the actuarial department of the Metropolitan Life Insurance Company and I hired him because Tom was a mathematician. I sometimes said that if you could pry his skull open, you'd find the inside filled with numerals and equations, like $E = MC^2$. I needed a figures man to back me up in my flights of promotional fancy and Tom filled the bill.

As it turned out, Tom was also a perfect example of the ideal mail-order "split personality" that Al Cole talked about; an individual who combined sales sense, a salesman's enthusiasm, and a copywriter's creativity with an accountant's cold-blooded practicality.

So all day long I looked around for Tom, but I couldn't find him. And I couldn't find anybody else who wanted to talk to me.

It happened that Wally and Lila were holding one of their very special cocktail parties that afternoon at their miniature hilltop castle called "High Winds." All the important *Digest* editors and top business department people, together with their spouses, were invited—perhaps 100 men and women in all—and the party overflowed into the warm sunshine on the Wallace's terrace. My wife and I had no choice but to be there.

When we arrived, a little late, we strolled up to a group chatting together. The chatting ceased when we approached and an uncomfortable silence ensued.

We went on to another group and another. We were like ghosts at a wedding feast. Nobody seemed to want to acknowledge that they even knew us.

Presently I spotted Tom, and I sidled up to him.

"We are in trouble," I muttered.

"Don't worry," said Tom. "I've got it all taken care of."

"What do you mean, 'taken care of?' Have you seen the returned books down in the warehouse?"

"Where do you think I've been all day?" Tom asked. "It's all right, I tell you. Everything will be fine in the morning."

"For God's sake," I said, "what have you done?"

"Well," said Tom, "I called MacIntyre." (The MacIntyre organization handled much of the *Digest* vast mailing and clerical operations at that time.) "And I told him to get ahold of every damned delivery truck on Long Island and send them up here to the *Digest* office tonight. Right now, they're loading those returned books on Mac's trucks, and they'll have them all out at his warehouse in Great Neck before the *Digest* offices open tomorrow morning, even if it takes all night. And I've arranged with the Post Office in Pleasantville to let Mac pick up all the mail bags of returned books from here on. Mac meets all the trains, and trucks the books out to his warehouse. From here on, there *are* no returned Condensed Books. We'll repackage the books and ship them out to the future new customers we'll pick up in the next three months. We'll make money on every returned volume."

And this was indeed what happened. The next day, Tom and I casually waved aside all inquiries about those returned books—we had planned for them all along, they were gone, and we were reselling them at a huge profit. The sun came out, and once again we were heroes.

Incidentally, although we did subsequently succeed in securing another 200,000 members, to whom we shipped our repackaged books, we also continued to have a problem with the sheer numbers of our returned books. On following volumes, we set our initial print orders well below anticipated sales, and "rolled" our sales efforts so that we could use returned volumes over again, but it never worked out exactly. Tom and I spent a fair amount of time over the next few years, trying to persuade the Seaman's Institute and other worthy organizations to fill their library shelves with the free Condensed Books we wanted to donate. But you can only put a modest number of books in the Seaman's Institute Library.

Meanwhile, with the help of John Caples, we ventured into print and broadcast advertising. We even made mailings to non-*Digest* mail-order lists (which, naturally, didn't pull nearly as well as our *Digest* subscriber list). We acquired a sizeable new wing in the *Digest* building, where the Book Club fulfillment department was housed, and we acquired a new Book Club fulfillment manager to run it.

In my last year at the *Reader's Digest*, we had *four million paying members* on all four volumes issued by the Club. We sold, and were paid for, 16 million books. The price had gone up by then to $2.89, so our total Book Club sales were over $45 million, and profits exceeded the $18 million total income that *Reader's Digest* had enjoyed when I joined up, 12 years before.

The *Reader's Digest* Condensed Book Club was (and remains) one of the most successful book promotions of all time. The Club's condensations, it was found, actually stimulated the sale of many of the complete books from which the condensations were made, and helped turn ordinary books into best-sellers. I, as well as the Promotion Department, got a certain amount of credit for success-fully promoting the Club, although the editorial skill that went into selecting and condensing the books is generally credited with most of the Club's success. Personally, I think it was the *idea* of the Club—put simply, "*Reader's Digest* Condensed Books"—around which the editorial selection and the promotion were both built, that explained the Club's huge success—that, and the wonderful *Digest* subscriber live list. And, of course, the *idea* went all the way back to Wally's original concept of condensations for pleasurable reading.

Still, it *was* my idea that the *idea* be given a new application!

A SUMMARY OF THE SECRETS THAT MADE THE READER'S DIGEST *BOOK CLUB SUCCESSFUL*

1. We had a *unique* product (a *"condensed"* Book Club) which offered five or more entertaining works of fiction in a single vol-ume, skillfully condensed by *Reader's Digest* editors at a very low price; a product which satisfied a human *need* for *entertainment*.

2. We offered this product to our huge *house list*. We were mining our own vein of gold. As we discovered when we started selling the Club *outside* the *Digest* list, the general public which did not know the *Digest* was not very receptive to the *Digest* Book Club.

3. We had a *bargain* offer that made it supremely easy to order:

Initially, the first book *free*; later, when "free" wore out, a 10¢ offer which was even "freer than free." We offered this first book with *no obligation* to purchase an additional volume. It was not necessary (as with Book-of-the-Month Club) to sign a "negative option" card if you didn't want a volume. The books were shipped automatically) "until forbid." You could cancel at any time, but you *had* to cancel to stop getting the books.

4. We *dramatized* the offer with physical "hot potatoes": a 10¢ *coin card*; a "shipping label" order form (you didn't even have to send in an order form—simply return the shipping label and we'd paste it on the book and mail it to you) and; later, a "two penny" mailing in which we sent the prospect two pennies, one to keep for luck and one to mail back to secure your first volume of Condensed Books.

5. Last but not least, we had a management that embodied the perfect mail-order "split personality": willing to seize on a new idea with the imagination to recognize its potential, careful to run cold-blooded test after test until the validity of the idea was established and then willing to invest (gamble!) millions of dollars on direct mail to make the project successful. When the *Digest* decided to mine its list, a huge investment *was* necessary. A full-scale subscriber mailing, even in those days, cost a couple of million dollars.

But, of course, working with the vast *Digest* list made it all seem easy.

11

Using Action Devices that Get Sales

The What, Why and How of "Hot Potatoes"

I've already cited a number of examples of "hot potatoes," with some explanations of what they are, and how and why they work, but perhaps it would be worthwhile to briefly summarize the concept at this point, before telling the story of the biggest single hot potato mailing I know of, and how the idea developed.

WHAT A "HOT POTATO" IS

A hot potato is simply a *physical* action device that represents a sales idea. For example, instead of telling the customer, in writing, "you can have a $5 discount if you send in your order by February 10th," you enclose in the mailing a *dated* $5 discount certificate— "offer expires February 10th." The certificate becomes an instant hot potato. It must be used before February 10th—or the prospect is throwing $5 away.

Once you have this simple principle in mind—the idea of using a *physical object* to force action—your choice of hot potatoes is limited only by your own ingenuity.

In brief, a "hot potato" gets attention, dramatizes a mail-order offer, makes it easy to order, and forces action.

There is also an element of "monkey see, monkey do" in a good hot potato. A punch-out token, which must be attached to the order card to claim whatever incentive bonus is being offered—a free issue of a magazine, a premium book, a discount—is a most effective hot potato. Sticking the token in the slot is somehow a compelling thing to do.

And, finally, the hot potato makes it easy to order. You don't have to write out terms, or sign a contract, or fill out an order form. You just stick the token in the reply envelope and you've made a purchase.

I've used "hot potatoes" for every conceivable kind of mail-order product—from staid insurance companies to Christmas gifts, magazine subscriptions, solicitations for worthy causes, club memberships, and catalog products. I wouldn't put out a mail-order mailing without some form of hot potato in it.

Now for a very specific example of a hot potato, and the story of how it developed.

On March 26, 1957, the front page of the old New York *Herald-Tribune* carried a news story with the headline, "Someone is getting one hundred million pennies."

The story went on to say, "The Chemical Corn Exchange Bank confirmed yesterday that one of its clients had asked to be supplied with one hundred million pennies—one million dollars worth.

"Just who the customer is and what the pennies are for, the Bank wasn't prepared to say. But such a quantity of pennies could, conceivably present something of a shipping and storage problem.

"The Federal Reserve Bank of New York, which would supply any such quantity of coins requested in this area, explained that pennies come in bags of 5000, which weigh 34 pounds apiece. This means that one hundred million would weigh in at 340 tons, and be delivered in 20,000 bags, roughly a foot square and 5 inches or so through the middle."

The mystery of the 100 million pennies aroused a good deal of journalistic curiosity and speculation. The *Wall Street Journal* said,

> We're as baffled as the next guy as to why anybody would want a million dollars in pennies. But that's the request made of a local bank by an undisclosed client. We have three working theories:
>
> 1) Somebody in these inflated times wants to make a million dollars really look like something;
>
> 2) A billionaire is about to play a practical joke on the tax collector;
>
> 3) A wealthy eccentric is tired of having the sales tax bust up his dollars.

Another newspaper columnist speculated that an indignant alimony payer was going to pay off his wife in pennies. Actually, 100 million pennies represented 10 percent of the United States Mint's production of pennies for that year (they churned out about a billion new pennies in 12 months—that quantity of new pennies was necessary in order to keep enough pennies in circulation). Nobody knew—I was told by the Mint—quite where a billion pennies a year could disappear to, but the Mint calculated there would be a shortage if the supply were not replenished each year by at least a billion new coins).

The story really goes back to the Spring of 1948, when I put out my first test mailing for *Reader's Digest*—and discovered the power of the "hot potato," the inclusion of an action device in a mailing.

Les Dawson, the *Digest's* Subscription Manager, who was in charge of *Digest* Renewal and Christmas efforts, had pioneered the use of such action devices. First he had included 1¢ postage stamps in his renewal efforts, in the same way that *LIFE* had used such stamps to get attention and induce action (a 1¢ U.S. Postage Stamp was *valuable*, and nobody in those days would have thought of throwing such a stamp away). Later Les had introduced *Reader's Digest* "Savings Stamps," which had a nominal value considerably higher than a penny; and he introduced other action devices.

Naturally, I took a page from Les Dawson's book. I used a 1¢ stamp in my first *Digest* mailing. I went on to savings stamps, on both *Digest* and *Digest* book and Book Club promotions. Then it occurred to me that an actual coin would be better than a savings stamp, and I came up with a beautiful, blue $1 plastic coin for the magazine, and a lovely $2 plastic coin for the Book Club.

The $1 coin said:

READER'S DIGEST

SAVINGS T0KEN

$1.00 VALUE

LIMITED TIME OFFER

ON A *READER'S DIGEST*

INTRODUCTORY TRIAL

SUBSCRIPTION

EXPIRES MARCH 1, 1952

I mailed out 20 million of these plastic coins in January of 1952, and they brought in about 1.5 million new *Digest* subscribers. This was a dramatic way of presenting Frank Herbert's old $1-off offer.

In those days, third class mailing envelopes (under the "Rules" in the Post Office's big Black Book) had only one window, through which the recipient's name and address were permitted to show. Les Dawson had the feeling that his postage stamps and savings stamps would be more effective if he could have them show through a second window. The U.S. Government actually used a double window envelope on checks it sent out; the second window permitted a serial number to be read on the enclosed check, without opening the envelope. Before I joined the *Digest*, Les had asked the Post Office for permission to use a double-window envelope on *Digest* renewal mailings, and had been denied.

I shared Les Dawson's belief that we should have a double window, and I saw my opportunity when a new Postmaster General took office, and announced he was going to "liberalize" Post Office rules and regulations, to facilitate and encourage the use of the U.S. Mails. I paid another visit to Washington, and shortly after the Post Office put out a new directive announcing that double windows would be permitted in third class envelopes.

Not a very earth-shaking development, and one that was little noted at the time by the mail-order fraternity, but it certainly revolutionized third class envelopes! We, of course, pounced on the new regulation, and from there on most *Digest* mailings were distinguished by double windows; my 20 million "blue plastic $1 coins" all peered forth enticingly from their own little plastic window on the envelope.

Over the years, I had come to the conclusion that, *if* you have a good offer, and *if* you have good selling copy, the most productive and immediate result-boosting change you could make in a mailing was the *appearance* of the mailing, and the *dramatization* of the offer. And of course my original test of all previous *Digest* mailings had convinced me that mailings quickly wear out; a *new* and *better* mailing was required each year, just to stay even.

So, every year, I struggled with the problem of finding new ways to change the look of our mailings and to dramatize the offer.

I went from 1¢ stamps to discount certificates ("valuable soap coupons"), to savings stamps, to coin cards (to send back payment on Condensed Books), to plastic coins, to shipping labels. Thinking up gimmicks became my principal occupation.

By 1955, my circulation department had expanded considerably, and I was becoming more of an administrator and less of a copywriter. I had even acquired a copywriter, Marie Hill, who helped with both *Digest* and *Condensed Book* promotions, and helped me puzzle over new ways to get attention.

One morning Marie came into my office with a fund-raising mailing someone had sent her for some worthy charitable cause. The mailing had a shiny new penny in it—"for luck," as the accompanying letter said. And Marie suggested that we should try out a penny in our *Digest* mailings.

Sticking a penny in a mailing just to get attention seemed a weak crutch to me. But it suddenly occurred to me that in my search for new attention-getting gimmicks, like savings stamps and plastic coins, I had gradually gotten away from the basic thing I was trying to sell: the rewards a reader would enjoy from a subscription to *Reader's Digest*. I had gotten away from the basic story of what a wonderful magazine the *Reader's Digest* was—the story told in the old Persian Poet letter.

That letter carried *Reader's Digest* circulation up from next to nothing to a circulation of more than five million. And the letter started out: "Dear Friend: An Ancient Persian Poet said, 'If thou has two pennies, spend one for bread. With the other, buy hyacinths for thy soul.'"

The trouble with the old Persian Poet mailing was that it did *not* dramatize the offer with a *physical* object. The offer was there but you had to read the copy, and the communication of ideas through the written word is always difficult. The obvious wedding of Persian Poet and pennies came in an instant flash. I fished out the old Persian Poet letter and modified it slightly. I put together a mailing with two bright, shiny pennies showing through a second window in the envelope. And the copy on the envelope said: "If thou has two pennies, spend one for bread . . . " On the letter inside, I

READER'S DIGEST "TWO PENNY" MAILING

The 100 million penny breakthrough mailing.

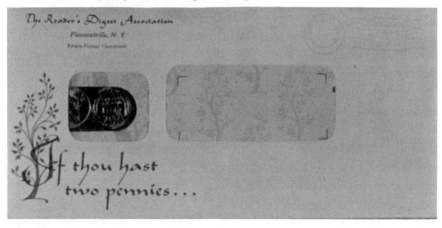

Reprinted by permission of *Reader's Digest*.

went on: "Keep one penny for bread," I said. "Or for luck. Send back the other penny as a down payment on a subscription to the *Reader's Digest*—a penny to seal the bargain! You'll get 8 months (a $2 value) for $1.01. You'll save 99¢. So the penny is worth 99¢ to you, *if you use it now*. We'll bill you for the balance of $1.00."

We tested this mailing in 1955. The test was extremely successful. It increased returns from about 6 to over 9 percent.

But the total return was potentially far greater than that. If you get a 9 percent pull on an initial mailing, one of the invisible laws of mail order says you can get a return of at least half the initial pull on a follow-up mailing. So I had, potentially, a promotional effort which could bring in a 13 percent response on the *Digest*, something like 2.6 million new subs from a 20 million mailing and a 20 million follow-up mailing.

Tom Knowlton, my assistant, had arranged with Chemical Bank, the *Digest's* regular bank, to secure 100,000 or so pennies— all we needed for our tests. Providing 100,000 pennies was no problem for a bank like Chemical.

But the initial *Digest* test was successful beyond all our wildest dreams! We decided that we would make a 20 million mailing the following year to secure new *Digest* subscribers. With 2¢ enclosed in each letter, this meant that we needed 40 million pennies. Even Chemical Bank admitted that this was a bit steep.

Tom Knowlton was a mathematician, and favored with an extremely logical, mathematical mind. He reasoned that the only place in the world where he could get 40 million pennies would be from the United States Mint. Accordingly, he got on an airplane and went to Washington to see the Director of the Mint, a Mr. Brett. The Director of the Mint was courteous, and friendly, but not too helpful. He explained that it was illegal for the United States Mint to produce coin of the realm for commercial purposes, or to sell or give any of the coins it minted to any purchaser except the Federal Reserve Bank. The Federal Reserve Bank, in its turn, distributed coins and currency only to member banks who, in turn, passed the money out to the general public.

"Well," said Knowlton, "if you were me and you had to get 40 million pennies, what would you do?"

Mr. Brett, somewhat amused, said that the greatest source of pennies, other than the Mint, was the penny gumball machine operators. There was a company in New York, he said, that gathered in the coins from subway gumball machines, gave them a mild acid bath to make them look new and shiny, and packaged them in rolls of 100, which they sold to the banks for $1.02 per packet. He suggested that we might try the penny gumball machine people.

Tom Knowlton looked up the gumball machine people, and a bargain was struck. For $1.03 per 100 pennies, plus the gift of a case of whiskey, we were able to corner the New York penny market.

Even so, it took us several months of hoarding to gather together the needed pennies. In the meantime it developed we needed another 20 million pennies. Tom and I had reasoned that, if pennies were so good for getting new subscribers for *Reader's Digest*, they ought to be equally good for getting new members to join the *Reader's Digest Condensed Book Club*. We made a test and we found that it worked—increasing the Book Club mailing results from 6 percent to an incredible 11 percent. So we decided to mail 10 million letters on the Book Club to *Reader's Digest* subscribers. In addition to the 20 million *Digest* mailing's 40 million pennies, this raised our total need to 60 million pennies.

In due time, we accumulated those 60 million pennies, and put out our 30 million pieces of mail. The cost of the 60 million pennies at $1.03 per hundred, was $618,000.

And the gumball machines came through!

As expected, the 60 million pennies did their job. Results on both mailings lived up to forecast. At the cost of $10 for each 1000 letters mailed, we were bringing in at least 50 extra new *Reader's Digest* subscribers to the magazine—a million extra new subscribers—and another million new subscribers to our book club membership rolls.

The next year—1957—we decided to mail again. Only this year we decided to mail a total of 40 million pieces for the *Reader's Digest*, 20 million in the spring and 20 million in the fall. In addition, we planned to mail another 10 million circulars on *Reader's*

Digest Condensed Book Club. Our total need was now 100 million pennies.

Once again Tom Knowlton thought of his friend down in Washington, Mr. Brett, the Director of the Mint, and Tom gave him a call.

"Remember me?" Tom asked. "I'm the fellow who wanted 40 million pennies last year. I'd like to see you."

"And I'd like to see you," said Mr. Brett. "Suppose you come here to Washington right away."

"He didn't sound too friendly," Tom said. "Maybe you'd better go down with me this time."

So Tom and I went to Washington. When we arrived at the office of the Director of the Mint, it was noon, so we invited Mr. Brett out to lunch. He carried a large, rolled up chart under his arm. As soon as we were seated, he spread the chart out among the luncheon dishes and wagged his finger under our noses.

"You said you were going to use 40 million pennies last year," he said. "You didn't. You used *60* million pennies! Look at this chart! Here's where you started hoarding pennies, and you kept it up right up to here!"

And he pointed to the figures on his chart.

"Do you realize," Mr. Brett said, "that I had to ship 60 million pennies into the New York area to prevent a coin shortage? And do you realize what that penny shortage could have done if I hadn't shipped the pennies in? An election year was coming up. And you know how sensitive bankers are. All we needed was for one banker to say to another one, 'Have you noticed there's a shortage of pennies?' The second banker would have said to a third one, 'Have you noticed the shortage of money?' Then all of them would have started hoarding currency. A financial crisis would have ensued. The country would have been thrown into a financial panic, and a Democrat would have been elected President. Now, how many pennies do you want this year?"

We told him that we wanted 100 million pennies.

"Well, if you will accept delivery in Denver, where the coins are minted, I could justify letting you have them on the basis of the fact that I'd save $20,000 in shipping costs that I'd otherwise have in getting 100 million pennies to New York," he said. "You go to Chemical Bank and tell them to go to the Federal Reserve and order the coins, and tell the Federal Reserve to come to me, and you'll get your 100 million pennies—F.O.B. in Denver."

So we thanked Mr. Brett and returned to Chappaqua, and Tom got in touch with both Wells Fargo and Brinks and asked them what they would charge to transport 100 million pennies half-way across the country. They came up with identical bids—$120,000. I was very indignant and called Mr. Brett.

"I think you misled me," I said. "You told me it would cost $20,000 to transport 100 million pennies from Denver to Chappaqua, and it works out it would cost $120,000."

He then asked, "How do you plan to transport these pennies?"

"By armoured car. Brinks or Wells Fargo."

Mr. Brett was delighted. "Well, the Mint transports them on open railroad flat cars," he said. "It's simply impossible to steal a hundred million pennies. Why, if somebody grabbed two bags of pennies—a total of just 10,000, worth only a $100—he couldn't run a hundred yards with them."

So we made arrangements with a trucking firm to transport the pennies by ordinary open flatbed trucks, out to the Long Island warehouse of the MacIntyre organization, where the mailings would be put together. The cost of the shipment from Denver was $20,000.

The MacIntyre Company put our 100 million pennies in a room in their warehouse—all 340 tons of them—and the floor of the warehouse collapsed.

Meanwhile, we went ahead with preparations for the mailing. There was a small technical problem which we had discovered when we made our big mailing the preceding year. Then, due to the fact that we were mailing out considerable "coin of the realm," which in its 60 million total was quite valuable ($600,000), we had taken the precaution of printing "Return Postage Guaranteed" on the outside envelope. We knew that we'd get a certain percentage of "nixies"—undeliverable mail—due to changes in address, deaths, inaccuracies of mailing lists, and so forth. We normally figured on a 4 percent nixie rate on a 60 million two-penny mailing, which meant we would get back $36,000 in pennies. Even though it cost us money for such returns, we calculated we'd be ahead of the game.

However, when the pennies actually came back, in the "nixie" envelopes, we found that extracting these pennies from the envelopes so we could use them again was beyond the power of the already overburdened *Digest's* fulfillment department. So we went to the MacIntyre organization.

"How much will you charge us to extract two pennies from an envelope?" we inquired.

The answer was, "Three cents."

This was the lowest bid we could find, and it was a losing proposition. Nevertheless, we gave the envelopes to the MacIntyre Company, and they gave us approximately $36,000 worth of pennies, for which they charged us $54,000.

The following year, when we proposed to mail 100 million pennies, Tom Knowlton, whose strong point was logic, had a brilliant idea.

"We'll leave the 'Return Postage Guaranteed' off the envelope," he said. "We aren't required to put that on, anyway. So the Post Office will keep the mail and destroy it, and we save the return postage costs *and* 1¢ per letter for getting the pennies out."

On an estimated 4 percent nixies—two million returned letters from a mailing of 50 million—we'd save $40,000 on returned postage due—plus $40,000 net loss on four million pennies we wouldn't have to recover.

So, we happily printed up 50 million envelopes without "Return Postage Guaranteed"; had the MacIntyres stuff the envelopes with pennies and brochures and letters and truck them down to the Great Neck Post Office.

And then the Post Office lowered the boom.

"These envelopes contain coin of the realm," they said. "Some of this mail will be undeliverable. It will come back to us, but you are not accepting these returns. What are we supposed to do with these four million pennies we'll have on our hands? Normally, we burn undeliverable mail. But we can't burn up coin of the realm— this would be committing a misdemeanor at the very least. So, your mail is unmailable, and you can't mail those 50 million letters with those 100 million pennies in them."

Tom and I then got on another airplane and went back down to Washington. This time we visited my old friend Ed Riley of the Post Office Classifications Division. Once again, I found myself explaining a dilemma, and once again Ed Riley made sympathetic noises, but was firm in backing the local Post Office's position.

However, by then, I was something of an expert myself on the Post Office and the rules in the Big Black Book.

"There are some 42,000 U.S. Postmasters," I said. "Suppose I wrote to each of them and guaranteed that we, the *Reader's Digest*, would accept and pay for all nixies, even though the envelopes don't say so. Would this be acceptable?"

Mr. Riley said that it would be, so we went back to Chappaqua, and I dashed off a letter to 42,000 Postmasters, and our mail went out, on time.

Now, both the mailings on the magazine and the Book Club contained two pennies, and we did indeed get back four million pennies in two million nixie envelopes. Net value of those pennies (after extraction) was $40,000.

We got the anticipated response on these mailings—9 percent on the two magazine mailings, about 3,600,000 new subscribers from a total of 40 million mailings mailed, and about 1.1 million Book Club members from the other 10 million Condensed Book mailings. Tom and I were very pleased with ourselves. There remained, of course, the small problem of getting those four million pennies out of the envelopes.

The February 8, 1958 issue of *The New Yorker* took up the story. Here's how *The New Yorker* tells it.

"Now, when the predicted 4 percent of the letters started returning, how much would it cost to get the pennies out of the envelopes? Some commercial firms volunteered to do the work for the *Digest*, one of them offering as much as 75 percent return of the money. But at that point, Raymond Wall, Director of the Mount Kisco Boys' Club, said he would like to take over the task and split the proceeds evenly with the *Digest*. The *Digest* agreed to the deal. The first *Digest* letters went out in September, and within ten days the nixies—the magazine's word for returned letters—

started coming in. The tide of nixies rose steadily throughout the fall and early winter and is now at flood, and when we visited Mr. Wall at the Club a few days ago, he told us that his only worry was the weight of the mail stacked on the Club House Floor. Every day, the Pleasantville Post Office, having counted the nixies in order to bill the *Digest* for their return postage, puts them in bags, and the *Digest* trucks them to the Club House, where every night fifteen boys and parents spend several hours ripping open envelopes and extracting pennies. The envelopes and the accompanying literature are thrown into waste baskets and eventually burned; the pennies are dropped into old coffee tins and mixing bowls, weighed, put in bags that hold exactly $50 worth (5000 pennies weigh exactly 34 pounds, 5 ounces) and delivered to the *Digest* which deposits them in its bank.

"The process of extracting the pennies from the envelopes has come to be known as 'husking,' and Mr. Wall compares it to opening clams. A good husker can husk up to 13 nixies a minute; this amounts to $15.60 an hour, or $7.80 for the Boys' Club, at the time of our visit, something over $7,000 apiece for the Boys' Club and the *Digest*. 'These pennies have been a Godsend to the Club,' Mr. Wall said. 'By the time we are through, sometime in the Spring, we will cut our mortgage in half, and all it will have cost us is the strength required to go through 90 tons of nixies.' "

A little later, *Saturday Review* ran a cartoon by Cem, showing some prosperous looking gents, gathered by a fireplace, with drinks in their hands, with the punch line below—"After I found the *Reader's Digest* lucky penny in my mailbox, the breaks started coming thick and fast."

In the August 1958 issue of *Top Secret* Magazine, along with a story about "How her husband tortures Gina Lolabrigida," there was an exposé of the *Reader's Digest* man who threw away 100 million pennies. The title of the story was "How the *Reader's Digest* Bought a Million-Dollar Headache—for Three Million Bucks," and it intimated that Walter Weintz, who was the Circulation Manager of *Reader's Digest*, was in deep trouble.

The only trouble I encountered came down from Canada. The Canadian Edition was by then an independent operating entity, which did its own promotions—always pointedly different from the ones we did at Pleasantville, and always, somehow, with better results than we were able to attain in America. These results were memoed down to Al Cole regularly. Al naturally compared Canada's results with my domestic results, and sometimes Al seemed to suspect that Canada knew how to do mailings better than we did in Pleasantville.

And presently, after my 100 million-mailing, came a memo from Canada. They had taken their standard mailing (which said nothing about either Persian Poets or pennies) and tested it with and without the enclosure of a penny. Sure enough, they had discovered that the addition of the penny made not the slightest difference in the results. The inference which could have been deduced from this test result was that I had thrown away a million dollars of the *Digest's* good money with my 100 million penny mailing.

Although I'm sure the Canadian Circulation Manager was expressing no intentional innuendos, one of the perils of being the Circulation Manager of the domestic edition of the *Digest* was the flack I ran into from the international editions, who always seemed to find ways to do things differently—and better—than what I did in Pleasantville. Since Pleasantville was headquarters, and London, Paris, Rome, Madrid, and Frankfort were thousands of miles away, the circulation managers of these editions were somewhat like a Russian in Siberia—it was difficult to get the home office's eye and receive proper appreciation for work accomplished. So it became a fairly common practice for these circulation managers to take each new mailing that I put out, and to test it against a mailing of their own manufacture.

Tested properly, my mailings invariably came out ahead.

But the foreign editions were not run by mail-order people, and the tests they ran were generally pretty unscientific. They were able to prove just about anything they wanted to, by fudging the tests just a bit this way or that way, and they sometimes did.

This was the principal reason why I had hired Tom Knowlton as my assistant; Tom was a numbers man who quickly untangled misleading test results and put his finger on the fallacy hidden in the cloud of garbled information. The first thing I had Tom do, after he joined the *Digest*, was to write a book on the Probability

Tables. Tom did so; the book ended triumphantly with a bit of unarguable arithmetic:

$$n = \frac{x^2 pg}{(xs)2}$$

Where n = size of sample
p = percent return
g = 100-P
s = measure of variation (sigma)
x = number of sigmas
xs = limit

At least one purpose of this book was to discredit the mailings from foreign editions. Fortunately, in the case of the Canadian two-penny test, Tom was able to quickly point out the error of the Canadian test.

The test reports that came in from the foreign editions frequently reminded me of a magazine my father subscribed to when I was a boy, called the *Journal of Mining and Metallurgy*. I liked to read it because it contained jokes, mixed in with its reports on ore recovery statistics and new lead and zinc separation techniques. An item that particularly impressed me was the story of a group of engineers who got into an argument about the relative intoxicating power of different alcoholic beverages—scotch, rye, bourbon, and gin. Being engineers, they made a scientific test, and sent a report on the results of the test to the *Journal*.

The engineers sat down one evening with a bottle of scotch, and—since they didn't like to drink straight Scotch—mixed it with water. They consumed the bottle and noted their results the next day. Very intoxicating.

The following evening they repeated the procedure, with rye— and to make their test consistent, they mixed the rye with water. They consumed the entire bottle, with the same results—drunkenness and a headache the morning after.

The next night they drank a bottle of bourbon (with water), and the following night a bottle of gin—and again, to keep their experiment down to a single variable, they had gin and water. Results were the same as on previous nights.

"Our conclusion," said the engineers' summary of their tests, "is that water is very intoxicating—because water was the only constant present in all experiments."

Mail-order testing is a science that requires scientific setting up, execution, and analysis. A bad test—slanted, consciously or unconsciously—can lead to dangerous, erroneous conclusions. But even a *good* test—analyzed with the help of personal prejudice—can be equally misleading.

THE SIMPLE ELEMENTS OF A SUCCESSFUL TEST

Throughout this and preceding chapters I've skimmed over the elements that make the difference between a successful and an unsuccessful test. I'll sum up these elements here.

First, my definition of a successful mail-order test: This is *any* test which gives you *reliable* results. That word "reliable" defines the most important element of a scientific test.

There are all kinds of mistakes, oversights, and shortcomings that can make a test unreliable. The wrong list, an inadequate test quantity, and the inclusion of more than one variable in a segment of the test are a few of the most obvious pitfalls.

Essentially, when you are making a test mailing you are trying to find out if a given product can be sold at a profit in commercial quantities. So, given a product which you believe has mail-order potential, the first problem is to seek out *lists* of people who *might* buy your product *in commercial quantities.*

Obviously, you can leave out lists that have only a few dozen or a few hundred names (unless, of course, your product has a *very* limited appeal, which may tell you right at the start that it's not a mail-order product, or unless the product has a *very* large margin: For instance, if you are selling around-the-world cruises or $150,000 foreign sports cars).

The first mistake made by most beginners (and many seasoned practitioners who should know better) is failure to test a sufficient number of lists. If you test only one list and the test fails you'll never know whether or not the failure was due to your list selection. But if you test a *spectrum* of at least 10 lists and all fail you can be pretty sure that your product, your offer, your copy, or all three, are no good.

And I would consider such a test result, on a *reliable* test quantity, a *success*. The test has given you a reliable "No" on your proposed project. It has saved you money. You would be wise to abide by the results.

Naturally, besides testing a number of lists, you need a statistically reliable *test quantity* on each list. In most cases, I consider a 5000 test quantity a bare minimum. So if you are testing 10 lists, and 5000 on each, right at the start you have a 50,000 test.

Next, you need to make sure that you are getting a genuine, legitimate cross section of each and every list. You get this, first, by putting your requirements in writing, and, second, by renting your list *through a responsible list broker*.

List brokers are an important element of the mail-order profession. These brokers have at their disposal the names and characteristics of hundreds of mail-order lists which are available for rental. The list broker can tell you how many names there are on a list, how the list was built, what the people on the list purchased, and what their ages, sex, occupations, financial status and interests are. List brokers will help you rent the kind of mailing lists that seem most suitable for your product.

Successful list brokers have many clients. In the course of a year they may rent thousands of tests on hundreds of lists. They know which list tests result in roll-outs, and which lists are tested but not followed up. So list brokers are walking encyclopedias of mail-order lists. They *know* a lot more about lists than any beginner possibly can, and their advice and services are well worth the commissions they receive on the list rentals they manage.

In setting up a list test you would probably want to specify an "every nth name selection." The broker can advise you. Brokers know which lists are on computer, what subsections of a list can be tapped, and how to get a fair geographic and demographic reading. These days list brokers themselves have their list of lists on computer, and you have only to specify the kind of lists you want; by punching a few keys the broker can give you every conceivable list answering your needs.

Another important point: You should definitely try for a *spectrum* of lists. A "spectrum" is a range of likely lists: big lists versus smaller lists, and lists that are precisely up your alley versus lists that *might* be.

A quick example: Suppose you are selling expensive, rubber-soled yachtsmen's boating shoes. An obvious list of prospects would be yachtsmen. But what about Coast Guard Registrations? Or state registrations? Or would you be doing better with lists of people who have previously purchased boating equipment (compasses, lorans, radars) by mail? Would sailboat buffs be better prospects than motorboaters? How would BIG yacht owners (yachts over 60 feet) compare with *small* Coast Guard registered boats (over 16 feet, under 24 feet)?

You could easily assemble 20 or 30 likely lists. Then your problem is to pick 10 of these lists which are sufficiently *different* to help you define your potential market through a set of tests.

One final footnote on the size of tests. Ultimately you are dealing with the U.S. mail. The U.S. Post Office is a *mass* medium. The Post Office mails billions of letters practically every day. A minor mistake here or there is bound to happen now and then. I've heard of *small* tests getting mislaid in supposedly empty mail bags; the bags might be sent from one postal distribution center to another and the second center, finding a few "old" third-class envelopes lodged in a supposedly empty bag, would have a natural tendency to dump those envelope "undeliverables." I'm pretty sure I've been jinxed once or twice by "undeliverable" mail that never got delivered simply because it was too small to bother with.

So by all means make your list tests at least big enough to assure that the tests won't be lost.

The third important element in any test, after product and list, is *offer*. Should you offer credit card privileges, insist on cash with order, or offer a 10-day free examination? Should you charge $10.00, $17.95, or $16.00 plus $2.89 postage and handling?

Should you offer a *deluxe* version of your product? (10 or 15 percent of the customers for any product will automatically check a "deluxe" offer; for instance, in medical insurance, $60 a day coverage vs. $40 a day; or on magazines, a two-year subscription offer vs. a one-year offer.) But offering a *choice* slows down a sale; would you be better off *without* a deluxe rider on your order form?

The only way to get the answers to such questions is through testing.

But you can't test *everything*. And many mail-order people waste a lot of time and money trying to do just that. They test pink envelopes vs. blue envelopes. They test six different prices, thereby reducing their individual test cells to an unreliable small quantity.

Which leads to the final, most important element of any test, and that's *judgment*. In setting up a test, you must be governed by common sense. And in analyzing results, particularly, you must be governed by good judgment. You must not let your emotions sway your interpretation of test results.

Done right and interpretated correctly, mail-order testing is an invaluable tool—one which is scarcely duplicated in any other field of marketing. It's the science which enables some mail-order practitioners to make millions. But the most important element, human judgment, is the weakest link in the chain, and so it behooves us all in the mail-order business to check, refine, study, and learn with each test we make.

To illustrate my point, I'll mention a brief encounter I had with a marketing executive of a large corporation. This executive had gone to work, right out of MBA school, for a very large and successful mail-order company. In about ten years he reached the top of this corporate ladder, at which point things started going sour. Someone commented to me that this company had, in effect, a whole navy of licensed sea captains at the helm, none of whom had ever been to sea in a storm. And when things got rough, none of them knew what to do.

But one of them did call me in for a consultation. He explained the problem. Sales were off. What should be done?

Out of my vast wisdom (since I really didn't know precisely what was wrong with their sales, or what they might do to solve their problems) I suggested a test.

"Oh, we never make tests," this mail-order executive replied.

"You don't?" I said. "Why on earth not?"

"Because we don't need to," he replied. "We've been in this business long enough so that we know all the answers without testing. We know what works and what doesn't, and why."

"Then I guess I can't help you," I said. He agreed, and that was pretty much the end of the story except that, subsequently, he was one of the thirty or so vice presidents who were let go when the corporation had a much-needed housecleaning.

The story of 100 million pennies had another sequel which took place in 1980, more than 20 years after the *Digest* mailing. By this time I had become a mail-order consultant, and had taken in as my partner my oldest son, Todd Weintz. The two of us were serving assorted magazine clients, among them Litton Industries, whose Medical Economics division had decided to publish a new magazine about the future, which they called *NEXT*.

The circulation manager of *NEXT*, Joe Kenna, was old enough to remember the *Digest's* penny mailing. "You haven't done a penny mailing for twenty years," Joe said. "Neither has anybody else. So let's try in on *NEXT*."

So we did. We tested a straight, introductory offer—"Yours for half-price"—and against it tested a Penny Sale offer (the same half-price offer, really, plus a penny)—"Six issues of *NEXT* for the regular price, and six more issues for 1¢, and here's the penny."

The penny mailing doubled returns. We went out with a big mailing and got 300,000 customers to send in their orders. The offer we used was the standard so-called "soft offer": "Send no money. We'll send the first issue on approval. If you aren't delighted, write 'cancel' on our bill and forget it."

We believed, from previous experience, that we would get about 60 percent payment, and 40 percent cancellations and bad debts (a far cry from the 96 percent payment I got on the 1948 *Digest* mailing); this was the current state of consumer sophistication relative to magazine introductory offers.

At the same time, we tested the same 1¢ offer on another Litton publication called *Hudson Home*. This publication was a very worthwhile how-to-do-it periodical that Litton had purchased but never promoted; it had about 15,000 circulation.

We had no trouble laying our hands on a few thousand pennies for the test mailings on both these publications. In fact, the Mint made them available to Litton's bank.

The results showed that we could secure a 6.5 percent response on the *NEXT* mailing, and about 8.5 percent on a big mailing for *Hudson Home*. So we went ahead with both.

But in each case we used the "soft offer": "Look at the first issue—then cancel if you wish." We predicted a 40 percent cancellation, at most, for both publications.

In fact, 80 percent *cancelled*, or failed to pay, on *NEXT*. And better than 80 percent *paid* on *Hudson Home*!

So Litton killed off *NEXT*, and the name of the other magazine was simplified to just plain *HOME*, and a big mailing went out on it. This was a penny mailing. We got in about 200,000 paying subscribers. We laid plans for a follow-up mailing. But, the Mint then announced that no more pennies would be available.

Then, one Sunday morning, Todd was reading the *New York Times* and came across a little humorous article about "the only product that a penny will still buy." This was a penny gumball, purchased from a gumball machine. And the article gave the name of a company in Chicago which manufactured these machines.

On Monday morning, Todd called up the company's president. Could he supply pennies? No, he only manufactured the gumball machines, which were purchased and serviced by a number of big individual gumball distributors throughout the country. He gave Todd their names and phone numbers. Todd called them all up, and they said they'd be glad to sell *HOME* pennies for a small mark-up.

So once again, we were in the gumball coin business. Gumball dealers in Atlanta, Dallas, Los Angeles, and Minneapolis sent truckloads of pennies—for $1.04 per hundred. Trucks came daily to Metromail's plant in Nebraska, from all over the country, loaded with copper pennies.

We put out a two million mailing, and secured nearly 300,000 additional subscribers to *HOME*, boosting the circulation to about 500,000.

It was, however, a nerve-wracking business for all of us—Joe Cece, the *HOME* Circulation Director, Todd, the publisher of *HOME*, and me. The publisher had a silver plaque inscribed which he presented to Joe Cece. It said, in plain English: "We don't want no more penny mailings no how never again."

It occurred to me that I had, long ago, used blue plastic coins for *Reader's Digest*, so I instituted a search for a plastic coin manufacturer. Several were found, but their price in every case was prohibitive; 5¢ to 10¢ per coin, which was more than we could afford to pay. Then the Weintz Company's Art Director discovered an aluminum gadget manufacturer who offered to make us aluminum coins for about 1¢ apiece. Moreover, these coins looked much more like a genuine, valuable coin than did my old *Digest* plastic coins.

The aluminum coin said:

HOME

$1.95

VALUE

SAVINGS

TOKEN

LIMITED OFFER

THIS TOKEN

IS WORTH

$1.95

ON A HOME MAGAZINE

INTRODUCTORY TRIAL

SUBSCRIPTION

We tested this coin and to our delight it pulled even better than the authentic U.S. copper penny! So Joe Cece ordered a big mailing—about two million letters—using the aluminum coin.

Unfortunately, an unforseen hitch developed on aluminum coins. The original penny mailing had the penny pasted (with rubber cement) to a coin card, so that it showed through the appropriate envelope window.

Our mailing house, the Metromail organization, had modified its Phillipsburg inserting machines so that the machine would drop a spot of glue on the coin card, then drop the copper coin on the glue spot, where it stuck—all done at no extra cost by high-speed machines.

But when we went into mass production on the aluminum coins, it was found that these coins, being aluminum, were much lighter than the copper pennies and, instead of sticking, they bounced!

The production of this mailing became a slow, painful nightmare. (The *test* of the aluminum coins, done on an experimental, hand-fed basis, had failed to reveal the problem flaw in the aluminum coins.)

The mailing, however, was a success. And it was decided to make an additional mailing the following year.

"But no more aluminum coins!" said Joe Cece.

I then recalled that one of the *Digest's* efforts, perhaps 30 years before, in the evolution of *Digest* mailings toward copper pennies, had been a rather crude coin card with a printed punch-out token. In the succeeding 30 years, the printer's art had evolved enormously, and it was now possible to *print* an embossed coin with a beautiful metallic silver surface right on the coin card. So we tested that.

And the *printed* coin card actually pulled better than the aluminum coin!

I believe the reason (I can always explain, on Monday morning, why something unexpected happened in a mailing Friday night) was that the aluminum coin was, to a certain degree, an amusing "collectible"—something to put in your pocket and perhaps use to try to fool a coin machine or turnpike coin box. The *printed* token had no such possible use. It was a simple "hot potato"—use it, or lose $1.95. It worked.

With these three updated versions of the old *Digest* penny mailing—a penny, an aluminum coin, and a cardboard token—we took *HOME* to a respectable 600,000 circulation base. Then Litton sold it to Thompson International, and Thompson sold it to Knapp Publications, and The Weintz Company went on to other things.

Perhaps I should add one final note on my *Digest* hundred million penny mailing. This was the last major mailing I made for *Reader's Digest* before leaving the Digest Association and setting up shop as a consultant. The mailing pulled 9 percent.

"Let's see them beat *that*," I said to myself as I cleaned out my desk and strode off into the wilds of mail-order consultation.

The next year the *Digest* put out its first sweepstakes mailing. And the mailing pulled 14 percent.

"They won't pay," I said.

Actually, payment on the sweepstakes subscription orders turned out to be a bit better than on the previous non-sweepstakes effort. Evidently, people felt that, if they didn't pay, they'd somehow lose their chance to win a big $100,000 sweepstakes prize.

"They'll never renew," I said.

At the end of the year, the *Digest* used a sweepstakes renewal series. And renewals were better than ever before.

"Well, now what will they do for encores?" I asked.

This was in 1960. Since then the *Digest* has used nothing but sweepstakes and circulation has grown from the 12,134,283 average net paid total it attained during the last six months of 1958, under my promotional management, to a fairly constant total of 17 or 18 million.

Sooner or later, of course, the sweepstakes will run out. Last year, I noticed, the *Digest* has stuck a real, authentic nickel in their sweepstakes mailing, as a simple attention-getting package opener. It seems weak to me.

Maybe they should try a new, inflation-era version of the Persian Poet mailing.

"If thou hast two nickels, spend one for bread. With the other, buy hyacinths for thy soul . . ."

A SUMMARY OF ADVICE ON THE USES AND ABUSES OF HOT POTATOES

This chapter wraps up what was probably the most important "discovery" I have made in 40 or so years of learning the mail-order business. The "discovery" (which, I repeat, was most certainly not first discovered by me) was that a good "hot potato" can generally increase the response of *any* mailing by at least 25 percent, usually 50 percent, and sometimes 100 percent.

That's the good news. The bad news is that, as response goes up, quality is apt to go down. *Not necessarily*: The *Digest's* "sweepstakes" secured subscribers who were actually better than my "penny" subscribers. But this is a pitfall to watch out for. On a "free examination" offer, for instance, a hot potato may bring in a host of free-loaders who have no intention of paying.

A hot potato should have a *perceived value* which induces action. For instance, if you send in a sweepstakes entry form, you may win a million dollars (while you're at it, better sweeten your chances of winning by purchasing the product). If you throw away the sweepstakes entry form, you may be throwing away a million dollars.

This is why *Reader's Digest*, Publishers Clearing House, and other big sweepstakes users customarily get a *50-percent* response on their mailings. Of course, most of the 50 percent may be "NO" entries but there'll also be a lot more "YESES" than there would be without a sweepstakes.

Finally, a hot potato that is *related* to the product you're selling naturally helps sell that product. A "token" offering a free book about preventing high blood pressure, on a mailing promoting PREVENTION magazine, will probably increase returns more than would, say, a free book about woodworking. A $1.00 discount token on a subscription to HOME that is good on HOME, and HOME only, puts pressure on the reader to subscribe to HOME.

The last chapter on hot potatoes has still to be written as ingenious mail-order practitioners find new ways to present their offers with the help of *physical* action getters. Knowing about the general principles involved may make it easier for you to be the next "brilliant discoverer" of the power of the hot potato!

12

"War Stories" from a Consultant's Diary

Some Clients I've Served And The Lessons They Taught Me.

In a way, the 12 years I spent working for *Reader's Digest* were, for me, like the time Adam spent in the Garden of Eden before the Fall. I was working in a protected environment, where everything I did usually came out right, and I could do no wrong. I had a great product, a great customer list to mine, and things were perhaps a little too easy. I was pretty innocent.

Then I decided to leave *Reader's Digest* and strike out on my own. And I discovered a new world, where success no longer came quite so easy. I discovered that the mail-order business had numerous endemic problems, many of them unfamiliar to me. The experience of working on these problems was most educational.

However, the one big lesson I learned was the fact that the old mail-order basics still applied, whether I found myself working for magazines, book clubs, insurance companies, politicians, or non-profit fund raising organizations.

So in this chapter I'd like to illustrates some of the lessons I learned after I became a marketing consultant, and some of the basic principles I rediscovered, with "war stories" about some of my actual experiences with some of the clients I've served over the past 30 years.

The experiences also answer some of the questions I'm frequently asked, by beginners and sometimes by ambitious veterans in the mail-order field. Just what is a "direct marketing" or "mail-order" consultant, anyway, and what does he or she do to earn a living? How does one become such a consultant, and what are the rewards and penalties of a marketing consultant's career? And why would anyone become a consultant—if there is any logical reason for such a move?

In 1958, I was, according to my own evaluation, riding high at *Reader's Digest*. I had an interesting job, reasonable pay, lifetime security, pleasant associates. However, there were a few serpents in my Garden of Eden.

For one thing, the *Digest* was changing rapidly from a small, close-knit outfit of entrepreneurs into a giant departmentalized organization. Memos and financial forecasts, and MBAs and lawyers and meetings were beginning to jam their sticks in my wheels. After years of freedom from big-company committee decision-making, I found the change irksome.

So the time came for a decision. At 42 I could still start a new career. If I waited to see what happened after Al Cole retired, the age factor would be beginning to work against going out on my own.

These considerations helped me to a decision. But basically I think my real reason for leaving the *Digest* was that I didn't *like* being a big wheel in a successful, departmentalized corporation. I wanted some excitement. It seemed to me that if I left the *Digest* and hung out my shingle as a "mail-order consultant"—whatever that was—I'd have all the uncertainties I could ask for. So I quit.

Al was very nice about it. He reasoned with me over a period of weeks, after I told him of my intentions. I had a final session with Wally, who asked me what it would take to make me stay, and hinted at big things. I said my mind was made up, so we shook hands and he wished me luck.

Then Al announced that my first client would be *Reader's Digest*, and as I was now a company rather than an individual, my income would be substantially increased; he would pay me a monthly retainer, and he handed me a two-year contract, spelled out by the *Digest* lawyers. I signed it, and I was in business.

When I first hung out my consulting shingle, I had many doubts about where my clients would come from, or whether any would come at all. I need not have worried. From the moment I opened my doors, an unending procession of mail-order operators marched in, each announcing in turn his or her availability as a client and his or her willingness to be serenaded.

There were all kinds. The Texas millionaire in the pointed $500.00 boots who flew his own plane to New York to see me, and who wasn't interested in the details of the budget for his new publication—just the bottom line total for two years (which he paid without argument). The old man who refused to tell me what his mail-order idea was (it was worth a fortune, he said, and I might steal it from him) but who wanted me to write up a test proposal, finance the test, and meet with him regularly. He was difficult to get rid of.

And then there were junior executives in various mail-order companies who summoned me preemptorily to their offices, quizzed me at length about my qualifications, methods of operating, and fee structure—and then announced that it sounded like a pretty soft way to make a living and they thought they'd have a fling at it themselves.

There were innumerable dreamers—the mail-order business has more supposed ways to get rich quick than any field except possibly the stock market and wildcatting for gold, oil, or uranium, and mail-order seems to attract adventurous souls.

There were also hard-headed businessmen with practical problems. And there were entrepreneurs and speculators.

The worst were the free information seekers: men—or women—who actually had going mail-order businesses, wanted and asked for both advice and copy, but had no intention of paying for either. There were also the competitive bid seekers, the "pricers" who had no intention of buying, but who wanted to keep informed on the market. And, the "That proves we don't need it" boys who—at management's request—called me in for an interview so that they could then report they had investigated my services and found them wanting.

However, there were also legitimate (and paying) clients. My second client (after *Reader's Digest*) was a triple: three related corporations, Simon & Schuster, Pocket Books, and Golden Press. Leon Shimkin, the business head of these three organizations, was a friend of mine. After the success of *Reader's Digest* Condensed Books, Leon had come to see me with the suggestion for a new *Digest* enterprise. The *Digest*, through its books, was in the business of culture mixed with entertainment, said Leon. So why not sell musical records—the works of great masters? This would be a logical extension of the *Digest's* editorial services. In fact, why not set up a joint venture between S & S and the *Digest*: they'd provide a big $18.00 album of great recordings by great masters, and the *Digest* would sell this album to its culture-conscious eager-for-self-improvement readers.

As it happened, I had already decided that musical recordings were the logical next field for *Digest* expansion, and I had previously presented the idea to Al in a memo which Al had under consideration. I suggested to Al that the S & S musical album would be a good way to get our feet wet.

Al thought the idea had merit—but objected to having Simon & Schuster, a book publisher, as partners in a musical venture.

So I told Leon we were going to go it alone, and the *Digest* made arrangements to secure a set of classical recordings from RCA—by RCA Victor performers—paying RCA for production and royalties, but keeping the profits after these costs entirely in the *Digest's* pockets.

I put out a test—one of my last mailings before leaving the *Digest*—and it was a success. We ended up with a big mailing to the 10 million *Digest* list, which sold a million record albums at a round figure of $18 million—of which one-third was profit.

Leon was philosophical about our decision to go it alone, and we stayed friends. So when I left the *Digest*, my first visit was to his office at Simon & Schuster. I reminded Leon of my vast success selling *Digest* books and records, and offered to do the same for him—for a retainer. Leon accepted, and between Leon and *RD* I was assured a steady, adequate income for the year ahead.

My third client was Sam Josefowitz, and my fourth was Time Inc.

Sam Josefowitz was a mail-order entrepreneur who had made millions with what I believe was the first record club ever started in America, which he named the Concert Hall Society.

Sam had seen my *Reader's Digest* "until forbid" mailing on the Reader's Digest Condensed Book Club, and he lifted the offer bodily for use in his Concert Hall promotions. With this offer— "your first album for 10¢"—he quickly built the rolls of this record club to a million members, and he then sold the club for, I believe, $3 million.

Sam went on to do a vitamins club, which he called Vitasafe, and which he promoted with the same successful 10¢ sampling formula, automatic shipment, and "until forbid." He promoted his vitamin club with some sexy, highly suggestive (but very effective) ads. The inference of the ads was that you'd be a better husband, or wife, if you took Sam's vitamins.

The FTC didn't like Sam's promotional approach. They fined him $18,000 for false and misleading advertising, and slapped a cease-and-desist order on him. (Much vitamin advertising today, incidentally, is a lot more suggestive—and a lot more misleading—than Sam's ads were in the 1950's, although not nearly as entertaining.)

So Sam sold his vitamin club, again for several million dollars, and retired to Switzerland, where he built a company doing 80 million in annual sales of mail-order products, principally books and records, but including body-building machines, silver candelabras, and other assorted merchandise. He sold these products through subsidiary companies that he set up in England, France, and all over Europe.

Shortly after I left the *Reader's Digest*, I received a call from Sam.

"Walter, I hear you are going to be a consultant," said Sam. "How about being a consultant to me?"

I told Sam I would be delighted.

"I tell you what," said Sam. "I'll make you a proposition. We will agree to have lunch once a month for the next year. I will buy the lunch. And I will pay you $1,000 per lunch. You do not need to prepare for these lunches. I will do the preparation. I will think about my problems, and then we will talk. If I get one idea from you in the course of the year that is any good at all, I will renew the agreement. If not, we will terminate the agreement, and we will still be friends. What do you say?"

"I don't know, Sam," I said. "Let me think about it."

A few days later I got back to him.

"I have a better proposition for you," I said. "I will have lunch with you 12 times this coming year, once each month, and *I* will buy the lunch. Furthermore, I will prepare for these luncheon meetings, instead of coming to them cold. I will study your problems. In order to do so, of course, it will be necessary for me to visit your offices in London and Paris and Amsterdam and Lausanne. You will pay my expenses. Maybe we better have our lunches in some of these places."

So over the next few years I had lunch with Sam and his various staffs at regular intervals—in London, Paris, Amsterdam and Frankfurt. Sam paid the expenses for these trips, as well as my consulting fee. And we discussed the local problems with Sam's resident managers.

"Our problem is that the sort of thing that you do in America would never do with *us*," said the English staff. "We simply can't use high-pressure tactics to sell our products, the way Sam did in America. It isn't done, you know."

"Frenchmen are inclined to be deceptive," said the Paris office. "They make promises they never intend to keep. They buy our products—and never pay for them. That's our problem in France."

"In Germany, the law says you go to jail if your competitor says you are competing unfairly," said the German staff. "German laws are very strict. How can we make sales, when we are afraid of making claims that would put us in jail?"

My fourth consulting client came through Dick Coffey, who was then Circulation Promotion Manager of *LIFE* magazine. Dick called me up and invited me in for a meeting.

"I understand you're a hot-shot writer, and very expensive," said Dick. "So I'll make a bargain with you. I'll pay you $25,000 to write me a test mailing for *LIFE*. If the mailing fails, our arrangement terminates. If it beats everything else that I and my staff and our ad agency can come up with, I'll renew the contract for another year. And I'll pay you $25,000 a letter—so long as your letters beat everything else we can put out."

Dick was a tough, down-to-earth promotion man. After I joined Dick as his consultant, I heard about an exchange he had with one of the Senior Vice Presidents of Time Inc., over a mailing I did for him. This officer objected to the tone of my mailing. He was a well-known shouter, and he started yelling at Dick.

Instead of agreeing that I should be fired, Dick said, "Don't shout. The last time anybody yelled at me I was in a POW camp in Germany, and the guy that did the yelling was a guard with an automatic weapon poked in my belly. I made up my mind then, nobody yells at me again, unless he's got a gun—and you haven't got a gun."

"Besides," said Dick, "this guy works for me, not you, and I'm the only one in my department who decides who I fire or don't fire."

I wasn't fired.

I put together a penny mailing for *LIFE*, which was a frank adaptation of the *Reader's Digest* technique, but different. *LIFE*'s trademark was their brilliant red masthead logo, so I produced a brilliant *LIFE*-red envelope. *LIFE*'s slogan—the slogan with which Henry Luce and Roy Larsen launched the magazine was:

> You are invited to see life . . . to see the world—to eyewitness great events.

You did this through the pages of *LIFE*. I simply put this slogan on the red *LIFE* envelope, and then cut a hole in the envelope in the shape of a human eye—put some eyelashes on the eye to make it realistic—and had a copper penny showing through the eye-window in the place of an iris. The penny was your "down payment" on a subscription to *LIFE*—so you could see the world.

The penny was appropriate. It was in character. It was an action device. And the mailing beat all the mailings that Dick Coffey's staff and ad agency could muster to test against it.

LIFE MAGAZINE PENNY MAILING.

This mailing for LIFE *demonstrates how a fresh application of familiar principles can make an exciting winner.*

Reprinted with permission of *Life* magazine.

Incidentally, beating those competitors each year thereafter was simple enough. A whole year would go by after a mailing went out, and then Coffey called for new proposals. The staff and the agency sat down and sought inspiration. Their mailings were original and often ingenious; they also tended to be smart-aleck. They started from scratch, without benefit of the experience I had been amassing through tests. They called attention to the skill of the writer, rather than the desirability of the product.

One of my favorite examples of the basic principle for writing good mail-order copy comes from an anecdote in an essay by Michel de Montaigne, the sixteenth century philosopher and sage. Montaigne tells the story of a debate, in ancient Athens, between the great orator, Demonsthenes, and another orator whose name I don't even remember.

The other orator spoke first, in flowering phrases and purple passages. When he had finished his oration, the audience cheered and said: "How wonderfully he speaks!"

Then Demonsthenes spoke, and when he finished his oration, there was no applause, but the audience rose up and said, "Let us march against Sparta!"

While the other writers were laboring to win applause, I was analyzing last year's results—and building on them—and by the process of "line-breeding" and "cross-breeding," developing a new mailing that used last year's strong points as a jumping off stage for writing an even more successful follow-up. I had at least a one-year start on everyone else, because I was the only one basing my efforts on test results—and the only one trying to make sales, rather than have everyone say, "How wonderfully he writes!"

I worked for Coffey for a number of years, with success and mutual admiration, and this led to my work for Time-Life Books.

Time-Life Books didn't exist at the time I started working for Dick Coffey. But one of the first mailings I made after leaving *Reader's Digest*, for my new client Simon & Schuster, involved Harry Abrams—and also Time Inc.

The Abrams Company published beautiful books of art reproductions, which Harry frequently sold to Book-of-the-Month Club for Club premiums. One such book which Harry created was a magnificent, deluxe edition of the King James Bible, illustrated with full-color prints of great religious paintings by Michaelangelo, Raphael, and other Renaissance masters. He called this edition the Masterpiece Bible.

Harry felt that this Bible would be a great mail-order product. (The King James Bible was, and is, the largest-selling book published—in spite of the efforts of various Protestant churches to get rid of King James and foist off modern-language versions of the Bible on the Bible-reading public.)

But Harry lacked two essentials for mail-order sales. To begin with, he didn't have a *list* of customers he could mail to, and in the second place, he didn't have the *money* to finance a huge mailing, which would be necessary if he had any hope of selling a substantial number of his expensive Bibles.

So Harry persuaded Leon Shimkin to take Simon & Schuster into partnership with him, and Leon persuaded Time Inc. to enter a joint venture, selling Bibles to the *LIFE* subscriber list. Harry would produce the product, Leon would finance the mailing, so that *LIFE* risked absolutely nothing. And the mailing was made to *LIFE's* huge, mail-responsive subscriber list.

And, as Simon & Schuster's mail-order consultant, I produced the mailing. It was a big, glossy, expensive job—done *LIFE* style. And it worked. We sold (as I recall) approximately 350,000 copies of the Bible, at a price of $39.95 (plus postage and handling), thereby giving *LIFE* a good demonstration of the gold that lay hidden in their subscriber list.

Not long thereafter, Jerome Hardy, who was a vice president of Doubleday, convinced Time Inc. that they should set up a separate division of Time Inc. for the specific purpose of utilizing their big mail-order lists to sell books, which the Time-Life editorial staff would create, and with Jerry as the head of the book operation.

Jerry and I were friends, and Jerry now approached me.

"I understand that you are a consultant to Dick Coffey and Time Inc.," said Jerry. "That means you are a consultant to me."

So Jerry proceeded to create Time-Life Books. In this project he was assisted by Norman Ross, who was appointed the Editor, and by me.

The three of us would convene at Stonehenge, a very expensive suburban restaurant which had private cabins in which its guests could hold meetings, and Jerry would beat out ideas and plans for projected book properties, again assisted by Norman Ross and me.

Jerry's idea for book projects was quite different from the *Reader's Digest* one-shots and the *Digest's* Condensed Books. Drawing on his experience with Doubleday's continuity programs, Jerry envisioned similar programs: a series of *related books*, shipped at 60-day intervals, the series comprising a set, when completed, and each set covering a given subject. The sets all bore the imprint of *LIFE* magazine: oversized picture books, with easy-to-absorb, educational essays, accompanied by full-color illustrations on almost every page.

I created the successful mailings for the earliest of these series; the mailings were extraordinarily productive, and Time-Life Books was in business.

The first series was the *LIFE Nature Library*. By this time in my mail-order career I had evolved my theory about the importance of outside mailing envelopes into a pretty firm conviction. The first book in the *Time-Life Nature Library* was a book about "Life in the Sea." Accordingly, my problem was to dramatize, with the envelope, the concept of life in the sea.

LIFE NATURE LIBRARY "FISH" MAILING

The first Time/Life mailing for "Life on Earth" book series.

Reprinted with permission of Time-Life Books, Inc.

I solved this with an oversized, 9 × 12″ envelope, with a big, circular, glassine window. The envelope represented the inside of a bathysphere. From outside the bathysphere (but, of course, inside the envelope) a big, goggle-eyed fish peered at the reader. It was unusual, attention-getting, dramatic—and effective. For many years this envelope continued to sell Nature Libraries for *LIFE*, and it was certainly one of the most successful mailings *LIFE* ever made.

My problem with the *LIFE World Library* Series was somewhat different. The first book in this series was about Russia. How do you dramatize a book about Russia, on the outside of a 9 x 12″ envelope? I considered pictures of the Kremlin, of bearded Rus-

TIME-LIFE MAILING FOR "WORLD" SERIES

Reprinted with permission of Time-Life Books, Inc.

sian peasants, of dreary Russian landscapes, but none seemed to fit. So I simply printed "RUSSIA" in big, red block letters on the back of the envelope, covering the entire 9 x 12" area. The effect was startling, and it made the envelope stand out in the mail box.

In those days, full color envelopes, and 9 x 12" envelopes, were almost unheard of. Such envelopes, for Time-Life Books, naturally commanded notice in the mail box. They also happened to reflect the image of *LIFE* magazine. They were "in character."

Again, this was an enormously successful mailing, and helped launch a second multimillion dollar project for *LIFE*.

Very shortly after Jerry got Time-Life Books division started, Joan Manley, who had been his assistant at Doubleday, joined him at *LIFE*. Presently Jerry moved up to a senior Time, Inc. spot as a corporate VP of Time Inc. and as publisher of *LIFE*, and presently Joan took over the book division. I worked for Joan as I had worked for Jerry, and admired her greatly.

In the interim, Jerry continued to conceive book projects faster than I could write mailings for them, and I finally protested.

"It's not that I mind doing all these mailings," I said. "I'm getting paid to do them. But even if only half of them turn out to be successful, you'll never have the editorial staff or the money to produce them all. So what are you trying to do?"

"Some of these projects will probably flop," Jerry said. "But we don't know in advance which ones. If I tested only one project, and it happened to be one of our losers, Time Inc. might lose interest and close the whole book division down. This way, I've got so many projects going that some of them are bound to be successful, and I've got so much money invested that they can't back out."

I worked for Jerry and Joan for a number of years during the development of Time-Life Books, and then a conflict of interest developed which made it necessary for me to choose between two clients. I chose the other client, and for a number of years no longer worked for Time Inc., although my relationship with the organization remained cordial.

Meanwhile, with Leon Shimkin and Golden Press, I had a most successful record album experience. This was on an album of children's records, called "The Golden Record Library." Using the

GOLDEN RECORD LIBRARY MAILING

A colorful, off-beat mailing that reflected the personality of the product—successfully.

Golden Library name, and mailing to easily identifiable lists of parents of young children, who had previously bought children's products by mail, we made millions of mailings and sold hundreds of thousands of sets. Again, we used colorful, off-beat envelopes (although these measured only 6 x 9″).

Another early experience I had in my new career as a consultant involved *McCall's* magazine. *McCall's* had a gifted but obstinate young editor, Otis Wiese—who considered himself a genius and, whenever *McCall's* management disagreed with his editorial approaches (which was often) was in the habit of resigning. Management then had to abase itself and gratefully accept Otis' reenlistment—each time with the understanding that they would keep their sticky fingers out of his editorial pie thereafter.

Naturally, management did not like this. *McCall's* circulation was not doing well, and when a magazine does poorly, the editor is blamed. Then Herb Mays, the Editor of *McCall's* rival publication, *Good Housekeeping*, who was also gifted and difficult to get along with, left Hearst Publications. And Otis Wiese made the mistake of presenting *McCall's* with another of his resignations, over some more-or-less trivial matter. This was an untimely error on Otis Wiese's part. Much to his astonishment, management accepted his resignation. His editorial staff then presented *their* resignations. Much to *their* astonishment, management let *them* go, too—and ushered in Herb Mays as the new editor of *McCall's*, with a clean slate to do as he liked to get *McCall's* going again.

Herb Mays was definitely an editorial giant—one of only three or four I've encountered in all my years of working as a magazine consultant. He transformed *McCall's*, which up to then had been a rather drab, housewifely housekeeping manual, into a colorful, exciting, interest-packed magazine for modern women. He took advantage of the revolution in printing, brought about by modern, high-speed offset four-color presses, to fill the magazine with beautiful full-color illustrations that enlivened the text.

In response to this new editorial technique, *McCall's* newsstand circulation took off. But, oddly enough, *McCall's* subscription circulation stood still. So the Circulation Director, Russ Tippett, who was a friend of mine, invited me in to see if I could do anything about subscription sales.

At this point, Tom Knowlton had left *Reader's Digest* and joined forces with me as my partner, and we had given a summer job to my son, Todd. Tom and I did the contact work on *McCall's*, and Todd was given the hard task of redoing *McCall's* promotion.

We began the assignment by examining the promotional material that *McCall's* was sending out—renewal efforts and prospect mailings. I had a meeting with the man in charge of this activity, and it was an uncomfortable one. He had worked for *McCall's*, as its creative circulation writer, for many decades, and he made no bones about the fact that he deeply resented my intrusion into his field. For my part, I wasn't happy in this role, and I tried to launch a joint, face-saving project, but he would have none of it.

I asked him for samples of *McCall's* renewal mailings and outside mailings, and he handed me a half-dozen drab, cheap third-class-mail envelopes. These were conventional No. 10 envelopes—standard business mail. Their only distinction was that they were all of a repulsive, dull pink color.

I asked the promotion man why these envelopes were pink, and he replied, with some hauteur, "because pink envelopes don't cost any more than white envelopes."

I asked him, then, if he had ever tried pictorial envelopes.

"Yes," he said wearily, "we did that in 1922. Pictorial envelopes don't work."

I asked if I could see one of these envelopes that didn't work, and he produced a pink, No. 10 envelope which was distinguished by an illustration consisting of a small black circle with a tail on it—what appeared to be a crude pencil drawing of a pollywog—with a copy line beneath it.

The copy line said: "One year from today . . . will your mirror show you a more beautiful you?" I realized, on reading this line, that the pollywog was actually a mirror.

The reasons for the failure of this mailing—even in 1922—were obvious. The copy appeal was presented in a round-about, difficult-to-follow way, and the illustration was a hindrance rather than a help. The beauty appeal, while a strong feminine copy hook, wasn't necessarily the right appeal for a woman's service magazine like *McCall's*.

But the most important reason for failure was the fact that this mailing had been tested in solitary splendour—win or lose—with no alternate approaches tested against it. There had been no benchmark against which to measure the success or failure of the pollywog mailings, and this violated the first rule of mail-order testing. I could scarcely believe that this was the case.

"Have you ever tried any other pictorial envelopes since 1922?" I asked.

And the answer was "Of course not!"

It is always rather easy, in hindsight, to see the flaws in someone else's activities—especially when those activities have been demonstrated to be failures. In this case I felt I had some justification for suggesting a change in approach. Herb Mays had changed the whole character of *McCall's*. The promotional mailings reflected none of this. They were build around the old-fashioned, downbeat, dreary-housekeeping theme of the old *McCall's*.

So I suggested that we should at least *try* a new full-color promotional package. The circulation promotion man refused flatly to have anything to do with such a piece of idiocy. He pointed out that a full-color envelope would cost four times as much as a plain pink envelope. He threatened to resign. He blocked the idea of a test until finally his boss, Russ Tippett, the Circulation Manager, put his foot down. Then, indeed, he retired, and we were able to go ahead with a test.

Herb Mays was throwing money into full-color feature articles that were absolutely dazzling. I remember that I was particularly impressed with a two-page photographic spread he ran in one issue that summer, at the peak of the home gardening season. This was simply a full-color picture of a bunch of tomatoes, hanging on the vine, dotted with cool, morning dew—the photograph made you want to pluck the tomatoes off the page and eat them.

It happened that I had lunch with Herb Mays when the issue came out, and I remarked on the tomatoes. "Two pages in *McCall's* cost an advertiser $100,000," I said. "Nobody but you would have thought of using $100,000 worth of space on a picture of some tomatoes."

Herb Mays laughed. "That's just part of the story," he said. "Do you know that I spent the better part of one week with a photographer, working exclusively on getting that picture? But don't you think it was worth it?"

I certainly did. It was this kind of dramatic visual editorial treatment that I felt should be dramatized in the mailings we did for *McCall's*.

I told Todd, "Get a current copy of *McCall's* and put together a mailing that projects the new *McCall's* image."

Todd examined the current issue. It happened that the big feature in this particular issue was a section on little girls' dresses— with page after page of adorable pictures of little girls dressed up in attractive costumes. One of the most striking pictures had a lovely little girl standing in a field of bright, colorful poppies.

Todd simply took this picture and made an envelope out of it. Then he did a colorful brochure which showed other pictures from

McCALL'S "TULIP GIRL" MAILING

A pioneer in dramatic envelopes.

Reprinted with permission of McCalls, Publishing Co.

the new *McCall's*, illustrating other features of the magazine—
entertaining, home decorating, women's fashions, and so on—
and did an accompanying letter that extolled the color and variety
of the editorial matter, the lively, helpful articles on every one of
the modern woman's interests, which could be found in every
issue of *McCall's*.

We tested the mailing and it more than *doubled* response—from
less than 3 percent response overall on a multimillion mailing to
more than 6½ percent overall.

The interesting thing was that the "Tulip Girl Mailing," as it got
to be named, was indeed more expensive than the old pink envelope efforts. It cost perhaps $50 extra for every 1000 letters we
mailed. But with more than 30 *extra* orders secured from each 1000
letters mailed—and each order worth an immediate $6—we were
taking in $180 extra income for a $50 added cost.

This was, of course, the least of it. We did a big mailing for *McCall's* and added a million circulation at a single fell swoop.

At the same time we doctored *McCall's* renewal efforts, without adding to the cost. We pointed out the excitement of Herb Mays' new *McCall's*. We changed the renewal offer to an "authorized continuing subscription." Instead of saying, "Your subscription is about to expire," we said, "You can have your subscription *continue* without interruption, so long as you wish." And we kicked *McCall's* circulation up from 4 million to 8 million in the course of a few mailings.

The "Tulip Girl Mailing" pioneered full-color envelopes. It helped usher in the new era of direct mail that ended plain white transmittal envelopes and replaced them with full-color promotional envelopes, which are now pretty standard in the direct mail industry. Except, that is, for those mail-order operators who tested pictorial envelopes back in the 1920s or 1930s and found out they didn't work!

But such practitioners of direct mail are becoming scarcer and scarcer as the years go by.

One other educational experience that I went through in my early days as a consultant seems worth recounting. This involved Al Cole and the Popular Science Publishing Company.

Even after he left *Popular Science* officially to join *Reader's Digest* in the mid-1930s, Al had remained one of the major stockholders of Popular Science Company, the publishers of *Popular Science* and *Outdoor Life* magazines. As such, he continued to wield pretty much full control over all *Pop Sci's* activities, right up to 1958, when I left the *Digest*.

Shortly thereafter, Al called me up. *"Pop Sci* is having some troubles," he said. "I want you to go down and talk to the President and find out what's wrong and fix it."

As it happened, the Circulation Manager of *Pop Sci*, Gene Watson, was a good friend of mine, and a direct mail operator whom I respected. I was reluctant to step on Gene's toes by barging in on his territory, and I had other things to do, so I neglected to follow up on *Pop Sci*. But after a week or two, Al called me again.

"Have you gone down and talked to the President of *Pop Sci*?"
I admitted that I had not.

"Well, do it," Al said.

Again I procrastinated. But after another week or so, I received a call from the *Pop Sci* President himself. He told me that Al had insisted that he call me up and make a date to discuss certain circulation problems *Pop Sci* was having. Reluctantly, I agreed to a date.

However, I then called Gene Watson and explained my situation, and asked him if I could drop by his office before talking to the President of *Pop Sci*. Gene said this was all right with him. When I got there, I asked what the problem was.

"It's pretty simple," said Gene. *"Pop Sci* magazine has an ABC guarantee of an average of one million circulation per issue. In the current six-month period, we're running short by a total of about a million copies—about 175,000 copies per month. We'll have to publish this fact in our next pink sheet statement, and probably give all our advertisers a rebate. And that's not so bad as the black eye we'll get for missing a guarantee. It could be very damaging to *Popular Science.*"

"Holy smoke!" I said. "This is a serious problem. How on earth did you ever get in a situation like that?"

"Well, we put out a big five million promotion mailing that we expected to pull 5 percent, and it only pulled 1½ percent," said Gene. "So we're short by about 175,000 subs. And that's why we're missing our guarantee."

"That was a catastrophe," I said. "What did the test pull?"

"There wasn't any test. We mailed five million pieces of a new mailing without testing it first."

"Good gosh," I said. "You're an old mail-order hand, Gene. You know better than to make a five million roll-out of an untested effort. Why did you do it?"

"Because the President of *Pop Sci* ordered me to do it," said Gene.

"Well," I said, "Your mailings have always been pretty successful. Who wrote this effort?"

"He did," said Gene.

I took a quick look at the sample Gene showed me. It was evidently written by an ad salesman, touting *Popular Science* magazine as a great, successful publishing venture, with lots of readers who had a very satisfactory average income and other praiseworthy demographics. It said nothing that would make me, as a do-it-yourself workshop type of reader, want to subscribe to *Popular Science*.

"I think I had better not keep my date with your President," I said, and I got out of there.

Later that day Al called me again.

"Did you see *Pop Sci*?"

"Yes, I did."

"Well, what is it?"

"Al," I said. "You are the head of the Popular Science Publishing Company and they have a problem which only you can fix. If you don't know what that problem is, I can't tell you about it. You'll have to find out for yourself."

"Then I damn well will," said Mr. Cole.

A few days later he called me again.

"I want you to go down again to *Pop Sci* and work with Gene Watson on that problem," he said. "They have a new president."

Gene and I got together and Gene put out another huge mailing (which he had previously written and tested) which pulled a huge hunk of countable ABC circulation—double what he needed to get his one million circulation back, with enough excess to wipe out his previous shortage and give him an average of one million over the entire six-month period.

The Chairman of the Board of Popular Science Publishing Company was Godfrey Hammond, a wonderful, big-hearted, genial man who was several years Al Cole's senior—he was then in his early 70s. The two of them had worked together in the days when Godfrey was head office boy at *Pop Sci*, and Al was his first assistant. I had known Godfrey for some time—we were on the S-M News Company Board of Directors together—and Godfrey now retained me as a regular consultant to *Popular Science*.

Along with his genial nature, Godfrey had an explosive temper, and he also had a serious heart condition, which made it necessary for him to watch his health closely. His wife, Irma, was constantly worried about Godfrey's tendency to indulge in occasional rich foods and strong drinks. Godfrey's temper and health problem finally reached the point where he actually blacked out on occasion when his temper got the best of him, much to everybody's alarm. Godfrey then had a pacemaker installed, which he said did wonders for him. "Now I can get mad whenever I want to, without blackout," said Godfrey. Irma had reason to be concerned about him.

Still, Godfrey continued to operate along lines that suited him. Once a month Godfrey, Gene, and I would hold a very informal meeting. Gene would report briefly on his activities, Godfrey would tell some jokes, and I would listen, and then we would all repair to a nearby Jewish delicatessen which served cocktails as well as lunch, the crowning feature of which was a Black Forest chocolate cake dessert. Godfrey would have two martinis and a huge slice of Black Forest cake, and we were all very happy.

Presently Godfrey officially retired, but he kept me on as his consultant, and for some time Gene and I continued to hold monthly meetings with him, always topped by the self-same lunch. It finally dawned on me that Godfrey's only reason for retaining me as his consultant was to have an excuse once a month to get away from Irma's watchful eye and come to New York and have lunch, complete with two martinis and Black Forest cake. Godfrey was terrified of offending Irma, whom he dearly loved, and I was Godfrey's escape hatch.

It was one of the most pleasant consulting arrangements that I have ever enjoyed.

Looking back over those early years, I found that being a consultant—one fortunate enough to have clients—was a lot more exciting and demanding than I had anticipated it would be. In place of the one job and one boss I had enjoyed at *Reader's Digest*, plus the competent staff to back me up, the unlimited budget in which to bury mistakes, and the leisurely 12 months to work out the single annual subscription mailing that was the core of all our activities, I now had six or eight clients, each with three or four executives who considered themselves my bosses, and all with half-a-dozen or so vital mailings that they simply *had* to get out in the next 30 days.

It was necessary for me to have lunch with each of my 20 or 30 bosses, individually, at least once a week, spend a half-day a week with each in an important meeting, talk to all at least once a day on the telephone, write at least one major mailing apiece (or a half-dozen billing or renewal letters, or conversion efforts), and get in at least one major memo plus a test proposal or two per month, for all of them. Many of these projects I was working on were truly major undertakings, like Jerry Hardy's launching of the *LIFE* Books program, or *McCall's* shift-over from field-sold subscriptions and five million circulation to mail-sold subscriptions and 8½ million circulation; one of these projects by itself could have been a full-time job. And, as each of the 20 or 30 individuals who represented these clients lived in the innocent belief that I had no other clients, and was his alone, I led a pretty fast life.

Now, one of those questions which I've often been asked since I became a consultant—and not always in a polite manner—is, "What on earth does a mail-order consultant *do*?"

In other words, just how do you justify your existence?

I once got a cinder in my eye, which required emergency assistance, and I went to a local doctor whom I didn't happen to know, in Pound Ridge, New York—one of New York City's outlying "bedroom communities."

"What do you do for a living?" the doctor inquired as he poked at my eye.

"I'm a consultant," I said.

"My God," said the doctor. "Everybody in Pound Ridge is a consultant. Doesn't anybody around here work for a living?"

Indeed, a very common sub-family of the species *consultant* is the alcoholic who got fired, can't get or hold a job, has some calling cards printed and sets up shop as a consultant. If you ask him who his clients are, he's apt to be a bit vague.

Some other consultants simply give advice—and some I know more than earn their fees with nothing more than the advice they give, which may save or earn their clients millions of dollars.

In my case, I've made a career out of helping clients solve marketing problems by providing advice and ideas for direct marketing promotions, and then *executing* those ideas. In other words, I think up marketing plans to help sell products, and then create the mailings: plan the offer (price, terms, free trial, cash or credit card or bill me, as appropriate), decide on the components (letter, brochure, plastic card or what have you), and write the copy, get an artist to lay the mailing out, and submit copy and layout to the client. Usually, there's a good bit of interchange and interaction along the way; we propose and the client objects; the client proposes and we try to work it out.

Next, the Weintz Company produces the mailing (or the client produces it, if the client happens to have a production department). We select and order lists, get type set and photographs taken, order lettershop production, and see the mailing into the mails.

Finally, and one of the most important ingredients of our "mail-order consulting" service, we help analyze response. Did test A pull *significantly* better than test B, and if so, would it be profitable if we did a big roll-out (at an appropriate, big-volume, substantially reduced per-thousand cost)?

Another question that sometimes arises is, "Where do your ideas come from? At least one answer to that question was provided for me by Frank Scully, then President of Funk & Wagnalls Encyclopedia.

For a number of years, the Weintz Company worked for Funk & Wagnalls as their direct mail consultants, and Frank Scully and I developed an amiable relationship. From time to time we had lunches, at which we discussed the state of the world and the frailities of mankind, and we exchanged views about such other matters as interested us. On one such occasion Frank remarked to me:

"Walt, do you know what a consultant is?"

"No," I said. "Tell me about it."

"A consultant," said Frank, "is a man you ask him what time it is, and he borrows your watch, tells you the time, and then keeps your watch."

"That's very funny," I said. "If you feel so badly about your watch, why haven't you asked for it back?"

"I have," said Frank, "many times. But you always give me somebody else's watch."

There is a lot of truth buried in Frank's cynical observation. Naturally, a consultant learns from experience, and he transfers the learning he has acquired working for one client to the solution of other clients' problems. Since all mail-order enterprises have much the same basic problems of product, market, promotion, and finances, and as the underlying principles that apply in one case are apt to apply in another, it is to be expected that similar problems often call for similar solutions.

Also it is a fact that consultants are apt to learn as much from their clients as their clients learn from them—if they have good clients. One way to identify a good consultant is to locate one who has a good client list—and see if he has a provable track record of successes for those clients.

An example of the *perils* of consulting was my experience with the National Liberty Life Insurance Company of Valley Forge, Pennsylvania, one of my very first (and longest-lasting) clients.

Shortly after I left *Reader's Digest*, I received a phone call from Lynn Mapes, a young *Digest* ad salesman who was a good friend of mine.

"I have a problem," said Lynn. "There's a fellow who wants to run a third cover and flap ad in the January issue of the *Reader's Digest*. Our price for such an ad is $180,000, and I'm afraid to sell it to him."

A third cover and "flap" ad was the inside back cover of the *Digest* with an extra flap added, which turned the back cover into a three-page ad.

"Doesn't he have the money?" I asked.

"He has it. He's given me a certified check for the money."

"Who is he?" I asked.

"He's an insurance agent who is also a born-again Christian, and he's selling a health and accident insurance policy for folks who don't drink. The only place he's advertised up to now was in a religious publication called 'Sword of the Lord.' He's seen one of those famous Harry and David ads for Fruit-of-the-Month Club— the ad with the headline 'Imagine Harry and Me Advertising in Fortune.' He thought this was great advertising, so he used a headline for his ad in *Sword of the Lord* that said 'Imagine Nancy and Me Advertising in *Sword of the Lord*.' Nancy's his wife. The ad worked, so he thinks it will work in the *Digest*. His name is Arthur deMoss."

"Well, why are you worried?" I asked.

"In the first place, I'm afraid a corny ad like that wouldn't work for him in the *Digest*, and he'd lose his shirt. We don't like our advertisers to lose money. And in the second place, the ad wouldn't be appropriate for the *Digest*—it would give *us* a corny appearance, and our other advertisers wouldn't like it. I told him you could help him do a *Digest* ad that would pull its head off, and he wants to meet you."

I met with Art deMoss and persuaded him that a "Nancy and Me" advertisement wouldn't be effective in the *Digest*. We worked up a more conventional ad, that bore down on the fact that Art's insurance rates, for non-drinkers, were lower than the regular health and accident insurance rates which covered both teetotalers and drunks. The ad had a coupon; it was a typical mail-order advertisement.

Art was that rare bird, a man who was born with the right mail-order instincts—and a split personality. He had an intuitive knowledge of what would entice customers to buy. He was imaginative, inventive—and cold-blooded.

"If you don't drink, why should you pay high insurance rates to help cover the medical expenses of folks who do?" Art's advertising copy said. "If you don't drink, we can give you lower rates."

It was pretty easy to build our ads around this theme. In due course, Arthur deMoss ran his third-cover-and-flap ad in *Reader's Digest*.

"How much can you afford to pay to secure a new policy holder?" I asked him.

"One hundred dollars," said Art.

Dividing $180,000—the cost of the ad—by $100, I calculated that he needed 1800 sales to make his ad pay off. Actually, the ad pulled 30,000 inquiries, and then converted to about $3 million in premium sales.

For a number of years thereafter, I was Art's direct marketing consultant. I helped him with ads, and I helped him with direct mail. There was then a shibboleth in the insurance business, to the effect that insurance mailings had to go out in plain, white, No. 10 envelopes, with no writing on the envelopes, because if you mentioned the word "insurance" on the outside of the envelope, the recipient would throw the envelope in the waste basket without opening it.

Insurance mailings of the kind Art was using (which were the universal rule at the time) pulled about two-tenths of one percent—two *inquiries* for each 1000 letters he mailed.

I argued that if the message inside the envelope was so negative it would put off most recipients, disguising the message in a plain envelope wouldn't be much help. The customers might open the letter out of curiosity—but on finding it to be about insurance, the mailing would probably still end up in the waste basket.

Therefore, I said, it is necessary to make the *benefit* of the insurance protection so obvious, so needed, and so important that it could be blazoned on the outside of the envelope itself—and the message would be so compelling that it would force recipients to open and read.

I had great difficulty getting this idea across. Art's business grew rapidly, and he expanded from being an insurance agent to the ownership of his own insurance company. He hired a considerable staff of insurance experts. These people all knew that the way to sell insurance is to put out the cheapest possible mailing (because returns are so low that an expensive, attractive mailing is uneconomical); and of course, the mailings went out in plain white envelopes.

I got beaten down whenever I presented an idea that was off the beaten track, and whenever I did manage to put a test in the works, Art's insurance experts managed to convert it into a "white envelope" effort which somehow didn't work. Naturally this confirmed what they had said even before the mailing went out: "It won't work."

Meanwhile, I myself went through some changes in my consulting business. I had started the business with the theory that I would have a little office in my home, take care of one or two clients, working at an easy pace one or two days a week, with the help of a part-time secretary and free-lance artist. The idea didn't work out.

So when my son Todd told me he was leaving J. Walter Thompson, the giant advertising agency, because it was too big and he didn't have sufficient opportunity to meet with clients and work

out their problems with them, I suggested that I knew a much smaller company that needed some help, and Todd came to work as my partner.[1]

At the time, in addition to Art deMoss (his company was the National Liberty Life Insurance Company) I had the *Atlantic Monthly* as a client. They were in Boston. And, as it happened, on Todd's first day at work, I had an appointment to see the *Atlantic*. As I made ready to catch a plane to Boston, National Liberty's new Marketing Director called up and ordered me down to Valley Forge, Pennsylvania.

I explained to Todd that this conflict of dates was a recurring problem for a consultant with more than one client, and this was one of the reasons why I had brought him in. So I said, "I'll go to Boston and you go to Valley Forge and find out what they want."

So we went off in opposite directions, and Todd reported in at the Marketing Director's office.

"Who are you?" this individual asked.

Todd explained about my previous engagement with the *Atlantic*, and asked what he could do to be helpful.

"When I tell a consultant to come see me, I don't expect him to send a substitute," was the response. "I'll tell you what you can do. You can go back and tell your father he's fired."

This experience on Todd's first day at work was no doubt an interesting introduction for him to one of the perils of consulting. That peril I would define as the Autocratic Underling, a stock character often encountered in large organizations.

For a while, National Liberty ceased to be a client. But then— before too long—the individual who fired us was in his turn fired, and Art deMoss asked us to come back to work for him. We worked happily on mailings for health insurance for non-drinkers—"special insurance for special people"—and continued to struggle to get Art to use proven mail-order techniques, such as envelopes with words and pictures on them.

The real breakthrough finally came in 1976 (after I had been working on the National Liberty account, off and on, for 18 years), when Art decided that one of the biggest groups of "special people" in the entire United States was veterans. As I recall, he determined that more than 60 percent of the men over age 50 were, at that time, veterans of the armed services. So the National Liberty staff put together a health and accident insurance program for veterans, and Todd did a veteran's mailing.

Somehow, we convinced the National Liberty people that a veteran's mailing required flags and uniforms and soldiers and sailors saluting—*on the envelope*—and we succeeded in selling National Liberty on a pictorial envelope. Todd put together an envelope that had the Stars and Stripes waving across it, with smiling veterans at attention saluting the flag. Art had decided that a commemorative medal would be appropriate as an action-inducing gift for veterans who signed up, so we had a medal designed, and had its picture showing through a second window in the envelope.

A subhead, under the picture of the medal, said:

YOUR GIFT
You can receive
this handsome
Bicentennial
Minuteman Medallion

But the most dramatic element of the entire envelope was the headline—which actually mentioned the word "insurance." The headline said:

ENCLOSED: Important information about
low-cost group insurance
for U.S. veterans!

The subhead said: "But your response is needed by midnight of . . ." and a *third* window in the envelope revealed a specific due date.

Obviously, all these pictures and copy necessitated a bigger than normal envelope, so we went to a 6 × 9″ size.

We had hoped that this mailing of Todd's would pull something over twice the normal response. And in fact it did.

I then said that since we were selling our Veterans Insurance at

NATIONAL LIBERTY VETERAN'S MAILING

An insurance mailing that dared to say "insurance" on the envelope—and got away with it.

Reproduced by permission of Veterans Life Insurance Company.

special *group* rates, it was perfectly obvious that a group *membership* card was in order.

I said the card should be an embossed, heavy, plastic card, like the plastic credit cards which had become a status symbol for the affluent, and like the cards we used for the Republican National Committee.

The idea of actually putting a plastic card with an individual's name on it in a mailing was met with almost universal scorn and many practical objections from the National Liberty staff. But we produced samples of the plastic Membership Card which had worked such miracles for the Republican National Finance Committee, and a test was finally arranged.

The National Liberty Production Manager had considerable difficulty getting plastic cards in the quantities he required—tens of millions at a crack; nobody had ever before asked plastic card manufacturers for such quantities. Also the prices he was originally quoted were outlandish: 60¢ per card ($600 per thousand pieces of mail). Yet somehow these practical problems were worked out. The plastic cards pulled a phenomenal return which I am not at liberty to divulge.

However, it is giving away no secrets to say that plastic cards became the workhorse of *all* National Liberty mailings. A plastic card manufacturer recently told me that National Liberty bought and mailed out more plastic "credit cards" per year than all other credit card companies *combined*—over 200 million credit cards in a single year!

Naturally, when you get a success like that, the word gets around. We were extremely careful not to talk about the success of plastic cards to National Liberty's competitors or to anyone else. But plastic card manufacturers were not so reticent.

The only wonder, to me, was why it took other insurance companies so long to get around to plastic card mailings.

Like every other over-used mail-order gimmick, I'm sure that plastic cards—which may be the ultimate "hot potato"—will eventually wear out. Competitors and imitators rush to capitalize on any new idea, and I can foresee the day when the postman will be staggering under his daily load of plastic cards. And then, as a certain reaction to an over-zealous use of a good thing, plastic cards will cease to pull.

In the meantime, National Liberty continues to test many alternate (and less expensive) ideas—and to mail out millions of plastic cards. And certain other clients of ours have discovered the power of plastic cards.

All of which brings up another peculiarity of the mail-order consulting business. In my time I have helped bring off quite a few mail-order successes. The question naturally arises:

"If you're so good, how come you never win any of those awards for excellence that the direct mail associations hand out every year?"

One reason is that we rarely enter our mailings in such contests, because most of our clients won't let us. When a mail-order operator latches on to an idea that works, he is not anxious to have a host of imitators wear his idea out.

And another reason is that the mailings created by the Weintz Company are not designed to win awards—their purpose is to make sales. Some of them are not pretty, and some of them are of the type that evokes derision at suburban cocktail parties. Our purpose—our only purpose—is to make sales at a profit for our clients.

Like Demosthenes, we are interested in results. Our aim is to get the recipients of a mailing to say,

"Let us mail in the coupon!"

Another illustration of the pleasures and perils of direct mail consulting (especially the pleasures) came early in my consulting career, with a phone call from the Chicago office of McCann-Erickson, one of the very biggest of all advertising agencies.

McCann, it developed, had the Encyclopedia Britannica advertising account, which was relatively large and lucrative. Britannica—that is to say, Robert Hutchins and his Editor-in-Chief, Mortimer Adler—had just launched "Great Books of the Western World," a 20-plus volume set of the "Hundred Best Books." Mortimer Adler had appended two volumes to the set, which he called the "Syntopicon." These volumes contained a ready index to the way the authors of the various great books had treated such subjects as love, marriage, death, patriotism, and other important matters. Without the necessity of reading one Great Book, you could leaf through the two-volume Syntopicon and discover what authors like Plato and Francis Bacon and Thoreau and other deep thinkers had to say on almost any given subject.

McCann had been advertising the Great Book series with satisfactory results. However, Britannica felt that the agency was also obligated to create a successful direct mail campaign for the series. McCann had tried this, and failed. The mechanics of advertising, which they knew so well, just didn't apply in direct mail.

So McCann asked me to prepare a mailing for them—at their expense. They felt that they needed such help to hang on to the Britannica account, and they were willing to pay good money for the help. How much did I think the creation of such a mailing would cost?

I suggested a fee of $35,000. McCann felt that this was a reasonable sum; after all, on an advertising campaign where the client spends $1 million, the agency collects $150,000 in commissions. The direct mail campaign Britannica was planning for Best Books would easily cost $1 million over all, and $35,000 for a creative fee, for effective copy and layout, was well within their budget.

McCann told me that their space ads for the Great Books Program were very successful, and they couldn't understand why the direct mail mailings failed. I asked to see samples of both.

The ad—a full page in full color—had a large photograph of an ancient Greek statue's head—an impressive stone character with a portion of his nose broken off. The illustration took up the upper half of the advertisement. The head was placed against a handsome red background, and the headline said

"What on Earth is a
SYNTOPICON ? "

The subheads then asked

How can it change your life?
How can it strengthen your beliefs, give you confidence?
How can it affect the way you think, live—and progress?

The copy then went on to explain that a Syntopicon was a key that unlocked the treasures of the Great Books of the Western World, so that they could be enjoyed without too much effort or reading.

By contrast, McCann's direct mail piece had a small (No. 10) plain white envelope, no illustration, and a brief letter. It simply didn't take advantage of the opportunities for full-scale salesmanship that direct mail offered. It was an advertisement (and not a very good one) compressed into a mailing package.

It took no great genius to put together an effective mailing. I simply took the Greek bust on the red background, and the headline "What on Earth is a Syntopicon?" from the successful ad, and made a *big* 9 × 12" envelope out of these elements.

Inside, I packed a 4-page letter and an oversized "bedsheet" flyer that listed all the 100 Great Books and described the plea-

ENCYCLOPEDIA BRITANNICA "SYNTOPICON" MAILING

A mailing that dramatized the product—promised personal advantages—and forced the reader to open the envelope to find out what, how, and why.

sures and cultural benefits that reading (or just owning) these books would give their proud owner. I packed the 9 × 12″ envelope with a couple of thousand words of sales talk, and numerous pictures of happy families enjoying their Syntopicons. And I handed this 9 × 12″ Syntopicon mailing to McCann-Erickson together with my bill for $35,000.

"But all you did was take our idea and make an envelope out of it," the McCann account executive protested.

"No, what I did was to use your idea to create a dramatic, show-stopping mailing," I said. "This will beat the pants off the thing you've been using, and it will have the double advantage of bearing the authentic stamp of McCann-Erickson creativity, since it is indeed your own ad turned into a mailing. Try it and see what happens."

So McCann presented the mailing to George Collins, Britannica's marketing vice president, and George liked it. The test mailing went out, and the public liked it. It was a great success; it brought in responses at a most favorable level. And McCann was happy to pay my $35,000.

Although in the case of Great Books, I was called in because I was needed, and the person who called me in recognized his need, I have sometimes been called in for an interview with a prospective client for exactly the opposite reason—because someone wanted to prove that I was *not* needed. My old employers, *The Saturday Evening Post* and Curtis Publishing Company, are the best example of this strange phenomenon I can think of.

When I was learning the magazine mail-order business at *Reader's Digest*, under the tutelage of the circulation manager, Frank Herbert, I was puzzled by a form letter, recurring samples of which arrived in my mailbox from time to time, from Curtis.

This was a dingy little envelope, in which was enclosed what looked like a bill. This bill was the only enclosure, except for a reply envelope, addressed to Curtis, which had a box in the upper right-hand corner, with the legend "Place postage stamp here."

The copy on the bill was approximately as follows:

"This is not a bill. If you wish to subscribe to *The Saturday Evening Post*, return this form with the following payment: (check or money order): Three years . . .$." (I don't remember the exact price quoted, but it was over $20 for a three-year sub.)

This mailing baffled me. It seemed to violate all the rules of mail order that Frank Herbert was busy teaching me. So when one of these form letters arrived, I took it in to Frank and I said, "I can't understand this. Here is *The Saturday Evening Post*, one of the most successful of all magazines, putting out a mailing that to me appears to be absolutely stupid. The mailing must be good, or Curtis wouldn't be mailing it. What is it I don't understand?"

"You are wrong and you are right," said Frank. "The *Post* is *not* one of the most successful of all magazines, and this *is* a mailing that's absolutely stupid. The fact is, Curtis doesn't understand modern magazine selling, and—you watch—they're probably going out of business."

It took some years for Frank's prediction to come true. In the meanwhile, I left the *Digest*, became a consultant, was called in by Curtis, and got a further insight into their promotional genius.

The circulation executive who called me in asked me how I did my consulting work, and I explained that I reviewed a client's problems and then came up with proposed solutions, which the client tested. For some reason the circulation executive didn't seem to be much impressed with my approach.

"Our mailings are so successful that we really don't need any help," he said. "I just thought I'd see you to find out why any magazine would pay good money for an outside consultant. Probably they don't have Curtis' know-how."

I asked if I could see the successful mailing that he was so proud of. He produced the familiar, dingy little bill mailing that I had first encountered years before. I asked him how many of these little bills he sent out, and he mentioned some astronomical figure—millions of bills, which he said he sent out *every month*.

I asked what percentage of return he was getting, and he mentioned a figure of about one half of one percent—five orders for every 1000 bills he mailed.

"But since we only accept 3-year subs, and the price is over $20.00, and our mailing is so simple and inexpensive, we make a profit on every subscription we sell," he said—with great enthusiasm, I must add.

"Well," I said, "I won't charge you for this, but I can tell you how to cut your mailing quantity in half, and get the same response, with one simple change."

The executive manifested mild interest. "How's that?" he asked.

"Instead of mailing out a fixed quantity every month of the year, concentrate your entire mailing in January. It's the best mailing month, and you'll get at least twice as many orders from each January letter than you'd get from the same mailing in June."

The man laughed. "Obviously, you don't understand circulation economics," he said. "By mailing every month of the year, we keep our mailing department busy all year. Also we get new business every month of the year, so the fulfillment department has an even flow of work. If we mailed only in January, we'd have to build up to two huge departments, and the expense of keeping these two departments idle for the other 11 months would bankrupt Curtis."

"Then why don't you get an outside mailing house, and use seasonal, part-time fulfillment help, like *Reader's Digest* does?"

"Because we can do mailings much cheaper in-house than the outside supplier can," he said. "And besides, we've got such an investment in buildings and mailing machines and files and equipment that it would be throwing millions of dollars away if we tried to change our system."

I shook hands with him and took my departure. I'm sure he was pleased to have his estimate of mail-order consultants confirmed, and to have proof (which he could mention to his superiors) that Curtis was doing a great job and had no need for outside help.

And, in a way, I was pleased, too. I was confirmed in my opinion that Curtis didn't know what they were doing, and would probably soon go out of business.

Which, of course, they did. There were plenty of other reasons why Curtis went under, but one of them surely was their direct mail operation.

The problems a consultant is called upon to solve are frequently unexpected. Sometimes the client doesn't even reveal his or her real reason for the assignment to the consultant. I recall an assignment I got from the Los Angeles Times-Mirror Company, which had just purchased the Matthew Bender Book Publishing Company. I was asked to look at Matthew Bender's mail-order operation and to give the Times-Mirror a report.

Matthew Bender sold legal books to lawyers—for $100 to $200 or so *per book*—by mail. Lawyers needed these books to conduct their cases and handle their business, so the acceptance rate on Matthew Bender's books was phenomenal. Indeed, Matthew Bender was in the habit of sending out new volumes, as published, without an order or any previous announcement, accompanied by a bill, to lawyers on their list. And the lawyers paid for this unordered merchandise. They had to—or Matthew Bender would have cut them off.

I studied the Matthew Bender operation, and found it good.

The mailings, list maintenance, copy, follow-ups, billing—everything seemed very professional to me. And I so reported.

The Times-Mirror then went ahead and fired the people who were handling the mailing operation, as they had intended to do all along, and brought in a new crew. I deduced that my real assignment, which I had muffed, had been to report back that the promotion department should be fired, and I had fallen down on that assignment.

The new director of promotion called me in immediately upon his installation. He picked a pencil up from his desk.

"You see this pencil," he said. "I use it as long as it serves me. When it wears out, I break it—like this—and throw it in the waste basket."

He disposed of the pencil.

"And that's how I treat consultants," he said. "I thought we should have an understanding. I use consultants as long as I find them useful, then I toss them out."

"Not this consultant you don't," I said. "I resign." And I departed.

Reading over the preceding pages of this chapter on the pleasures and perils of mail-order consulting, I find that I've dwelt at some length on the perils, but I've touched only lightly on the pleasures.

The ultimate question that I am asked about my curious mode of earning a living is, "Why would anyone *want* to be a mail-order consultant?"

And my answer is, of course, "For the fun of it!"

An aspiring young business executive who sets his or her foot on the bottom rung of a corporate ladder, and through diligence and brains rises to the top, tends to become extremely expert in a limited field. The people he or she works with will change over the years, as fellow workers come and go, and corporate problems change with the changing times. Also, as the junior executive rises to the top, the problems become more weighty and complex. And of course, by hopping from one corporation to another in the course of his climb, the businessman gets a change of faces and problems.

However, all this does tend to be in slow motion. A consultant, on the other hand, may deal with 10, or 20, or 50 different companies in the course of a year. And nobody hires an expensive consultant unless they have serious problems. So a consultant's life tends to be full of variety, excitement—and peril. This makes for a lot of fun.

Secondly, the ever-changing mix of people one meets makes mail-order consulting a fascinating profession—if you like people. Most of the mail-order executives I have worked with have been exceedingly smart. They have earned their positions of responsibility through brains and ability. The field of mail order is not tolerant of dummies and dunces. I can report that it is a pleasure to work with people whose abilities you respect. And, usually, such people are not only intelligent, but are possessed of active, inquiring minds, and outgoing personalities. They are good company. *Great* company!

One exception to this general rule may be the rising tide of MBAs who, in recent decades, have increasingly littered the business landscape. These individuals (this is, of course, only a personal opinion) tend to have set rules of logic for the creation of mailings. Such rules, of course, tend to stifle creativity.

One such MBA, not long ago, handed me an assignment for a single mailing he wanted executed—and with it a four page thing he called a "Zero Base Mailing Creative Directive," which listed 67 rules he wanted me to follow in creating my mailing. These began with Rule No. One: "Convince the prospect that he or she should purchase this product." And went on, "No. Two: Do not finish the first page of the letter with a completed sentence. Always have the sentence continued on page two and have the line 'Continued on page two' at the bottom of the page. No. Three: Always end your letter with a P.S. The P.S. is the most important part of the letter."

There were 67 such rules. The MBA's rules for the letter I was supposed to write were actually longer than the proposed letter.

I try to be a model, respectful copywriter when dealing with MBA's, so I said, "Of course. I will write you a letter and I will follow all 67 of your rules," and I got up to go.

But the MBA wasn't having any of that.

"Oh, no you don't," he said. "You can't write the letter just yet. First you have to write me a critique.

I said, "What's a critique?"

"It's an outline showing me how you are going to incorporate my 67 rules into your letter," he said. "After I read your critique, if it is satisfactory, you can then write the letter."

I was reminded of a poem I once read, about a centipede—one of the species of hundred-legged bugs—and someone asked this centipede how he decided which of his hundred legs he moved first whenever he started to walk.

"Well," he said, "that's easy. I just . . ."

"No," he said, "I don't either. What I do is . . ."

"No, come to think of it, the first leg I move is . . ."

The upshot was that the poor centipede got so confused trying to think which leg he moved first that he finally had a nervous breakdown and had to be sent off to the psychiatric ward in the hospital to recover.

This was how I felt about the MBA's 67 rules. If I tried to remember 67 rules to follow I would never get the letter written. The MBA and I parted company. My version of the encounter is that I quit. He says I was fired because I didn't know how to write mail-order copy.

Another, much more pleasant business phenomenom I've noted over the years (as compared to the rise of the MBA) has been the steady rise of female executives in the mail-order business. More and more, over the years, I've found myself working with and for extremely competent women who have earned top executive positions because they were and are absolutely top executives. Joan Manley, who became Group Vice President of Time Inc., is probably the outstanding example in the publishing and mail-order field of such a woman. Patsy Bogle, whose last position was Vice President and Promotion Manager of World Book, managed a number of million-dollar mail-order projects without ever, to my knowledge, getting ruffled. Sandy Corpora, Creative Director of Rodale Press, has been responsible for much of the creative output which has made Rodale so successful.

And Blair Bergstrom, Circulation Director of *Harvard Business Review*, combines in one person the two characteristics that make a top mail-order operator—cool good judgment with great creative ability.

To sum it all up, the interesting people you meet and work with, if you are lucky enough to be a mail-order consultant, comprise one of the pleasures of such consulting, and not the least enjoyable of these associates (in my experience at least) have been the women executives I've worked with.

SUMMING UP: A CONSULTANT'S PRIVATE VIEW OF HIS MANY MAIL-ORDER CLIENTS

Now, how can I summarize the lessons I've learned from the several hundred mail-order clients I've served over the past 30 years?

What significant differences in different clients' approaches contributed to their successes—or their failures?

First, I'd say that *all* my clients have been *intelligent*. This isn't crass flattery. None of them got to positions where they had important decisions to make without ability and brains.

Second, what separated the *successes* from the *failures* (and, though I hate to admit it, we have had our share of failures) seems to me mostly to have been the difference between an open and a closed mind: the conviction, held by some mail-order operators, that they *knew*—without testing—what was right and what was wrong, all too frequently led to disastrous results.

So: the *humble* clients tended to succeed—the clients who had no need for testing tended to fail.

Naturally, I blamed the failures on the *fixed* minds of the clients. Probably, I should have blamed myself—for going along with preconceptions.

The lesson? Whether you are a consultant or a client, you should certainly try to avoid getting a swelled head!

---

[1]My original partner, Tom Knowlton, had gone on to become Vice President and Advertising Director of Book-of-the-Month Club, and, subsequently, Executive Vice President of Wunderman, Ricotta, and Klein, the big mail order advertising agency.

13

On Your Own

*How to Start (and Run) a Mail-Order Business,
With Examples Good and Bad*

It's been my experience that mail-order consultants are generally not consulted by firms that have established, successful, going mail-order businesses . . . or at least, firms that *think* they have such a business. Consultants are called in either when the fire whistles go off—or when a new product is being launched. So my work, over the past 30 or so years, has largely alternated between marketing infant products (or businesses), and rescuing (or trying to rescue) products that have run into trouble and seem about to go over the hill.

I believe these two sets of problems are surely of major interest to any reader who has gotten this far in my book, so I'd like to cite some real-life examples here and point out how you can apply the lessons I learned to your own products.

I'll start with my own experience.

One of the questions I am sometimes asked at direct mail conventions and meetings is, "If you're so good at helping other people launch successful mail-order products and projects, why haven't you launched your own?"

Sometimes the question is put more bluntly: "If you're so smart, why aren't you rich?"

The question has also occurred to me from time to time, and when I was 50 years old I had reason to face up to it. I suffered a heart attack which put me in the hospital for six long weeks, with plenty of time to brood over my own shortcomings and the direction my life was taking.

And I remembered Arthur White.

"Now if you were like Arthur, " I said to myself, "you would turn your adversity into an opportunity and get rich. He had polio and was crippled for life, and he became a millionaire.

"Can't you figure out a way, with a mere heart attack, to do the same?"

The reason for my illness was clear to me: I hadn't been taking care of myself, and I was much, much too fat. Also, I reasoned, the United States was filled with millions of businessmen like me, who didn't take proper care of their health, whose essential health problem was obesity, and they were all skating down a slippery road to a disabling heart attack and possible early death. Heart attacks were, next to cancer, the second largest killer of the American male, as I knew.

So far, so good. I would have to lose 50 pounds myself, and in the process I decided I might as well help those millions of other businessmen who needed the same help. And, at the same time, help myself get rich.

So when I left the hospital I founded something which I called "Calorie Counters Anonymous" and set out to sell it by mail.

This was before the days of Weight Watchers. I reasoned that the only way to lose weight was by reducing caloric intake, and the only way to do that was by systematic calorie counting. So, with the help of a Simon and Schuster editor, Bill Clifford, I put together a series of 12 little pocket notebooks, each with 30 pages, with space for notation of daily caloric intake, and with interesting light calorie suggestions for the three daily meals: strawberries for breakfast, lots of lobsters and fish, and not too much of anything, especially martinis.

We planned to send these pocket books out on a monthly basis, accompanied by a newsletter which Bill would write. I got prices on the package, and found that I could produce and ship 12 booklets, with the newsletter, in the mail for a cost of $6. I threw free "cents-off" coupons provided by low-calorie food producers, like gelatin desserts, into each mailing—such freebies were easy to obtain.

My thinking was that I would sell my package for $12—$1 a month. With a cost of $6, I'd have $6 left for promotion and profits. (This was a somewhat lower margin than I thought desirable, but was the best I could do.)

I made a test mailing, and found that I got subscribers for a sales cost of $3 each. Response on the mailing averaged out to about 5 percent—a substantial and satisfactory return. With a product cost of $6, a promotion cost of $3, and a $12 price, this left me $3 gross profit, before overhead, on each starting customer. I calculated that I could mail six million homes and get 300,000 customers on whom I would have a margin of $600,000. I could do this every year and I would indeed be rich.

However, before calling up all my regular mail-order clients and resigning their accounts, I decided to track the performance of the initial test group. My mailing had utilized the usual mail-order "soft offer": send for the first booklet on approval, then pay or cancel. I made what I thought would be a reasonable allowance for cancellations and bad debts—10 percent overall. This tied in to my experience at the time on other products I'd helped promote.

We tested a total of 20,000 letters, and got an overall response of 1000 customers. One interesting fact which immediately emerged from the test was that female lists pulled while male lists didn't. Evidently those millions of overweight businessmen I was going to save from heart attacks just didn't care if they did die. On the other hand, women were very weight conscious—not because of any concern over health, but because of *looks*.

The second thing I discovered, almost instantly, was the reason why fat people are fat. Or at least this was how I interpreted my findings. Fat people are fat because they lack character. They have no will power. They can't keep their good resolutions.

Instead of a 10 percent loss due to bad debts and customer

cancellations, I got 60 percent cancellations and bad debts. For every 100 starters, I found, 30 would cancel, and 30 would simply not pay.

Thus, my actual cost per net *paid* sale was not $3.00, but $7.50. Added to a product cost of $6.00, this made my total out-of-pocket cost $13.50 for every $12.00 sale I made. Not a very profitable basis for launching a new business!

In fact, with a bit of fine tuning, I still believe that Calorie Counters Anonymous could have been made into a reasonably profitable mail-order business. My wife and children and I ran the Club for a year off the kitchen table, before we abandoned it, and results on those customers who stayed in were remarkably good. We received scores of letters from delighted customers who found the system lived up to its promise: an easy way to lose weight, and enjoy it.

The head of the Department of Home Economics of a western state university volunteered a letter stating that this was the only effective weight-losing technique she'd ever encountered.

In short, the response was good, but the project needed (1) a higher price to make it profitable, and (2) a big infusion of money to make it a success. The trouble, as with the Giant Squab projects of my youth, was venture capital. If I had had a couple of hundred thousand dollars to spare, and the time to spend it intelligently, I could have tested various refinements: different prices and offers, different lists, more economical fulfillment, and assorted devices to increase my margin and secure full payment up front.

However, I did not have the kind of venture capital such testing would have required. I didn't have the time to spare for such a project, from my basic business of earning money to put food on the table. So after a year we bid goodbye to Calorie Counters Anonymous, and that's why I'm still a consultant.

But the experience explains, in my opinion, the failure of many other promising new products. Perhaps the most frequent cause of such failures is *inadequate capitalization.*

Nowadays, you can't launch a new mail-order product on a shoestring. The days when Sam Josefowitz could start a $3 million mail-order business with a $5,000 investment are pretty much gone forever.

Quite a different example of the perils and rewards of starting a mail-order business, which Todd and I became involved in, was the Center for the Study of Democratic Institutions. This Institution was a very liberal Think Tank, founded by Robert Hutchins, the originator of "Great Books of the Western World." Hutchins was also the youthful President of the University of Chicago. His idea in founding the Center was to provide a sort of Athenian, Socratic meeting place, where important thinkers could gather to work undisturbed, to think, and to exchange important ideas.

Hutchins assembled a most impressive group of genuine important thinkers, including himself: Linus Pauling, two-time Nobel Prize Winner; Bishop Pike; Harry Hopkins; journalists John L. Perry and Harry S. Ashmore—to mention only a few. Occasional visiting scholars, scientists, historians, and writers added color to the scene.

The Center purchased a magnificent, colonnaded Grecian estate on a hilltop overlooking the Pacific Ocean, in Santa Barbara, California, to serve as its residence. The Resident Fellows of the Center were free to pursue their specialties without direction or constraint—to write books or papers, or simply to think. The Center provided surroundings, quarters, facilities and financial support so that the Fellows were free of all distraction.

Their only regular activity was to meet once a day, at 11:00 A.M., to talk about great ideas and geopolitical problems that were currently occupying their minds. Their dialogues—exchanges of ideas, which were all tape-recorded—lasted from 11:00 to 12:00, after which the Fellows had lunch together and thereafter were free to pursue their private activities.

Originally the Center was funded by a substantial grant, "The Fund for the Republic." Very shortly, the Center went through its grant and felt the need for additional capital. And this was when Todd and I came into the picture.

One day, in our New York office, there appeared a young man named Dick Gilbert, who announced that he represented the Center. He had heard that Todd and I were magazine consultants, and he told us that the Center was interested in starting a magazine. The members of the Center were churning out interesting and provocative ideas at their daily 11:00 meetings, but their audience for these Socratic dialogues was limited to themselves. The Center felt their thoughts merited a wider hearing, so they proposed to publish a journal which would mix Center dialogues with occasional articles, written by the Center members, and by others whose thoughts interested the Center's directors. Sale of this magazine would bring in much-needed revenue.

Dick Gilbert explained that the Center didn't want a huge circulation for its magazine—their aim was 15,000 subscribers. In fact, he doubted that a wider audience would be suitable, because the intended material of the Center magazine was expected to be a foot or two over most readers' heads. The magazine would not take advertising. The Center was prepared to take a reasonable loss on the publication, although they hoped, instead, to make a prudent profit. They hoped to secure a $6 annual subscription price for six issues per year—a total income of $90,000 on the 15,000 subscriptions.

So, said Dick Gilbert, could we help?

It should be noted that I personally am not particularly of the Liberal persuasion—how, then, it might be asked, could I justify working for the Republican Party on the one hand, and the Center on the other? Were we, as consultants, simply hired gunslingers who went to work for the highest bidder? The answer is that Todd and I sincerely believed in both institutions—or we wouldn't have worked for them. The Center was a genuine "Think Tank" where important, innovative ideas were examined and explored. We liked their ideas, just as we liked the basic principles that we thought the Republican Party stood for.

In its time, the Weintz Company has turned down a goodly number of prospective clients. Some we have refused because we simply did not believe they had a product which could make it in the marketplace, or because they were underfinanced and were, we thought, doomed to failure. Others we turned down because we didn't like them or their proposed assignments. One example of a questionable account that comes to mind was a tobacco public relations group that wanted to pay us an amazing amount of money to create and put out a series of mailings to the medical profession on the health advantages of cigarette smoking. We would have liked the money, but the job didn't appeal to us. We turned them down flat.

In any event, we told Dick Gilbert it seemed to us (drawing on our previous Republican Party experience) that the kind of people the Center was after would much rather be *members* of the Center itself, rather than mere *subscribers* to the Center magazine.

"Just imagine," we said, "what a privilege it would be for the ordinary liberal man or woman in the street to *join* the Center itself as a Fellow *Member*, along with such celebrated intellectuals as Robert Hutchins, Linus Pauling, Rexford Tugwell, and Bishop Pike!

"And," we said "just imagine how interesting and stimulating it would be, as a Center member, to receive not only the Center's magazine and Proceedings, which would convey the substance of many Center Fellows' private round table discussions, but also to receive occasional papers written by the Center's Fellows."

These Center Fellows, it should be noted, were all exceedingly literate, and they did pour out a remarkable quantity of serious writing.

So our suggestion to Dick and the Center was simple and obvious: that they should make a mailing which would invite selected individuals to *join* the Center, and to receive the new Center magazine as just one of the privileges of membership, instead of merely inviting them to *subscribe* to a magazine.

However, we said, a membership in such an organization obviously carried a higher price tag than did a subscription to a mere magazine. We suggested a hierachy of membership: a Founding Member, with a membership fee of $1,000 or more a year; a Supporting Membership, for $500 or more a year; Sustaining Membership of $100 or more; a Contributing Membership of $50 or more a year; a Participating Membership of $25 or more a year; and an Associate Membership of $10 or more a year.

Dick Gilbert and the Center decided to hire us. So Todd and I put together a half-dozen very impressive, 9 x 12" four color envelope mailings, each projecting the personality of the Center through a different visual image.

Actually, we simply picked up the proposed covers of the Center magazine, and made envelopes out of them. on the theory that magazine editors always try, through their magazine covers, to project the personality of their magazine most accurately and favorably, therefore making covers excellent mailings. One envelope, for example, pictured the Trojan Horse, with a cut line "I FEAR THE GREEKS, EVEN THOUGH BEARING GIFTS." Another pictured, in somewhat abstract fashion, an artist's impression, in brilliant tones of red, of the human brain. However, in each case the copy line on the envelope was the same:

You Are Invited

To Become A Member of

THE CENTER FOR THE STUDY

OF DEMOCRATIC INSTITUTIONS

and to receive

THE CENTER MAGAZINE

This was a good example of the old principle of "mail order with kid gloves on." It was, we felt, refined and elegant, but it also got directly to the point.

Inside the envelope was a Table of Contents listing assorted articles from the projected Center Magazine, which set the intellectual tone of our appeal: "The Reluctant Death of Sovereignty," by Arnold Toynbee; "Violence and the Home of the Brave," a discussion between Stringfellow Barr, Bishop Pike, and others, on the wave of violence then sweeping the country (this was in 1967); "East-West: The Beginning of a Dialogue," a discussion of the Cold War confrontation between Eastern and Western Europe, by Herbert Marcuse and Franz Cardinal Koenig, Archbishop of Vienna. There were some 16 articles of this general type.

Our next problem, after creating the copy and layout for test mailings, was (as is usual in mail order) to locate *lists* of liberal-minded individuals who would likely have heard of the Center in the first place, and, in the second place, be likely to want to join.

This was surprisingly easy to do. One of the curious facts about the mail-order business is the availability of lists of individuals with almost any kind of human characteristics imaginable. As I've noted before, lists can be rented from the list owners for a reasonable one-time rental fee.

And if you seek up-scale, well-to-do intellectuals of a liberal persuasion, they are as easy to locate as the fat people to whom I tried to sell my "Calorie Counters Anonymous" service.

We tested a number of our test mailings on a number of such lists, and all the tests were remarkably successful. The upshot was that we did *not* secure the 15,000 $6-a-year magazine subscribers, for a total income of $90,000, that the Center originally hoped to secure; instead, we brought in over 100,000 *members*, who contributed an average of better than $15 each. Our total income for the first year topped $1.5 million.

The Center was a most enjoyable account—one of those which makes a consultant's life worth living. Not only did they pay us well, but their location, in Santa Barbara, made frequent cross-country plane trips necessary; and because this involved such long-distance trips, we were treated like visiting royalty (with all expenses paid) on each visit. Trips to Santa Barbara, and sojourns at the Santa Barbara Biltmore, were more like vacations than work, because the job we'd been hired for was completed at a single stroke with our initial test mailings, and thereafter the work was all down hill. The people we worked with at the Center were without exception pleasant company. Occasionally, to save Todd and me from undue wear and tear, the business staff would meet us for lunch in Los Angeles. We'd fly out in the morning, have lunch, and fly back the same day. It was all rather like our idea of what a consultant's life should be.

However, with the Center's prosperity came problems for the Weintzes. The size of the membership operation required that the Center gear up to handle their memberships in a businesslike way. A fulfillment manager was hired. This individual, in addition to his knowledge of how to set up a fulfillment operation, was also an expert on lists and mailings—and was puzzled about the Center's need for expensive mail-order consultants.

This little problem was complicated by an internecine squabble among other business staff members. Unfortunately—for us and, as it turned out, for the Center—the group that employed and sponsored Todd and me lost out, and the group that supported the fulfillment manager won. Todd and I were fired.

Subsequently the Center settled down to mailing inexpensive, and also remarkably dull and uninspired, fulfillment department-type letters. The results were predictable. Membership and income quickly dwindled.

The decline of the Center had nothing to do with the effectiveness of the mailing and renewal program we had set up. Indeed, I believe it had nothing to do with the character of the Center itself; the Center was still fulfilling its purpose and doing it well. Rather, the decline was a demonstration of the public's remarkable lack of response to pedestrian sales efforts. Our "expensive" promotion and renewal programs were closed down, and sensible, low-cost, ineffective programs substituted. The result was the near-demise of the Center for the Study of Democratic Institutions.

What are the lessons to be learned from the Center experience?

I believe the reason for the ultimate failure of the Center's mail-order program was pretty clear: They had a successful formula, but they failed to stick with it. The minute they became successful in mail order, they decided that conventional mail-order methods were beneath them. They switched to dignified, restrained, inexpensive—and ineffective—mailings, which naturally failed.

The reason, perhaps, goes a bit deeper; and I've seen the same disease strike other successful mail-order businesses. This is what I call "corporate pride." The president of the company is embarrassed to go home to his family in Westport, where—at Friday night cocktail parties—he must run the gauntlet of friends who are amused by his way of making a living. He decides to start operating on a higher plane. Pretty soon he goes out of business.

Tenacity is one of the outstanding characteristics that distinguishes the most successful mail-order people I've known. The good ones are bull dogs. They have the judgment to quickly abandon a weak or floundering project ("I don't believe in throwing good money after bad," as Walter Thayer once commented to me just before he closed down the New York *Herald-Tribune*). But when they get a formula that works, they stay with it until they find something *better*.

This doesn't mean that such successful individuals don't continue to *test*. They engage in a constant search for "something better." But until they *do* prove to themselves that they *have* found a more profitable copy idea, or offer, or price, they stick with the one that's making the money.

They don't substitute *opinions* for facts.

Another experience which Todd and I went through as partners in the mail-order consulting business involved Max Geffen. Maxwell Geffen, multimillionaire and entrepreneur extraordinary, was, at the time we went to work for him, well over 80 years old, but still exceedingly active. And sure of his own judgment, as he had every right to be.

I had known Max slightly, going all the way back to my original tenure at Schwab & Beatty, when Max had started a magazine called Book Digest—a whole magazine of book condensations, similar to the single book condensations that appeared in the back of each issue of *Reader's Digest*.

Max asked Schwab & Beatty to promote this publication, which we did, but for some reason—probably poor editorial quality—it foundered.

Max also owned a small book publishing firm, the David McKay Company, which specialized in sports and game books. At Schwab & Beatty, I wrote many little ads for those books, in the process collecting quite a library at no cost to me, on fly fishing, boxing, chess, wrestling, and related matters.

Later, when I helped start *Reader's Digest* Condensed Books, Max persuaded Book-of-the-Month Club to help him test a rival condensed book club, called Omnibooks. It is interesting to note that this failed. I believe the basic reason why Max failed and the *Digest's* Club gained more members than any other book club in America was simply that Max didn't have the *Digest* subscriber list to work with, as, of course, the *Digest* did.

Subsequently, Max started a magazine which *did* succeed: *Medical Health Care News*, a publication which was distributed *free* to doctors, whether they wanted to receive it or not. The magazine made millions for Max and he eventually sold it to McGraw-Hill for a rumored $23 million in McGraw-Hill stock; Max thus became one of the largest shareholders in McGraw-Hill.

The simple secret of Max's success with this publication was the fact that the American Medical Association—the ethical and powerful physicians' association—frowned on patent medicine products (so-called over-the-counter "proprietary medications") and would not accept their advertising in the *Journal of the AMA*. So, proprietary marketers had no way of advertising directly to doctors. Max solved their problem by setting up his publication as a rival to the *AMA Journal*, filling it with patent medicine ads and mailing it *free* to every registered physician in the country.

Now Max called me in and told me that he was going to get rich all over again by publishing a *consumer* magazine which would do the same thing for consumers that *Medical Health Care News* did for doctors.

The AMA had a consumer publication called *Today's Health* which, of course, did *not* accept advertising for aspirin or cold remedies, or any brand-name medications.

"So I will start a consumer publication called *Family Health*, fill it with proprietary drug ads, and the money will roll in, just as it did for *Medical Health Care News*," said Max.

"All I need is a guaranteed ABC circulation of one million subscribers to start," he said. "I must have a million circulation in order to interest these big-money proprietary drug advertisers. And you and Todd are going to get it for me.

"Furthermore," said Max, "I will make it easy for you. I have arranged to secure Morris Fishbein's book, the *Home Medical Encyclopedia*, which we will give as a free premium with a $16 subscription to *Family Health*. And I have arranged with one of the major drugstore chains—a company with hundreds of stores—to mail to their charge account customers and offer them the opportunity to subscribe to *Family Health*, get Fishbein's expensive book free, and charge the whole transaction to their drugstore account. All you have to do is put this proposition in a mailing and we'll get our one million circulation."

Max had hired Dick Parisi as his business manager. Dick was an experienced professional mail-order man, a graduate of the Mc-Kinsey marketing consulting firm, who had also headed the *Christian Herald Magazine* and book circulation operation. He was also a former Vice President of the J.K. Lasser accounting firm, which made a specialty of auditing magazine accounting. So Dick knew a great deal about mail-order promotion, especially the figures side of the business. Dick's job was to supervise our production of the *Family Health* mailing and take care of the details of putting the mailing out, in addition to functioning as the financial head and business manager of *Family Health*.

While welcoming Max's account, we—Todd and I—objected strenuously to Max's promotion plan. To begin with, we doubted that the drugstore charge account list would prove productive or that, when the chips were down, it would even materialize. These were people who bought drug sundries at a drugstore, not folks who had purchased health-related items *by mail*. In a nutshell, they weren't mail-order buyers. More than that, we felt it unlikely that a drugstore customer list would turn out to be a practical source of names on 5-up Cheshire labels—the normal mechanism for addressing mailing envelopes.

On the other hand, the idea of a *premium*—the Fishbein book—sounded reasonable. We suggested then, that Max let us *test* the premium offer plus two classic mail-order alternatives: a "half-price introductory offer"—a $12 one-year subscription for $6—versus an "everybody wins" sweepstakes offer.

We proposed that, in addition to the drugstore customer list, we test a great many other mail-order lists: lists of women with children (our publication was "*Family Health*"); lists of health faddists—people who had bought diet pills, or books on heart disease, by mail; and tests of women who had subscribed to one of the women's service magazines, such as *McCall's*, on the assumption that it is the woman of the family who is interested in and responsible for *family* health.

Very reluctantly, Max agreed to the tests, and under Dick Parisi's supervision, we put together quite a complicated test of lists, offers, and mailings. Dick was a stickler for detail, and there were a thousand details in these assorted mailings where questionable decisions or minor mistakes could be made. Since this was, for Dick, a win-or-die situation—if the mailings failed, he'd be out of business—he examined and re-examined, and questioned everything we did. We were accustomed to working with large clients who had competent staffs to look after minor details, and we frequently dropped a detail or two. By the time the tests finally went out, relations between Dick and me were more than a little strained. Then the mailing results came in.

As we had anticipated, the "millions of names" of drugstore charge customers turned out to have an actual grand total of less than 100,000—considerably fewer than were needed to get Max his one million starting subscribers. And the names we did secure for testing proved to be completely unresponsive to mail-order blandishments.

Also, Max's premium offer (the free Fishbein book) proved to be even more of a dud than we had anticipated. It pulled an *average* of about 1½ percent on the top mail-order lists we tested.

In contrast, our half-price offer (12 issues for $6) pulled about 5 percent overall—enough so that, by mailing 20 million names, we could secure one million subscribers. The trouble was that we didn't have 20 million good health-oriented mail-order names in hand.

However, the sweepstakes mailing, which we had forced down Max's and Dick Parisi's throats, pulled 12½ percent. By mailing 8 million names, we then secured precisely one million net paid subscribers.

Dick Parisi and I became fast friends.

But—as with one previous Weintz client, ATLAS magazine— there remained the problem of getting the advertising revenue needed to support a consumer magazine; the problem of securing the millions of dollars in patent medicine advertising that Max had expected to fall from the heavens. Max knew everybody in the proprietary drug field, so he had felt it unnecessary to hire a staff of Madison Avenue ad salesmen. He went out personally to visit the heads of the big pharmaceutical firms, and offered them the opportunity to advertise their wares in a consumer publication that was precisely perfect for their needs.

This was a mistake. The pharmaceutical presidents then turned Max's proposals over to their marketing and advertising Vice Presidents, who in turn consulted their Madison Avenue ad agencies. And these organizations put their media departments to work on their problems. These individuals were accustomed to being wooed by handsome ad salesmen with elaborate flip-overs, loaded with demographics, readership statistics, and three-martini lunches. The media people resented being told, by somebody who handed the order down second hand from a client president, that *Family Health* might be a good advertising medium for their client's product. And they successfully sabotaged the whole idea, as so frequently happens when decisions are left to media departments. *Family Health's* manna of advertising revenue failed to fall from the heavens.

But the real reason for *Family Health's* failure to attract advertising was that Max Geffen had failed to identify his *real* competition. He was *not* offering an alternative to the AMA's publication, *Today's Health*, as he thought he was. He was, in fact, going into competition with television.

And on television you can show interesting action photos of stomachs dissolving under the impact of acid indigestion and the quick, vivid neutralization of that acid when the appropriate brand-name anti-acid is ingested. You can show action pictures of hammers striking an agonized headache sufferer's head and the hammer dissolving when the sufferer takes just two brand-name analgesic tablets. You can show hands swelling to giant proportions and turning red-hot from arthritis, and tiny anti-arthritic granules racing to the rescue, right through a picture of the stomach, up a shoulder, down an arm, into the very tips of the sufferer's fingers.

You can't show action like that in printed ads, even in a publication like *Family Health*!

For a number of years, Dick Parisi managed to stave off *Family Health's* economic disaster. He rented the subscriber list to other mail-order companies. He sold medical health insurance to his subscribers using a "third party endorsement" technique which was exceedingly effective and profitable. He performed miracles of financial juggling which he had learned at J.K. Lasser.

But eventually Max Geffen decided that enough was enough. He sold the business, with an attractive tax-loss carry forward, to a new owner. Dick and the Weintz Company departed.

THE LESSON TO BE LEARNED FROM FAMILY HEALTH

Max Geffen was essentially a financier and as such, he made certain that he started *Family Health* with adequate capital. But he still went astray in the financial area. He counted on income from advertising which never materialized.

For any would-be mail-order entrepreneur, the lesson is still one of financing: You must be sure, before you launch your project, that you have adequate cash in hand to see you through the birth and early stages of your new mail-order product or project. This is where the accountant half of the mail-order operator's "split personality" comes into play. Either you have the money you need, or you do not. And if you don't have the money, forget it!

*   *   *   *   *   *   *   *   *

Years later, in 1982, Avon Products, which had had great success selling Avon Fashions by mail, decided to expand their mail-order operation. They hired Dick Parisi to start a new division called Great American Magazines, which was to sell subscriptions to most U.S. magazines at great discounts, in direct competition with Publisher's Clearing House.

Dick then hired the Weintz Company as his direct marketing agency. And we put together a sweepstakes. The keynote of this sweepstakes—the one distinctive feature which set it apart from Publisher's Clearing House and other sweepstakes—was the inclusion of a little plastic card. The card peeked through a second window on the big, garish 9 x 12" envelope, and the copy on the envelope said (among other things):

THIS CARD MAY *ALREADY* BE WORTH

ONE MILLION DOLLARS TO YOU!

The difference between the plastic card, and the mailing we tested without the plastic card, was put succinctly to me by Dick Parisi:

"Without the plastic card the test would have failed, and we'd have lost, $1.5 million. With the card we have the start of a successful business."

A WORD ABOUT SWEEPSTAKES

The subject of sweepstakes, as an action-getting device, is almost worthy of a separate chapter and it would take a pretty long chapter to go into all the intricacies and pitfalls involved in putting

GREAT AMERICAN MAGAZINES MAILING

A successful sweepstakes mailing that combined an irresistible offer with a plastic card "hot potato" to induce immediate action.

Reprinted with permission of Great American Magazines.

out a sweepstakes that is actually effective. However, I've illustrated the basic principles, with examples, in previous sections of this book, so here I'll simply sum up the salient features of this "hot potato" device.

1. A good sweepstakes will, as a rough rule of thumb, increase the pull of any mailing by at least 25 percent—more likely 50 percent, or even 100 percent. Or more! For example, the difference between Max Geffin's *premium* mailing for *Family Health*, and his *sweepstakes* mailing, was the difference between 1½ percent and 12½ percent. The sweepstakes mailing was *7 times* as good as the premium effort. On an 8 million mailing, the sweepstakes pulled

one million *paid* subscribers. In contrast, had we rolled out with the premium mailing, we'd have secured only 120,000 subscribers!

2. The big *drawback* of a sweepstakes mailing is the legal obligation: you have to *distribute all prizes*. If you offer a million dollars in prizes, but get only 1000 responses from a 100,000 test, and you decide to abort the effort then you still have to distribute that million dollars among the 1000 respondees.

In fact, in New York and Florida, you must post a bond guaranteeing payment of all prizes. Failure to do so would make you liable for mail fraud, a serious offense.

3. Prizes must be sufficiently large to arouse action-inducing avarice. Nowadays a first prize of a compact automobile will scarcely arouse most individuals to action. A million dollar first prize definitely *will* do some arousing. Just think: "I know the odds against me are great. Still, just suppose I *am* the winner, and fail to claim my prize."

I can think of a couple of sweepstakes I've been involved in which were *not* successful. Each taught me a lesson. One was a sweepstakes for *My Weekly Reader*—an educational magazine for young readers. We offered a grand prize of *a four-year, paid-up college education for your boy or girl*, to parents who subscribed to *My Weekly Reader* on behalf of their child. The response was abysmal, and the *lesson* that sweepstakes taught was that parents get a lot less excited about an education for their child, some time in the distant future, as opposed to *cash*—right now—FOR THEMSELVES.

A second failure I presided over was a sweepstakes for the Republican National Committee. This was in 1976, an election year, so, as an inducement to secure contributions, we offered two *free* tickets to the Republican Convention, along with suitable side trimmings—meeting VIPs, going to convention parties, and so on.

Some inducement! The response told us plainly that going to a Republican Nominating Convention, even for Republican partisans, was not much of a motivator. The Managing Director of the Republican Finance Committee had to spend several days shepherding the winners around, and she told me later that there would be no more such penny-pinching prizes.

So, unless you can work out a *very* attractive small prize—something absolutely unique—you are definitely much better off with a BIG cash prize and the bigger the better. Indeed, I would say that these days a $50,000 grand prize is just about the minimum.

4. Sweepstakes mailings are the ultimate in razz-me-tazz. You're doing a "circus" type of mailing, and this calls for a circus type of presentation. Bells, whistles, plastic cards, mystery "rub-off" prize announcements, "Instant Winner" extra cash prizes, laser and impact personalized printing, giant, oversized envelopes—all are part of the menagerie you should consider enlisting in your effort.

In brief, a sweepstakes mailing will probably *not* be effective unless you *do* go in for a circus approach. Certainly it will be nowhere near as effective if you present it in a dignified, refined package.

And there's a second lesson in this necessity for using a circus approach to package a sweepstakes mailing. If you have the kind of product for which a sweepstakes mailing would not be appropriate, then by all means, don't use sweepstakes. The appropriateness of the mailing style is an important consideration whenever you make a mailing. *Appropriateness* is a prime consideration when you start thinking about using a sweepstakes to promote your product.

* * * * * * * * *

Another interesting example of a start-up business, and what to do and what not to do to make such a new business successful, was a beauty club project that I became involved in.

I had been doing some consulting work for the R.H. Donnelley Company, old friends of mine from my *Reader's Digest* days, and one day I received a call from the president of Donnelley, Ham Mitchell, who invited me to his New York office.

"We've been working for a year on an idea for a beauty club, but we can't seem to make it go," Ham told me. "See what you think of it."

The basic idea seemed very good to me. Donnelley owned the famous Donnelley mailing list—about 60 million consumer names, neatly stored away on computer. The principal use which they made of this gigantic list was to rent it to "cents-off couponers" for "co-op mailings."

Donnelley would announce to the food and drug trade that they were about to make a mailing to 20, 40, or 60 million households, and anyone wishing to get some cents-off coupons into the hands of consumers could have a coupon inserted in the mailing package for a modest sum—$12 to $15 or so per thousand. These mailings went out over the signature of "Carol Wright," a fictitious character who shared other consumers' enthusiasm for bargains.

The Carol Wright mailings were stuffed with such coupons—20, 30, or more coupons to a mailing. The "redemption rate"— coupons which consumers took to the supermarket and used to help finance their purchases of couponed products—sometimes ran as high as 30 percent. So Donnelley had no great difficulty getting participants in their mailings, and they had proof that Carol Wright mailings worked.

"So," said Donnelley, "what's to keep us from sticking an extra *Carol Wright* coupon in some of these Carol Wright mailings—at no cost to us, obviously, as an extra coupon can ride free, if it's our own? Anything we sold by this method would be sold at little or no selling cost, and could be very profitable."

Accordingly, Donnelley started to participate in their own Carol Wright co-op mailings. They set up a department especially for this purpose, and by the time I came along they had successfully sold quite a number of items at a profit: jade-colored glass earrings, ladies wallets, scarves, salt and pepper sets—inexpensive novelty items that were good impulse-sales getters. The Carol Wright program was successful. The appeal of its products (like the appeal of all its participating co-op products) was strictly to women.

So someone suggested: Why not start a beauty club—and promote it through Carol Wright co-op mailings, at virtually no selling cost to Donnelley?

The idea of the club sounded good. Most American women spend hundreds of dollars every year on cosmetics: lipsticks, rouge, nail polish, perfume, hair care products, and skin creams of a thousand varieties. Each month, Donnelley told me, the Carol

Wright Beauty Club would offer its members a $5 package of cosmetics on a "negative option" basis. The Club would be organized along the lines of the Book-of-the-Month Club: You join the club and pay $1 for an introductory gift, then every month you receive a notice of the upcoming "selection"—a manicure set, or a skin cream package, and so on—an interesting, different beauty-care package each month. And unless you said "No," you subsequently received (and were billed for) the package.

Since the mark-up on cosmetics is simply astronomical—a lipstick that in those days cost 10¢ to produce would sell for $2 to $5—and since there would be no sales cost to speak of (the Club would send out inexpensive flyers in the Carol Wright co-ops) and the Carol Wright name would be recognized and trusted by millions of consumers, the proposed Club seemed destined to thrive.

What, then, seemed to be the hang-up?

The hang-up, I quickly discovered, was arithmetic. I waded through elaborate sets of projections. These showed that a handsome kit of cosmetics could be put together for a couple of dollars; the cosmetics cost very little, but the packaging—the pretty bottles and compacts and so on—was very expensive, and ran the cost up substantially. And the postage ran the cost up further; cosmetics did not share the book club advantage of mailing at low, low "book rates."

In addition, the book club "negative option" method of selling products to members is quite expensive. Each month the club must send an advance notice of its upcoming "selection" to all members, and give members a chance to say "No, I don't want this month's selection." The resulting bookkeeping—sorting out acceptances and refusals—involved a lot of clerical expenses.

The figures I examined showed me that, after paying for an introductory "gift" on which the Club might expend two or three dollars, there was only a dollar or so in margin on each monthly "kit" that the Club proposed to put out. And after overhead (bookkeeping, billing, product procurement, design, and shipping), the Club stood to lose perhaps $2 on each kit it shipped out.

Thus, if the average member accepted five kits in the course of a year, the Club stood to lose $10 per member plus two or three dollars invested in member acquisition. The Club stood to lose $12 total in the first year on a new member!

On a modest 100,000 membership, this would amount to a $1.2 million out-of-pocket *loss* in that first year.

I suggested several perfectly obvious changes. First, the product cost had to be somehow reduced. One of the basic marketing ideas behind the Carol Wright co-op mailings was *sampling*. Food, drug, and household products participated in the co-ops partly to stimulate immediate sales and partly to get *new* customers to *try* their products. They actually *paid* Donnelley for participation in thise co-op mailings.

"So," I said, "let's offer beauty product manufacturers an opportunity to *sample* their products *at no cost*. We'll send those products out to women who actually *pay* for the privilege of trying the products—members of a beauty club, women who are so concerned with the serious problem of feminine beauty that they pay good money to get beauty products they can *try*.

"And," I said, "we won't even charge the beauty product manufacturers for participation in our Club."

This way we got the products for nothing, instead of paying for them. This largely eliminated the problem of product cost.

Next, I said, we have to change the *concept* of the Club to adjust it to the *sampling* idea. Instead of putting together a series of kits—an eye make-up kit, a skin care kit, and a manicure kit—we'll send out packages of mixed *samples*: small *sample* packages of perfume, skin creams, mascara, soap, rouge, and lipstick, all mixed up together so that club members can *try* all kinds of exciting new beauty products and they can survey the whole "world of beauty" and discover for themselves the very products that would meet their individual beauty needs.

We toyed with the idea of calling the club the Carol Wright Beauty Club but were troubled by the identification of the Carol Wright name with supermarket products—breakfast foods, detergents, and toilet cleaning products. Then someone came up with the name of "The World of Beauty Club" which solved that important problem.

Next, I suggested that the 60 million recipients of Carol Wright mailings were not really *mail-order* buyers so if we went after them with the standard, book club "negative option" approach, and tried to sell them a beauty kit every month, we'd scare them off and our bookkeeping, on this approach, would be excessive.

Therefore, I said, we should try the successful *Reader's Digest* Condensed Book Club approach: Offer a sample kit for 10¢, then have an *automatic shipment* of the Club's selections every *three* months instead of once a month "until forbid."

By such an approach, bookkeeping cost would be greatly reduced, and the three-month interval between product shipments would give us ample time to *collect* $5 for each sample kit and to kill off "bad debts."

And I made one last suggestion.

"True, an insert in the Carol Wright mailings costs you nothing," I said. "But you are mailing to a *compiled* list, not a mail-order list. You have an audience of 60 million names, but how many are women who are (1) mail-order buyers and (2) would-be beauty queens?

"Shouldn't we, therefore, *test* a conventional mailing to good mail-order lists, *against* an insert in the Carol Wright co-op?"

It was very easy to lay our hands on millions of names of women who were extremely beauty conscious who were also previous mail-order buyers, and had desirable demographic characteristics as to age and income. For example, every woman who subscribes by mail to a magazine is, *ipso facto*, a mail-order buyer and if she subscribes to a magazine like *Redbook*, *Glamour*, or *Mademoiselle*, she's young, interested in *beauty*, and has expendable income.

Dozens of products, sold by mail-order advertising in such publications, had lists of customers they were eager to rent to the World of Beauty Club.

So we put together a couple of tests. One was a modest flyer, which could be added to any Carol Wright mailing and ride free of postage or mailing list cost. Such a flyer, in those days, cost about $25 per thousand—2½¢ each. We projected that we could certainly afford to pay as much as $5 or so to acquire a member, exclusive of the 10¢ "gift" package. Therefore, by simple arithmetic ($25 divided by $5) we needed only a 0.5 percent response from our Carol Wright mailing to make it successful. This seemed ridiculously low!

Against this, we tested one of my elaborate, expensive, conventional mailings: an over-sized, full color envelope, a 4-color brochure, a 4-page letter, and a *coin card* order form (the consumer joined the Club by inserting a 10¢ coin in a little pocket in the card, and mailing back the coin to become a member of the World of Beauty Club and to secure her 10¢ introductory gift kit).

This package, in the mail, cost perhaps $200 per thousand (against the Carol Wright insert's cost of $25.). Thus, we needed perhaps eight times as great a response—at least a 4 percent response—to make this conventional mailing package successful.

The results were as the reader may have anticipated.

WORLD OF BEAUTY MAILING

This mailing which cost $200 per thousand, pulled orders at one-fifth the cost-per-order of a mailing that cost $25 per thousand. (The secret was lists.)

Reproduced by permission of the World of Beauty Club.

On the Carol Wright mailing to a mass, 50 million non-mail-order list, where our offer was sandwiched in with as many as 20 other offers, we got about 0.2 percent response. We needed 0.5 percent. The mailing was a failure.

On the other hand, on the expensive, conventional package to highly selective lists of female mail-order beauty product buyers—a universe totaling perhaps 10 million against Carol Wright's 60 million—we got anywhere from 6 percent to 12 percent response—an average of at least 8 percent. We needed 4 percent. This 8 percent response was about five times as good as the "cheap" insert mailing, in terms of cost-per-order, and it was a perfect illustration of the difference the proper use of the basic mail-order principle makes in the effectiveness of a mailing: *List selection* is vital to the successful sale of any mail-order product (and, parenthetically, lists of mail-order buyers are better than plain, unclassified compiled lists of telephone subscribers or auto buyers).

But we still did not know how enthusiastically our trial members of the World of Beauty Club would respond to our product or how well they would "pay and stay."

Also, the Donnelley staff assigned to the World of Beauty Club had an enormous task on their hands convincing cosmetic manufacturers that they really *were* getting "something for nothing," when we included their product in our Beauty Kits and didn't even charge them for their inclusion!

To our delight, the cosmetic manufacturers were eager to participate. And the Trial Members of our Club—the several thousand that we brought in from our tests—paid and stayed. Before the year was out it was established that we had a winner. Very conservative calculations projected a profit on each member we brought in by our "conventional" mailing of at least $10.

(The calculations, for the benefit of those who are interested in such things, were as follows: An 8 percent pull on a mailing that cost $200 per thousand mailed—80 orders secured from a $200 expenditure—gave us a member acquisition cost of $2.50. The 10¢ introductory kit cost us about $2.50. Each additional kit cost us about $2, in the mail, including overhead—yielding a margin per $5 kit of about $3. With a $5 initial selling cost, (the cost of the mailing plus the cost of the 10¢ kit) if the *average* starting member took and paid for five kits, our profit was $15 minus $5 sales cost: $10 profit per starting member.)

With a calculated mailing universe of about 10 million women, we figured that we could conceivably bring in 800,000 members every year, and have a tidy $8 million annual profit.

In the second year we sent out substantial mailings and brought the total Club Membership up to 600,000 paying members. This gave the Club an income of $3 million four times a year—$12 million gross annual income.

Naturally, Donnelley's President, Ham Mitchell, was very pleased, as was everyone else in the World of Beauty Club operation. And I had a particular reason for being pleased, which goes back to the question at the start of this chapter: "If you're so smart, why aren't you rich?"

As Donnelley's Marketing Consultant, I was under contract, and I received a monthly retainer for helping out whenever I could. I made trips to Donnelley's Oak Brook, Illinois offices and to their offices in Los Angeles, where I applied my mail-order background to various marketing problems the Donnelley sales staff encountered. My retainer was generous, and the account was a lot of fun—helping to solve all kinds of interesting sales and marketing problems.

However, Ham Mitchell and Giles McCollum, who ran the Beauty Club, did not feel that my basic retainer compensated me for the work I was putting in on The World of Beauty Club. Donnelley had a very generous incentive system of rewarding its salesmen with commissions on income they brought in. Ham Mitchell and Giles McCollum said the same should apply to me on the World of Beauty. Therefore, they said, I should be a stockholder and part owner of the Club.

Accordingly, Giles wrote out a second contract, which gave me a handsome percentage of the ownership of The World of Beauty Club.

When we reached the point where the projected profits of the Club for the year ahead were about $3 million dollars a year on 600,000 paying members, I calculated *my* share of the pie would be some $60,000 a year—a good, steady income. And if Donnelley decided to sell the Club (as was hinted they might) I calculated that the sale could well be for 10 times earnings—$30 million dollars—which would yield me $600,000. So I was happy.

Unfortunately, Donnelley was owned by Dun & Bradstreet, which is essentially a financial and investment firm dealing in large financial transactions with major business corporations—a money company. And the President of Dun & Bradstreet was the Chairman of the Board of Directors of Donnelley.

As is the custom, the Board of Directors of Donnelley held a meeting, at which the Chairman of the Board presided, and the President of Donnelley reported on his company's activities.

The way I reconstruct what then transpired is as follows:

"And how is the World of Beauty Club doing?" inquired the Chairman of the Board.

"Just wonderfully," said Mr. Mitchell. "We now have 600,000 members, and we have just shipped out to them their current quarterly Club Beauty Kit—600,000 kits all told."

"Let's see," said the Chairman of the Board. "Those kits sell for $5 each, don't they? So that means you took in $3 million this month from the Club. Splendid, splendid!"

"Well, not exactly," said Ham Mitchell. "We took in $3 million in *receivables*. That is, you see, we shipped these kits on a bill-me-later basis. The customers *owe* us three million dollars, which we have every expectation that they will pay."

"You mean to say you actually have 600,000 accounts receivable? And these 600,000 customers owe us $3 million? You've actually extended credit for that much money to that many consumers—I presume you've made very extensive credit checks on every one of them?"

"Well, not exactly," said Mr. Mitchell. "You see, we haven't made any credit checks. It isn't necessary. We have simply tested membership performance and we know from experience how many customers will pay."

"You're telling me," said the Chairman, "that you have burdened Donnelley with $3 million in small, consumer accounts receivable, without a credit check? If anything happened to the economy, or if your product turned sour, Donnelley could easily lose $3 million. This isn't the kind of business Dun & Bradstreet likes to be in. Get rid of The World of Beauty Club. I don't care what you get for it as long as you recover the $3 million you have outstanding."

The upshot of that session was that Donnelley sold The World of Beauty Club—including its $3 million in receivables—for a wash. They were paid $3 million out of the income that the new owner secured—from the receivables that came with ownership of the Club.

By the time Donnelley's investments in the Club were paid off, there was no loss. But also, there was no profit.

And of course, The World of Beauty Club continued to be a highly profitable enterprise, worth millions—to its new owner.

Also, naturally, I was rather bitter against the Chairman of the Board, for robbing me (as I interpreted it) of $600,000.

However, the Chairman very shortly retired, and Ham Mitchell was promoted to President of Dun & Bradstreet. I like to think that The World of Beauty had something to do with the change.

SUMMING UP: WHAT YOU NEED TO START A SUCCESSFUL MAIL-ORDER BUSINESS

As the examples I've cited all demonstrate, starting any mail-order business involves investing money. It follows that you need ample working capital to turn your idea into a successful business. I have seen more mail-order projects ruined by insufficient capital than by any other element of the mail-order equation.

Assuming that you yourself are not prepared to risk several million dollars of your own money to test out the start-up of your mail-order idea, you have a serious problem. Where do you get that several million dollars?

This is, indeed, the most critical problem of the start-up.

You can look for an "angel"—a venture capitalist. These individuals and organizations exist, but they are hard to find, and usually they want at least 51 percent of your business—frequently much, much more. Also, they seldom will invest a penny in an untested idea. "Show us conclusive test results, and maybe we'll be interested," they say. This means that the initial investment, while it may be smaller, is still your problem.

You can mortgage your home, borrow from friends and relatives, or issue unofficial "shares" in the hypothetical business—all at great personal financial risk.

This is where great "pocketbook courage" is called for. The Chairman of Dun & Bradstreet had the money but lacked such pocketbook courage. Before I would encourage any budding entrepreneur to risk his or her life's savings, I would most earnestly advise him or her to consider the consequences if the test of the idea is a failure.

Then I would suggest that the idea be *tested*. If the test *does* prove encouraging, you can then go to the Venture Capitalists and strike a bargain. Later on, if your initial development is promising, you can go public. And, if all the steps you've taken along the way have been sufficiently prudent, you may then indeed become that fabled personage, a Mail-Order Millionaire.

Good luck. And don't forget about the need for the split personality!

14

The Ten Commandments for Creating Winning Mail-Order Packages

When I left *Reader's Digest*, in the fall of 1958, someone suggested that now, as I was "retiring," it would be appropriate for me to write a book about all my experiences as a mail-order operator.

This seemed like a good idea to me. The only trouble was that when I sat down to write I found I did not have enough material to make a book. I was 43 years old at the time and although I did not know it, half my mail-order career still lay ahead of me.

In fact, it has taken me another 27 years to finish the book which you now have in your hands.

However, in 1958, I did find that I had sufficient material for one good speech. I titled this speech, "The Ten Commandments for Creating Winning Mail-Order Packages," and I delivered the speech before a sizable audience at a "New York Direct Mail Day" convention in 1959, where it was well received.

In tucking together the final pages of this volume, I went back and re-read my 1959 speech and the curious thing about it is that

the "Ten Commandments" laid down then are the ten commande-
ments I'd lay down today for creating winning mail-order packages.

In fact, these are the principles I follow whenever I set out to
create a winning mailing, and all my experience of the past 30
years has simply confirmed my belief that if you put these "commandments" to work when you start creating direct mail, you're
on your way to success.

Certainly, I did not invent these rules. And I do not wish to
appear guilty of following my MBA ex-client's procedure of laying
down 67 Commandments which cannot be broken. At least, like
Moses, I've restricted my Commandments to 10.

In any event, these 10 principles—rules, precepts, guidelines,
or what you will—sum up everything I've learned in more than 40
years as a mail-order practitioner about *creating* winning mailings,
and as such I reproduce them here.

(And by "winning," of course, I do not mean "prize winning." I
mean mailings which bring a substantial profit to the company
that sends them out.)

In the preceding pages of this book, I've tried to demonstrate all
10 Commandments with numerous specific examples out of my
own experience. Here I'll spell out the commandments. They are
illustrated throughout the preceding pages of the book, with pictures and excerpts of actual mailings I've made (or Todd has
made) over the years.

THE FIRST COMMANDMENT: TEST

The tests I made for the Eisenhower-Nixon campaign, in 1952, are
a beautiful example of mail-order's ability to deliver reliable answers to a surprising variety of the questions that come up in
business. An "opinion survey" will tell you what people *think* they
will do. Focus groups tell you what people *think* they *think*. But
mail-order test efforts that contain a coupon and ask for an
order—what Claude Hopkins called "traceable results"—will give
you projectable answers to your questions about how many people will respond to your mailing, and which of several sales ap-

peals that you may be considering is the right one to roll out with.

Incidentally, I favor another of those mail-order "rules of three." I maintain that *one* test, of a single effort tested on a single list, will tell you only what *that* particular mailing would do if you rolled out to the entire universe of that particular list.

The test *won't* tell you what the mailing would have pulled if tested on other lists, nor will it tell you what other copy approaches, prices, or offers might have pulled.

So, if the test fails you have no way of knowing whether the failure was caused by a poor list selection, or a weak sales pitch, or if, indeed, your product was wrong to start with.

However, if you test *two* different copy approaches, you'll almost invariably find that one is better than another. And if you test them on a *spectrum* of lists—at least 10 different lists—you begin to zero in on your market.

Naturally, if *both* tests are failures, on *all 10 lists*, you have reason to pause and consider! So testing two mailing packages on several lists is clearly better than testing one package on one list.

But if you test *three* different package approaches, you gain an additional dimension. Frequently you'll find that Test "A" is better than "B," and "B" is better than "C." You then have a direction pointed out to you for future "line breeding and cross breeding"— away from "C," toward the elements embodied in "A."

Then, perhaps by combining the best elements of "A" and "B," and throwing "C" out entirely, you can create a package that is even better than "A" and test it for use in future mailings at the same time you are rolling out with "A."

THE SECOND COMMANDMENT: MOTIVATE

When you make a mail-order test, it is always important to keep in mind what you are trying to accomplish with your mailing. Are you trying to win a Direct Mail Marketing Association Echo Award or a Folio Gold Certificate? Or are you trying to please the boss and get a raise—or perhaps even get a lot of orders?

I believe that your objective should be none of these. To reach any of these objectives, you must first go one step further and *motivate* the reader of your mail-order piece to *respond* to your effort. This is the basic job of mail order—*motivation*. And that is my second mail-order principle. To succeed, you must motivate.

The fascinating question behind all mail order is, what motivates people to act? Why, for example, does a woman join a musical tape and record club? Is it to enlarge her family's cultural horizons? Is it to impress the neighbors with her cultural taste? Or to keep up with the Joneses? Or is it her inability to resist a bargain? Or is it simply to get some tapes and records for herself to enjoy because she genuinely likes good music?

And the problem is complicated because a woman may not *respond* to a direct appeal to her real motive. For instance, suppose she really wants music she herself likes and wants to listen to. If you begin your letter by saying, "Dear Music Lover: Now you can enjoy good music as never before" you might not get as many women to respond as if you begin, "Dear Music Lover: Here's a wonderful way to share your love of good music with your family by bringing beautiful recordings of great music into your home every month."

Or, you might try to give a woman some other rationalization to help her respond to your mailing such as, "Here's a new way to make your husband happy, and add a gracious touch to your family life."

Or you might do even better (in fact, probably much better!) if you said, "Dear Music Lover: Which *four* of these 123 great musical recordings do *you* want for only 89¢ (with a trial membership in our record club)?"

Which appeal is most likely to *motivate* the woman? That goes back to Principle No. 1. You *test*!

Very well, when we mail out a mail-order package, we are trying to find ways to *motivate* people. Now for the illustrations. At one time, early in my consulting career, *Glamour* magazine gave me a problem, which boiled down to this question: "Are women more interested in being *stylish* or in being *beautiful*?" There was a good reason for asking this question—*Glamour* wanted to sell subscriptions by direct mail. Which appeal should they use?

I reasoned that you can't ever be sure that these words, "style" and "beauty," mean the same thing to a woman as they do to a mail-order order *man*. When a woman gets her hair done up in the

GLAMOUR "PRETTY GIRL" MAILING

A mailing that lost because it **didn't** *motivate. (NOTE: The Crafts Club mailing shown on page 44, is a good example of* **motivation.** *It won because it* motivated *readers more effectively than did the mailing shown on page 43.)*

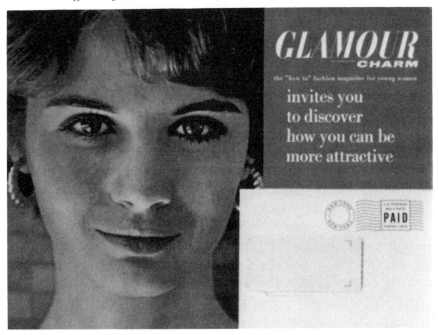

Reproduced with permission of Conde Nast Publications.

current style, does she think she is making herself *stylish* or *beautiful*? It's an interesting question.

Fortunately, it's very easy to find out not what she *thinks* she wants, but what she really *wants*. We put the question of "style" versus "beauty" to a group of women by sending them two mailings. One projected what we considered to be beauty—an envelope with a close-up of a pretty girl's face. Against this we tested what we thought was a *fashion* envelope—a full-figure picture of a girl in a red dress.

This second envelope said "clothes" rather than "hair, lips, eyes." It showed accessories, things a woman would notice.

And in the test, the girl in the red dress came out way ahead. Apparently she offered more women what they want than did the girl's face. We concluded that "style" was more important to the

GLAMOUR "RED DRESS" MAILING

A mailing that won—because it **did** *motivate.*

Reproduced with permission of Conde Nast Publications.

women we were after than physical beauty. At least, they were able to identify better with the woman in a red dress.

However, such generalizations can be dangerous! It may very well be that in another case a pretty, attractive woman (perhaps an older woman?) might have outpulled a stylish model. But in this particular test case we could say the test *proved* that a specific "fashion" effort outpulled the specific "beauty" approach tested against it.

THE THIRD COMMANDMENT: BEGIN WITH THE ENVELOPE

This brings us to my Third Commandment of mail-order. In both our *Glamour* mailings, the envelope was used to carry the main illustration and headline. This is because I believe, as I've indicated throughout this book, that the envelope is to a mailing what the top half of the page is to an advertisement. It is where the headline and illustration belong. I believe that if you have a message to tell, you should not wrap it up and hide it in a plain envelope which has to be torn open before your customer can get at it. The message should be outside where it hits the prospect in the eye, where he or she can't miss seeing it! So I say, contrary to what a lot of direct mail people seem to believe, that the envelope is the most important piece in a mailing. And my Third Commandment is that because the envelope is to a mailing what headlines and illustrations are to an ad, you should always begin with the envelope when you start creating a mailing.

The "Tulip Girl" envelope that Todd Weintz did for McCall's is a good example of an effective *envelope*, which set the tone for a mailing and gave it a dramatic start. The Time/Life Books' "Fish" and "Russia" mailings are other sound examples.

The "Syntopicon" effort we did for "Great Books of the Western World" is another good example of the effective use of an envelope. So is the Rodale Book Club effort I've illustrated earlier in the book, as well as the Veterans mailing Todd did for National Liberty Life Insurance Company.

Since the use of envelopes has been a basic theme throughout this book, I don't think it's necessary to elaborate the point further—except to say, again, envelopes are *important*. The creation of the mailing should *start* with an *envelope*.

THE FOURTH COMMANDMENT: THE BREAKTHROUGH PRINCIPLE

I believe that you can *double* the return of almost any mailing and that you can get drastically different and drastically better results if you apply what I call the "breakthrough" principle.

All of us who live in this age of scientific miracles are familiar with the term "breakthrough," which scientists use as a label for the dramatic discoveries and inventions that carry science forward in giant strides. Often a single discovery will bring about more progress, in a matter of days, than hundreds of previous inventions and developments have achieved in a dozen years. The jet aircraft engine and the computer microchip are just two examples.

The question is: How can a toiler in the mail-order field bring about the same kind of spectacular "breakthrough" results in his or her mailings that scientists are getting in their activities?

And the answer is, by doing something radically *different*. Not by changing from pink envelopes to blue envelopes, but by switching from No. 10 white envelopes to 9 x 12" Polybag containers. By radically changing the offer. By introducing new action devices, like savings stamps, shipping labels, and pennies. And by "zigging" when everybody else is "zagging!"

The best example of a "breakthrough" that I can give is the change in the "Persian Poet" mailing, where the single addition of two pennies to the basic Persian Poet mailing increased response from about 6 percent (which was uneconomical) to 9 percent, which was *very* profitable.

THE FIFTH COMMANDMENT: DRAMATIZE YOUR PRODUCT

To continue with envelopes, there are really only two sales messages you can put before your reader on the envelope. One is the *product*, the other is the *offer*. Of these two mailing elements, I believe the product is the more important. So it is the job of the envelope to put the *product* before the reader in a dramatic, breakthrough fashion whenever you can.

For instance, one of the first mailings I did as a newly fledged consultant was for Golden Press on a very expensive book about *antique automobiles*. How would you do an envelope about antique cars? The reproduction shows how I did it.

THE SIXTH COMMANDMENT: DRAMATIZE THE OFFER

Next, if possible, you want your envelope and your mailing to project the *offer* as well as the product in an exciting way. The very cluttered envelope for the "International Wildlife Encyclopedia," a

Weintz mailing I've reproduced on page 258, helped sell a half million sets of expensive encyclopedias because it dramatized the *offer* with a "Free Book" token.

THE SEVENTH COMMANDMENT: INCLUDE A HOT POTATO

The Great American Magazines plastic card sweepstakes mailing, reproduced earlier in this book, demonstrates the Seventh Commandment of mail order, which I call the "hot potato" Commandment. If you can dramatize the offer by putting something *physical* into the hands of the reader—something which he or she must do something with, like a shipping label or a coin card—you will increase your returns dramatically! A good "hot potato" can and

GOLDEN PRESS "RED CAR" MAILING

A mailing about antique cars which dramatized the product.

Reproduced with permission of Golden Press.

WILDLIFE ENCYCLOPEDIA—BABY SEAL

A *"Token"* mailing that dramatized *the free* offer.

often does double returns, compared with a conventional mailing effort.

Again, the *Reader's Digest* 2¢ mailing, which converted the old "Persian Poet" effort into a far more effective "hot potato" effort, is a good example.

The LIFE Magazine penny mailing was also successful because it had a "hot potato."

THE EIGHTH COMMANDMENT: LIST SELECTION

A perfect example of the difference *lists* make was the experience we had on the World of Beauty Club. Our tests proved that *mail-order lists* totalling 10 million names were more effective than a single 60 million list of telephone subscriber and auto owner names.

The availability and selection of proper mailing lists is absolutely critical to the success of any mail-order enterprise.

THE NINTH COMMANDMENT: COSTS

To be successful a mailing must pull orders at an acceptable cost per order and the COST/PRICE RATIO of the product itself must allow sufficient margin for a decent profit. If your mailing costs too much, your orders may cost too much. The same goes for your product. So although in general I'm an advocate of elaborate, expensive mailings, you should bear in mind that cost-per-order is the key to success, and one way to reduce order costs is to reduce mailing costs. In the end, all mail-order comes down to *arithmetic*.

FCL "POTS AND PANS" MAILING

This mailing for **upbeat** *cassette recordings by Norman Vincent Peale succeeded because it was* **in character.**

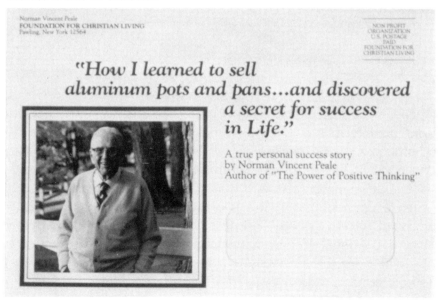

Reproduced with permission of The Foundation for Christian Living.

BRONX ZOO—"ANIMAL KINGDOM" MAILING

Another envelope that instantly projects the character—and the appeal—of the product.

New York Zoological Society
Bronx, New York 10460

Nonprofit Org.
U.S. Postage
PAID
N.Y. Zoological
Society

INSIDE:
A preview of a remarkable
new zoological
publication

Animal
Kingdom
MAGAZINE

PLUS
a sample center spread

R.S.V.P.

High Ridge Road
Pound Ridge, NY 10576

Reproduced by permission of The New York Zoological Society.

THE TENTH COMMANDMENT: KEEP IN CHARACTER

Finally, a mailing should be *in character*. This is my tenth and last Commandment. When you do a mailing for *Reader's Digest*, it must be different from a mailing for *McCall's* Magazine or *Organic Gardening*. Each has its own appropriate tone of voice. The Rodale Book Club mailing illustrated earlier in the book is quite different from the Foundation for Christian Living mailing I recently did for Norman Vincent Peale's cassettes, both of which are far different from the Animal Kingdom mailing. All of these are altogether different from the successful mailing for *Yankee* Magazine which Todd Weintz did recently, and it is different from the *Firehouse* Magazine effort renewal I did. All are different but all are *in character*.

A "frugal" New England mailing—very successful, very much in character.

Reproduced by permission of YANKEE magazine.

So much for my "Ten Commandments." But to conclude this book, I'd like to tell you the one overriding secret of mail-order success I've learned after all my experience. No matter what else you do you will fail in direct mail unless you appeal to *human nature*.

I said at the start of this chapter that the job of mail order is to *motivate* people. You do this by *appealing to human nature*. A good example of this principle is the mailing I made for the Republicans in 1960, over Spencer Olin's signature, to raise money. The Republicans needed a million dollars to balance their war chest before the national election. As you'll recall, we sent out one letter and raised the million dollars. This letter was *not* sent to a few thousand big party supporters. It went to hundreds and thousands of ordinary voters. Some of them weren't even Republicans. In fact,

FIREHOUSE MAGAZINE RENEWAL HEADLINE

A renewal mailing for **Firehouse** *magazine—aimed, obviously, at appealing to firemen, and very much in character.*

Reproduced by permission of *Firehouse* magazine.

The mailing that raised $1 million—by appealing to human nature.

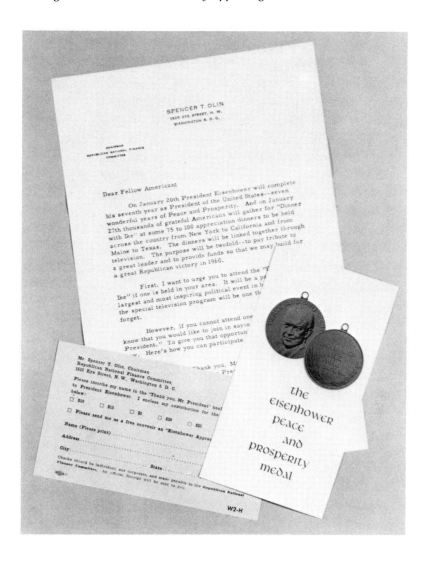

one of them was a Mr. Meyner, who was then Governor of New Jersey, a Democrat who immediately held a press conference and read the letter with great glee to the reporters. We held no press conference because we were too busy counting our cash contributions.

How did we get this million dollars in contributions? We did it by appealing to human nature.

Instead of simply asking for money, we *invited* the mailing recipient to *participate* in a heart-warming tribute to President Eisenhower on his last birthday in office. We *offered* a bronze medal as a free memento of Eisenhower's years. And we *offered* to inscribe the prospect's name in a book whose title was "Thank You, Mr. President," to be given to Eisenhower as a token of affection.

All that was necessary for our prospective participant was to send back his or her name and address on a handy reply card. The card carried space for a contribution. We subsequently inscribed 30,000 names in the book that was given to the President and we put a million dollars in the bank. We did this by appealing to human nature.

And with this, the basic secret of mail-order success, I have finished telling you everything I have learned from over 40 years of mail-order experiences. I hope that some of these experiences and some of this knowledge can be useful to you.

Index